Teaching Adult Immigra
Limited Formal Educati

Full details of all our publications can be found on http://www.multilingual-matters.com, or by writing to Multilingual Matters, St Nicholas House, 31-34 High Street, Bristol BS1 2AW, UK.

Teaching Adult Immigrants with Limited Formal Education

Theory, Research and Practice

Edited by
Joy Kreeft Peyton and
Martha Young-Scholten

MULTILINGUAL MATTERS
Bristol • Blue Ridge Summit

DOI https://doi.org/10.21832/PEYTON6997
Library of Congress Cataloging in Publication Data
A catalog record for this book is available from the Library of Congress.
Names: Peyton, Joy Kreeft, editor. | Young-Scholten, Martha, editor.
Title: Teaching Adult Immigrants with Limited Formal Education: Theory, Research and Practice/Edited by Joy Kreeft Peyton and Martha Young-Scholten.
Description: Bristol; Blue Ridge Summit: Multilingual Matters, [2020] | Includes bibliographical references and index. | Summary: 'This book aims to empower teachers working with adult migrants who have had little or no prior formal schooling, and give them the information and skills to help their students reach the highest possible levels of literacy in their new languages' – Provided by publisher.
Identifiers: LCCN 2019037510 (print) | LCCN 2019037511 (ebook) | ISBN 9781788926980 (paperback) | ISBN 9781788926997 (hardback) | ISBN 9781788927000 (pdf) | ISBN 9781788927017 (epub) | ISBN 9781788927024 (kindle edition)
Subjects: LCSH: Immigrants – Education. | Education, Bilingual. | Second language acquisition. | Native language – Study and teaching. | Native language and education. | Functional literacy. | Adult education.
Classification: LCC LC3719 .T42 2020 (print) | LCC LC3719 (ebook) | DDC 371.826/912 – dc23 LC record available at https://lccn.loc.gov/2019037510
LC ebook record available at https://lccn.loc.gov/2019037511
British Library Cataloguing in Publication Data
A catalogue entry for this book is available from the British Library.

ISBN-13: 978-1-78892-699-7 (hbk)
ISBN-13: 978-1-78892-698-0 (pbk)

Multilingual Matters
UK: St Nicholas House, 31-34 High Street, Bristol BS1 2AW, UK.
USA: NBN, Blue Ridge Summit, PA, USA.

Website: www.multilingual-matters.com
Twitter: Multi_Ling_Mat
Facebook: https://www.facebook.com/multilingualmatters
Blog: www.channelviewpublications.wordpress.com

The policy of Multilingual Matters/Channel View Publications is to use papers that are natural, renewable and recyclable products, made from wood grown in sustainable forests. In the manufacturing process of our books, and to further support our policy, preference is given to printers that have FSC and PEFC Chain of Custody certification. The FSC and/or PEFC logos will appear on those books where full certification has been granted to the printer concerned.

Typeset by Riverside Publishing Solutions
Printed and bound by CPI Group (UK) Ltd, Croydon, CR0 4YY.
Printed and bound in the US by NBN.

Contents

Saratu Ali Yunusa 1952–2020

Saratu was a member of the EU-advisory board and she was instrumental in encouraging us to imagine that interest in our modules could extend to teachers and tutors who work with adults gaining literacy in their home countries. She was an educator who served in Bauchi and Gombe states in Nigeria, in many capacities, from teacher, vice principal, principal, basic education consultant and coordinator, matron/caregiver in the Christian Orphans Foundation to Director of Education, and Chief Education Officer for UNICEF in ten northern states in Nigeria.

Foreword

Larry Condelli
American Institutes for Research, Washington, DC

The process of learning how to read fascinates us. We have experienced, observed and researched every aspect of the reading development process but still do not fully understand it. Our minds transform printed marks and electronic images of letters and characters into ideas, stories and knowledge that are the foundation of learning and communication, literature, science and, indeed, every human endeavor. As children, we typically experience learning to read as natural, almost effortless and over time, with practice and exposure, we master the process. We learn to comprehend thoughts from text, and that opens doors for our development and for all learning.

For adults, however, learning how to read is a much more difficult task. The difficulty is even greater for adults who try to learn to read in a new language. Fortunately, our literacy in our native language – along with oral language skills we learn in our new language – is transferable and a great help to us in learning the intricacies of interpreting new text. Imagine, however, the overwhelming challenge of learning to speak and read in a new language for adults who have limited or no literacy in their native language. This is the situation for adult migrants with limited education and literacy, the focus of this book. These adult learners are immigrants and refugees who come from countries where educational opportunities were limited. Consequently, they were never able to develop the basic reading and writing skills that form the foundation for acquiring literacy and for other kinds of learning. They face the dual challenge of learning a new language while also trying to develop the skills and strategies associated with decoding and comprehending print.

While there is voluminous research on how children learn to read in their native language, the learning process for adult second language learners with limited literacy is sparse. As world migration stresses Europe and the Americas to crisis levels, those who work with adult migrants, to improve their literacy and language skills and integrate them in their new countries, need research-based knowledge to understand how to teach these learners and help them improve their lives. In our current context, this volume arrives at a critical time to inform our world and offer direction for teaching and learning, and to offer new directions for further research.

The chapters of this book provide current and insightful research on the reading development process for low-literate adult migrants. As befitting this complex process, the book provides multi-disciplinary and international perspectives. Researchers from the United Kingdom, the United States, Finland, Germany, Turkey and Spain examine the reading development process from a psycholinguistic perspective, the social context in which development occurs, vocabulary and morphosyntax acquisition and examine multilingualism and perspectives on teaching of these processes. Each chapter brings to light new research and unique insights into the reading process and fills a void in previously unexamined areas for migrant adults with unique characteristics.

Part of the power of this book is its provenance, which reflects the authors' passion and commitment to this topic. The book itself also illustrates how knowledge can build over time through multiple approaches and different contexts through sustained commitment. The work represented in this book thus takes its place as a major contribution to the growing research in this area. In 2005, a synchronicity occurred among the handful of us working in the area of literacy development of low-literate adult migrants. On different continents, we were frustrated by the lack of professional journals and conference outlets to disseminate and discuss our work. If we were noticed at all, we were relegated to a forgotten corner of larger professional organizations dealing with second language acquisition and linguistic development. We also became aware that the migration of low-literate adults, in North America and Europe, was a growing and a common concern. Through email communication, our loose connection was tied together through a small conference, organized by Jeanne Kurvers, Ineke van de Craats and Roeland van Hout at the University of Tilburg in the Netherlands (Kurvers *et al.*, 2006; van de Craats *et al.*, 2015). From this first meeting, a new organization, soon to be known as LESLLA (Literacy Education and Second Language Learning for Adults; known as Low-Educated Second Language and Literacy Acquisition prior to 2017), was born.

From a small classroom in Tilburg with less than 25 researchers, practitioners, policymakers and students, LESLLA has grown to be a formal international and multidisciplinary organization, with over 200 members worldwide. Its mission is to support adults with little or no home language schooling or literacy, who are now learning to read and write for the first time in a new language, by sharing research findings, effective pedagogical practices and information on literacy policy and second language acquisition research and teaching. LESLLA is unique as the only organization devoted exclusively to the study of these topics as they relate to low-literate migrant adults. Through its annual conference, research by its members and website (https://www.leslla.org), LESLLA has built an impressive knowledge base of research in reading and oral language development and practice, as well as policy- and technology-based language learning.

In addition to the research and practice work, LESLLA has inspired several related projects. A team of European researchers created DigLin, an online testing program and basic course material for non-literate L2 adult migrants learning to read and spell in English, Finnish, Dutch or German (Cucchiarini *et al.*, 2015a). The software uses automatic speech recognition software to allow learners to read aloud and get feedback. More pertinent to this book, a second set of multi-year projects is directly tied to the LESLLA research community – European Speakers of Other Languages: Teaching Adult Migrants and Training Their Teachers, known as EU-Speak (https://research.ncl.ac.uk/eu-speak). Funded by the European Union, EU-Speak was conducted in three phases from 2010 to 2018.

EU-Speak was an international project with participants from the United States and the European Union, in which all of the authors of this volume participated. With little research in this field, there was, of course, little research-based teaching. The main purpose of the second and third phases of the EU-Speak project was to bring the research base to teachers, primarily through the development of six instructional modules. The modules were delivered worldwide to thousands of teachers and tutors of adult migrants with limited education and literacy. A survey of teacher needs, also conducted in the second phase of the project, informed the module topics, along with research conducted by other LESLLA members. As described in the introduction to this book, the module topics align with the book chapters, creating a unique convergence of researcher and practitioner materials to build a strong research base for teaching, where none existed.

It is within this context that the research described in this volume emerges. Each of the contributors to this volume is a prominent researcher in the growing field of teaching and learning of low-literate adult migrants. Collectively, they have built a body of knowledge from work under the LESLLA umbrella, through EU-Speak, and now in this new volume, which fills a vacuum by providing a strong research base for the difficult process of teaching and learning to read for the first time in a new language, research that just a few years ago did not exist. Following the approach of prior projects in this area, it has a multidisciplinary and multi-national focus, appropriate to studying the complexity of the reading process. The book takes us on an international journey, from underlying skills fundamental to reading, to social context and supports for learning, and directly to a discussion of teaching methods.

Two of the six substantive chapters address the most important underlying skills needed for reading and reading comprehension: vocabulary development and acquisition of morphosyntax. We learn from research done in Germany how children's prolific abilities in word acquisition before being literate can apply to adults with limited literacy. From work directly studying adult migrants with little or no formal schooling, we examine the processes of morphosyntactic development key to reading comprehension. Research in Spain provides a full overview of the reading skills development process, tying together the basics of reading skill development through a psycholinguistic perspective. Language and literacy, of course, occur in social contexts, and from Finland, we find an analysis of how learners' work and social contexts affect the literacy development process and learn methods to incorporate these contexts into teaching. From Turkey, our focus turns to the maintenance of learners' home/heritage languages. While learners, many of whom are parents, acquire their new language, they face the challenge of how or whether to become a monolingual household or maintain ties to the native language and culture with their children. Bi- and multilingualism allow maintenance of cultural connections that enable the generations to communicate, pass on and maintain cultural traditions.

All of the chapters include implications and strategies for teaching, but the final chapter, by researchers and practitioners from the United States, directly addresses this topic. This chapter includes specific strategies from different perspectives on ways to teach adult migrants at all levels to develop literacy proficiency.

A frequent lament of policymakers and administrators is that there is not enough research-based teaching. In turn, teachers observe that research is not presented in a helpful way that allows them to understand and transfer research findings into teaching approaches. This book is unique in that it addresses both concerns. It is unique in another way as well: It focuses on a unique group of learners, migrant adults with limited education and literacy, the needs of whom were, until recently, unknown and neglected.

Tying together research and practice alone would make this an impressive book. However, it also builds a strong foundation for continued research by providing a wealth of ideas and unexplored pathways. It serves as an invaluable resource for today and a guide for continued exploration and learning for the future.

Acknowledgements

We are highly indebted to those who worked on the development and delivery of the training and continued professional development modules on which the chapters in this volume are based. First and foremost, we are grateful to Yvonne Ritchie, who supported the EU-Speak project from its inception, as grant co-writer, including for the Erasmus+ funding for EU-Speak 3 (2015-1-UK01-KA204-013485 KA2). Yvonne was the project administrator and assistant manager of our dreams, and without her, EU-Speak would not have spoken so well. The idea for the project came from Bea Groves, who continued to support the project throughout by independently evaluating the first module offered and then by serving on the project's advisory board. Providing high-level technical support for the platform, the modules and their users was Gareth Cooper, assisted by Patrick Lawrence in bringing alive the appearance of the modules and by Enas Filimban on the final website (see https://research.ncl.ac.uk/eu-speak). Members of the LESLLA community from Canada, Italy, the Netherlands, the United Kingdom and the United States acted as outside evaluators for each module. Indispensable to the project's success were those project partners who participated in the forerunner of EU-Speak 3, EU-Speak and EU-Speak 2 (see the Appendix to Chapter 1 for the list of institutions) along with the many students at the EU-Speak 3 institutions who translated the modules into their native languages or acted as facilitators on the international discussion forum when each module was delivered.

EU-Speak 3 was served by an advisory board whose highly committed members had worked on EU-Speak or EU-Speak 2. Educator Saratu Yanusa further served on the board to widen the appeal of the modules to those working in adult education in developing countries, such as her native Nigeria. When the project ended in August 2018, a new board was established to manage the continued delivery of modules which, we hope, will be under the auspices of LESLLA.

The editors and authors of this volume are incredibly grateful to individuals who have contributed to this book, most importantly to our editorial assistant Katharine Miles, who made sure the book was complete, consistent and clear, and to second language acquisitionist Michael Sharwood Smith, who gives us a taste of his other talents in his cover painting. The independent reviewer of this volume spent considerable time going over it and offered numerous astute modifications, nearly all of which we have undertaken. Any remaining imperfections are, of course, ours.

Acknowledgements

Contributors

Kerstin Chlubek studied to become a primary school teacher and currently works as a research assistant for Dr Andreas Rohde at Cologne University (English Department II). She teaches university students who want to be teachers in primary or secondary schools for special education and works on her PhD in the field of second language acquisition. Her main fields of research interest are teaching English in primary school, morphosyntax in (second) language acquisition and cross-linguistic influences in the language acquisition process.

Nancy R. Faux, MA University of London, is now retired. She was the ESOL (English as a Second Language) Specialist for the Literacy Institute at Virginia Commonwealth University (VCU) for over 15 years. In her retirement she facilitates online courses for adult education teachers for the Literacy Institute. At VCU she coordinated professional development initiatives for ESOL teachers and programs throughout the state of Virginia. She was one of the founding members of Literacy Education and Second Language Learning for Adults (LESLLA) and worked on EU-Speak projects 2 and 3.

Belma Haznedar, PhD Durham University, United Kingdom, is professor of applied linguistics and bilingualism at Boğaziçi University, Turkey. Her expertise includes early childhood bilingualism, with reference to morphosyntactic properties of successive and simultaneous language acquisition. In recent work she has investigated literacy development in monolingual and bilingual children and created online materials for teachers working with migrant populations. She has published in internationally refereed journals and books and is co-editor with E. Gavruseva of *Current Trends in Child Second Language Acquisition* (John Benjamins, 2008) and co-editor with N. Ketrez of *Acquisition of Turkish in Childhood* (John Benjamins, 2016).

Pia Holtappels studied to become a primary school teacher and currently works as a research assistant for Dr Andreas Rohde at Cologne University (English Department II). She teaches university students who want to be teachers in primary or secondary schools for special education and works on her PhD in the field of second language acquisition. Her main fields of research interest are teaching English in primary school, the acquisition of written language (in a first and second language) and the use of written language in the Primary School Foreign Language Classroom.

Rola Naeb, PhD, Northumbria University, England, is a senior lecturer in Applied Linguistics and TESOL. She is the vice president of Literacy Education and Second Language Learning for Adults (LESLLA). Her main research interests are educational technology in second language learning for those with and without formal education and the linguistic integration of adult migrants. She has been involved in Grundtvig and Erasmus+ projects: the Digital Literacy Instructor, and phases 1 and 3 of the EU-Speak project. She is also one of the experts working on the European *Literacy Acquisition and Second Language Learning for the Integration of Adult Migrants* reference guide.

Joy Kreeft Peyton, PhD Georgetown University, is a Senior Fellow at the Center for Applied Linguistics, in Washington, DC. She has over 35 years of experience working in the field of languages, linguistics and culture in education. She collaborates with teachers and program leaders in K-12 and adult education to improve their instructional practice and study the implementation and outcomes of research-based practice. Her work includes implementing and studying approaches to writing that facilitate learner engagement and learning and promote academic and professional success. She has worked on the EU-Speak project and is now a member of the Board.

Andreas Rohde, PhD and German 'habilitation', Christian-Albrechts-University, Kiel, is full professor of English linguistics and second language teaching at the University of Cologne (since 2004). Since the 1990s, he has been involved in various projects evaluating bilingual kindergarten and primary school programmes, one of his major interests being second language word learning. More recently, he has been focusing on inclusive teaching of young learners. He was involved in the Grundtvig and Erasmus+ projects EU-Speak 2 and 3 (2014–2018). Since 2014, he has been a principal investigator in Zukunftsstrategie LehrerInnenbildung (ZuS), a project designed to enhance teacher education, funded by the German ministry of education.

Kim-Sarah Schick, PhD University of Cologne, studied to be a special needs teacher and did her PhD in the area of English language teaching for students with special needs at the University of Cologne. She is currently working in the English Department with Dr Andreas Rohde at Cologne University. She teaches university students who study to be teachers in special education, primary and secondary schools. Her main fields of research interest are foreign language learning in children with special needs, language impairment and foreign language learning, language learning strategies and foreign language word learning.

Johanna Schnuch, PhD University of Cologne, studied to become a primary school teacher for German and English. She worked as a research assistant for Dr Andreas Rohde at Cologne University (English Department II) and taught students who wanted to be teachers in primary or secondary for special education. She is currently doing her teacher training at a primary school. In her PhD she worked on the topic of language awareness in multilingual children. Her main fields of research interest are bi- and multilingualism, teaching English and inclusion.

Marcin Sosiński, PhD, University of Granada, is associate professor in the Spanish Language Department at the University. For over 15 years, he has been directly involved in teaching Spanish as a second language to immigrants, for several years in the charity sector. He contributes to the MA Programme on Spanish as a Second/ Foreign Language, where future teachers are trained, and he has been developing fiction materials for emergent adult readers with low oral proficiency. He was part of the Grundtvig and Erasmus+ projects EU-Speak 1, 2 and 3 (2010–2018) and also contributed to the Spanish DigLin website.

Minna Suni, PhD, is professor of Finnish language at the University of Jyväskylä, Finland. She is a specialist in Finnish as a second language. Her recent research projects have focused on second language learning and use in the workplace. Currently, she is a principal investigator in a project which analyses the development of adult migrants' second language resources in integration training and vocational education in Finland. She has also published on multilingualism and literacy skills of migrant school children; e.g. in the context of the Programme for International Student Assessment (PISA).

Taina Tammelin-Laine, PhD, University of Jyväskylä, works as a research coordinator in the Centre for Applied Language Studies at the University. Her research interests are L2 Finnish acquisition (reading, writing, speaking and listening) of adult immigrants with limited or interrupted earlier schooling, and assessment of L2 Finnish skills below A1 on the Common European Framework of Reference (CEFR). Her PhD thesis from 2014 is so far the only broader study on these learners learning Finnish as an additional language. She was involved in the Grundtvig and Erasmus+ projects EU-Speak 2 and 3 (2014–2018) and also contributed to the Finnish DigLin website.

Susan Watson, PhD, is ESOL Specialist for The Literacy Institute at Virginia Commonwealth University (VCU). She coordinates ESOL teacher professional development for publicly funded adult education programs in Virginia, ensuring that these efforts align with federal and state initiatives and guidelines. She is also adjunct faculty for VCU's School of Education, where she teaches in the adult learning and teacher preparation programs. Susan presents original work at local, national and international conferences on English language teaching and learning and adult literacy. She worked on the EU-Speak 3 project and is now a member of the Board.

Martha Young-Scholten, PhD University of Washington, Seattle, is professor of second language acquisition at Newcastle University. Since the 1980s, she has conducted research on the generative-linguistics-based L2 acquisition of morphosyntax and phonology, focusing on adults acquiring their L2 naturalistically. For the last decade she has been investigating the reading development of migrant adults with limited home language literacy. She has been involved in Grundtvig and Erasmus+ projects: 2013–2015, the Digital Literacy Instructor, as partner, and 2010–2018, as coordinator of EU-Speak. She co-directs with a creative writing colleague the Simply Cracking Good Stories project on L2 pleasure reading for adult beginners.

1 Introduction: Understanding Adults Learning to Read for the First Time in a New Language: Multiple Perspectives

Martha Young-Scholten and Joy Kreeft Peyton

1.1 Adult Migrants with Limited Education and Literacy

You may be well aware that there are adults with limited or no LITERACY among those who migrate to a new country. You may also know that the rates of illiteracy are slowly decreasing. Worldwide, 89.8% of males and 82.6% of females over the age of 15 are now able to read and write. However, 75% of the world's population, 750 million individuals over the age of 15, live in poor, rural areas or conflict-torn regions and have limited opportunities to participate in formal education and limited or no literacy in the language of their home and community. Two thirds of the 750 million are women (World Demographics Profile, 2018).

Educators who work to support adult MIGRANTS with limited education and literacy observe the myriad linguistic and literacy challenges that the learners in their classes face as they seek to adapt to their new country. Meeting these challenges is affected by a range of factors, from visa requirements and constraints to availability of basic skills classes and being taught by teachers and tutors who are specifically prepared to work with this population.

Educational provision for adults with little or no formal schooling or HOME LANGUAGE literacy is more similar than different worldwide. In most countries, for example, there is no formal qualification attached to the initial steps that learners take toward earning a qualification (e.g. Entry 1 in the United Kingdom). In some countries, unpaid volunteer tutors make an important contribution in one-on-one and small-group teaching, as well as in the classroom, and they may be responsible for their own classes.

Adult migrants who arrive in highly literate societies without the skills for living wage employment, who expect to support the education and well-being of their younger family members and to engage in the civic life of their community, need at least equal the attention from educators as those who arrive with years of schooling and high-level skills, who may be able to learn in formal educational programs, with trained, qualified teachers, and who have high standards for learning and achievement. Researchers, educators and policymakers have until recently paid far less attention to this group of ADULT LEARNERS. On this basis of similarities in educational provision and an urgent need to share accumulating knowledge, researchers and practitioners from the countries in which these adult migrants resettle have been collaborating. This means that the annual symposium of an organization dedicated to these learners, which was founded in 2005, Literacy Education and Second Language Learning by Adults (LESLLA, http://www.leslla.org), buzzes with the thrill of a Canadian, a Finnish, an Italian, a Turkish and a US teacher or tutor discovering how much they have in common and what they can learn from each other.

Research on these learners shows that, when compared with adult migrants with some home language and literacy, their progress in literacy development is much slower (Condelli *et al.*, 2003; Kurvers *et al.*, 2010) and can also be slower for oral language development (Tarone *et al.*, 2009). For decades, however, research has shown that adults can reach high levels of oral proficiency in a new language regardless of the age at which they are exposed to the language, the amount of education they have and the type of exposure that they have to the language (Hawkins, 2001). Educated adults have the advantage of knowing how to read and write in their native or other language(s), and this provides a bridge to literacy in a new language. First-time adult readers lack such a bridge. It turns out that their cognitive skills support them in laying a foundation on which to develop literacy, and they seem to follow a path similar to that followed by young children learning to read for the first time (Kurvers *et al.*, 2010; Young-Scholten & Naeb, 2010; Young-Scholten & Strom, 2006). However, so far, only a small percentage of adult migrants who start learning to read and write for the first time in their lives, but in a second language, demonstrate progress to higher levels, and the majority struggle to develop these literacy skills and remain at or even below A1 in the COMMON EUROPEAN FRAMEWORK OF REFERENCE FOR LANGUAGES (Kurvers *et al.*, 2010; Schellekens, 2011).

Oral language progress is also slower for those who are not literate, because the LANGUAGE INPUT that they can use is initially limited to listening. If they have no literacy skills at all, they will not be able to decipher environmental print. Older migrants may process oral language input more slowly than, and not remember things as well as, their younger counterparts (Tarone *et al.*, 2009), and they also spend less time in the classroom gaining oral language and literacy skills. In some countries, they spend considerably less time due to poor access to educational provision, work and family commitments or health issues. These factors are difficult or impossible to influence. What is possible to influence is the level of awareness, knowledge and skills relevant to their situation of the teachers and tutors who work with them. Research shows that the chances of success of migrant adult learners increase significantly when they are taught by well trained and knowledgeable teachers (Condelli *et al.*, 2010).

1.2 Terminology Used in this Book

In the chapters in this volume, authors interchangeably use the terms 'home language', MOTHER TONGUE, NATIVE LANGUAGE, FIRST LANGUAGE, LANGUAGE OF ORIGIN and HERITAGE LANGUAGE, to refer to the language(s) that an individual has spoken since birth or early childhood. We use 'migrant' throughout the volume, as does UNESCO (n.d.), to refer to individuals who resettle in a country other than their country of origin, regardless of their status (e.g. asylum seeker, refugee, chain migrant), and who have the expectation of remaining in the country. UNESCO uses 'adult' to refer to individuals 15 years and older and those who are past the age of compulsory or free schooling (UNESCO Institute for Statistics, 2016). Use of the term 'second language', abbreviated as 'L2', indicates any language (not literally the second language) acquired after early childhood, as has long been the case in the field of SECOND LANGUAGE ACQUISITION (SLA).

1.3 European Speakers of Other Languages: Teaching Adult Migrants and Training Their Teachers

The chapters in this volume emerged from the third phase of a project that ran from 2010 to 2018, *European Speakers of Other Languages: Teaching Adult Migrants and Training Their Teachers*. Surveys conducted during the second phase of the project confirmed the lack of opportunities that teachers and tutors have to gain such knowledge and skills (Young-Scholten *et al.*, 2015a), and between 2015 and 2018, six modules were designed and delivered twice to nearly 1000 teachers and tutors around the world. The modules can still be taken; information is available from the LESLLA website: http://www.leslla.org. Modules can also be delivered in hybrid or face-to-face mode by anyone who teaches or tutors adult migrants with limited education and literacy; contact the editors of this volume.

Criteria for choice of module topics to develop and offer were threefold: (1) practitioner need as revealed in a survey; (2) expertise of the EU-Speak 3 partners; (3) additional information, which included contributions to the LESLLA symposia and subsequent publications in the LESLLA proceedings, such as Vinogradov's (2013) proposition for the knowledge base shown in Table 1.1 (see also Vinogradov & Liden, 2009).

Six module topics emerged from this process that align with the chapters in this book. Key research (6), focused specifically on migrant adults with limited education

Table 1.1 Knowledge base of effective LESLLA instructors (adapted from Vinogradov, 2013: 11)

1. The refugee experience	6. Key research
2. Types of literacy-level learners	7. Components of reading
3. Literacy in childhood vs. adulthood	8. Balanced literacy
4. Emergent readers	9. Approaches to teaching literacy
5. Second language acquisition	10. Connections of L1/L2 literacies

and literacy, pervades all of the modules and chapters in this book. Here, we connect the chapter topics with the other numbered points on Vinogradov's list: *Language and Literacy in Social Context* (2, 8, 10); *Reading from a Psycholinguistic Perspective* (2, 3, 4, 7, 8, 9, 10); *Vocabulary* (4, 5, 7, 9); *Acquisition and Assessment of Morphosyntax* (5, 7, 9); *Bilingualism and Multilingualism* (3, 8, 10) and *Working with LESLLA Learners* (1, 2). The reader will note when delving into the chapters that research specifically on this learner group does not always exist, and it is often necessary to extrapolate from research on other learner populations.

See the Appendix and Chapter 5 for a description of the two surveys that led to the creation of the modules and of the countries where module participants live and work.

1.4 Literacy and the Acquisition of Linguistic Competence

This volume is, therefore, also intended to rouse readers to consider conducting their own research or working alongside established researchers to fill the gaps in what we know about this learner population. Unfortunately, the field of SLA has become less socially relevant than was the case some 40 years ago, when there was a flurry of research on migrant workers in post-industrialized countries in northern Europe, such as Germany and Sweden (see overview in Young-Scholten, 2013). Absence of an evidence base that such research would result in has serious consequences when advocating for more or specific types of educational provision for adult migrants with limited literacy. In the context of a now vast amount of research on the L2 acquisition of educated younger and older learners, there is almost nothing on the L2 acquisition of **LINGUISTIC COMPETENCE** by adults with limited education. When it comes to **READING**, there is much more research on the process of learning to read, and there is advocacy by organizations that aim to boost literacy. But researchers and organizations focus overwhelmingly on first-time readers in their native language and not on those learning a second language with no or limited literacy in their native language. Unlike older native language **EMERGENT READERS**, migrant adults are learning to read for the first time, but in a second language.

One long-standing issue in SLA is whether children and adults differ fundamentally in their acquisition of language, whether there is a **CRITICAL PERIOD** after which a language can only be effortfully 'learned' in classrooms rather than 'acquired' through mere exposure (Krashen, 1982, 1985). SLA researchers from the generative, **CHOMSKYAN TRADITION** assume that literacy is not one of the influences on, for example, the acquisition of **MORPHOSYNTAX** or **SYNTAX**. Another long-standing issue is that of the so-called **GREAT DIVIDE** in analytic ability between individuals who are literate and those who are non-literate. It was not until Tarone *et al.* (2009) took up this issue that these two ideas (the critical period and the Great Divide) were investigated with respect to migrant adults with limited literacy, when these researchers treated literacy as a variable in their study of Somali adults' acquisition of morphosyntax in English. Thus, Hawkins' (2001) conclusion that education does not determine one's ability to acquire linguistic competence in an L2 may be premature. This is important for practitioners, where the view one adopts will guide expectations of what learners are capable of.

Taking the research gap as a challenge for the field of SLA overall, Tarone *et al.* (2009: 1) note that because 'we know next to nothing about [non-literate learners'] processes of oral second language acquisition', theories are insufficient. They examined how more moderately literate vs. low-literate 15- to 27-year-old Somalis whose US residence ranged from three to seven years responded to the researcher's ORAL RECASTS of questions they had produced. Results showed that those with moderate literacy were significantly better at recalling and accurately repeating recasts and at including INFLECTED VERBS in their recasts. The authors conclude that ALPHABETIC LITERACY has an undeniable effect on the acquisition of L2 morphosyntax, and they also consider whether and if so, how, literacy might influence WORKING MEMORY CAPACITY (see also Gathercole & Baddeley, 1989; Reis & Castro-Caldas, 1997 on non-literate NATIVE SPEAKERS; Juffs & Rodríguez, 2008 on second language learners with limited literacy).

Considerably more research is needed before solid conclusions can be drawn about the influence of literacy on the acquisition of linguistic competence. Also rare are studies that look at the linguistic competence of literate vs. non-literate native speakers of a language. One example is Mishra *et al.* (2012), who describe their study of very low-literate and high-literate adult Hindi speakers in Uttar Pradesh, India, from the same Dalit community. They used a technique referred to as EYE TRACKING, in which they presented the study participants with a visual display of objects and played sentences to them. While participants were listening to the sentences and looking at the display, the researchers measured for each sentence where their eyes moved and watched to see if they anticipated what was going to come next by moving their eyes. The eye tracking showed that the participants with limited literacy were significantly slower at using the cues in the sentences to look at the objects in the display and to anticipate what would come next. However, in the analysis of their results and in their critical review of claims made about the influence of literacy on the mind and on language, Mishra *et al.* note that it is not clear whether literacy *per se* affects individuals' ability to use cues to anticipate information or whether it is because reading allows for faster processing (250 wpm) than listening to spoken language (150 wpm).

The dearth of basic research on adult migrants with limited literacy has consequences for what practitioners believe learners are capable of. Laborious, systematic observation and experimentation have given us wonderful stories about the capabilities of living organisms, from babies to crows. But laborious, systematic observation and experimentation on these learners' acquisition of linguistic competence is, to date, rare. For those who benefit from this volume and would like to expand their knowledge of these and other issues, Wright *et al.* (2018), *Mind Matters in SLA*, is a good place to start. Hawkins (2018) is another volume dedicated to applying cutting-edge ideas to the exploration of all aspects of the acquisition of morphosyntactic and syntactic competence in a second language. Another source is the OASIS project, which is dedicated to providing accessible summaries of SLA research (https://oasis-database.org/about).

1.5 Chapters in This Volume

As mentioned above, the chapters in this volume follow the topics of the online EU-Speak modules offered to practitioners.

In Chapter 2, *Language and Literacy in Social Context*, Minna Suni and Taina Tammelin-Laine describe the contexts in which adult learners with limited education and literacy live and learn, the impact that this has on their learning and ways that practitioners working with these learners can serve them successfully. They provide examples of research and practice primarily from Finland, the context in which they work, and other Nordic countries. Readers will notice commonalities with their own situations, confirming the premise that practitioners working with this group of learners are similar across countries in many ways.

Chapter 3, *Reading from a Psycholinguistic Perspective*, is the first of three chapters that focus on aspects of the linguistic competence that underpins reading comprehension. Marcin Sosiński describes the process of reading skills development, including how these link to phonological, phonemic, morphological and syntactic awareness, and pedagogical approaches that can be used to promote learning to read words and longer texts. While there is some research that focuses on the population of migrant adults with little or no formal education, much of the research discussed in this chapter comes from studies of children learning to read.

Chapter 4, *Vocabulary*, by Andreas Rohde, Kerstin Chlubek, Pia Holtappels, Kim-Sarah Schick and Johanna Schnuch, covers vocabulary and details how learners without literacy, young children, effortlessly amass an impressively vast store of words before they begin to learn to read. Although there is limited research on the vocabulary development of migrant adults, the research presented in this chapter is highly relevant to learners who cannot yet learn words from context during reading, cannot yet use text-based dictionaries and do not have the written-text-based strategies that educated learners have at their disposal. The chapter concludes with applications and implications for teachers and tutors.

Chapter 5, *Acquisition and Assessment of Morphosyntax*, by Martha Young-Scholten and Rola Naeb, covers a second aspect of linguistic competence that is fundamental to learners being able to comprehend text: morphosyntax. Morpho- refers to FUNCTIONAL MORPHOLOGY – words, PREFIXES and SUFFIXES that mark grammatical functions, such as tense; and grammatical relations between words, such as SUBJECT–VERB AGREEMENT. Syntax refers to word order. Nearly all of the information presented comes from research on adult migrants, some of whom have had little or no formal schooling.

Chapter 6, *Bilingualism and Multilingualism*, by Belma Haznedar, focuses not only on adult migrants but also on their families and communities. Since many of these learners are parents, supporting them in supporting their children's education is an important concern. A focal issue in children's education is whether they will eventually end up monolingual in the new language, without the skills to talk with older family and community members or read in their parents' home language, their heritage language, thus cutting them off from their linguistic origins, or whether they will grow up to be bilingual or even multilingual. Supporting learners' home languages and giving younger community members access to those languages as the MAJORITY LANGUAGE of the wider community begins to take over when children start school is an important process, about which teachers and tutors need to be aware. The chapter closes with practical ways that practitioners can become involved with the maintenance of learners' home/native/heritage languages.

In Chapter 7, *Teaching and Tutoring Adult Learners with Limited Education and Literacy,* Nancy Faux and Susan Watson describe the skills and attitudes needed for teaching and tutoring second language reading and writing to migrant adults with limited education and literacy. It provides specific INSTRUCTIONAL strategies that teachers and tutors can use to help learners at multiple levels of proficiency develop literacy practices and be engaged in learning and in the communities in which they live.

1.6 Conclusion

It is our hope that this introductory overview and the chapters in this volume will provide you, practitioners, students, trainers, program directors and researchers working with adult migrants with limited education and literacy, with a strong base in established ideas and new research and that it will yield practical implications to guide work in supporting these learners to reach their potential.

Appendix: Information Informing Development of the Online Modules

The chapters in this volume emerged from the third phase of a project that ran from 2010 to 2018, *European Speakers of Other Languages: Teaching Adult Migrants and Training Their Teachers.*

The aim in 2010 was to explore the various aspects of basic language and literacy support that are relevant to the rates of progress in learning to read made by adult migrants with limited education and literacy. This involved workshops in the partner countries on curriculum, instructional approaches and techniques, materials, assessments and teacher training and professional development across the European Union, with its range of languages, cultures, systems of education and education provision and policy. Institutions involved in the first phase of the project were Newcastle University (lead); Workers Education Association; VUC Fyn (Denmark); Universities of Amsterdam, Cologne, Granada, Leipzig and Stockholm (Grundtvig 2010-1-GB2-GRU06-03528).

The project partners agreed that the best way to positively influence the educational outcome of these learners would be to address the inadequacy of teacher and tutor training and continued professional development (henceforth T&CPD). In the second phase of the project (EU-Speak 2), the need for specialized T&CPD was established through international surveys of practitioners and LESLLA experts (Grundtvig 539478-LLP- 1-2013-1-UK-GRUNDTVIG-GMP). This phase involved Martha Young-Scholten, Newcastle University; Paula Bosch, ITTA University of Amsterdam; Belma Haznedar, Boğaziçi; Larry Condelli, American Institutes of Research, Washington, DC; Joy Kreeft Peyton, Center for Applied Linguistics, Washington, DC; Marcin Sosiński, Universidad de Granada; Rola Naeb, Northumbria University; Taina Tammelin-Laine, University of Jyväskylä; Susan Watson and Nancy Faux, Virginia Commonwealth University. The result was a set of LESLLA-specific knowledge and skills that teachers need to have, which fed into a curriculum to be implemented in the languages of the teachers and tutors, not only in English. The surveys confirmed the lack of opportunities that teachers and tutors have to gain such knowledge and skills (Young-Scholten *et al.*, 2015b). At the end of the second phase, an online module was designed by the project team at the University of Cologne and piloted in versions in the project languages as a free six-week T&CPD module. The third phase of the project, EU-Speak 3, ran from 2015 to 2018 (Erasmus+ 2015-1-UK01-KA204-013485). Institutions involved in this phase were Universität zu Köln, Boğaziçi University, Universidad de Granada, University of Jyväskylä, Newcastle University, Virginia Commonwealth University and Northumbria University. Five more modules were added. Each of the six modules was offered twice to nearly 1000 teachers and tutors around the world. The modules can still be taken in online, hybrid or face-to-face forms by anyone who teaches or tutors adult migrants with limited education and literacy. (Information is available from the LESLLA website: http://www.leslla.org.)

The map below shows the countries in which the teachers who took the modules live and work. The highlighted countries are the EU-Speak 3 partner countries.

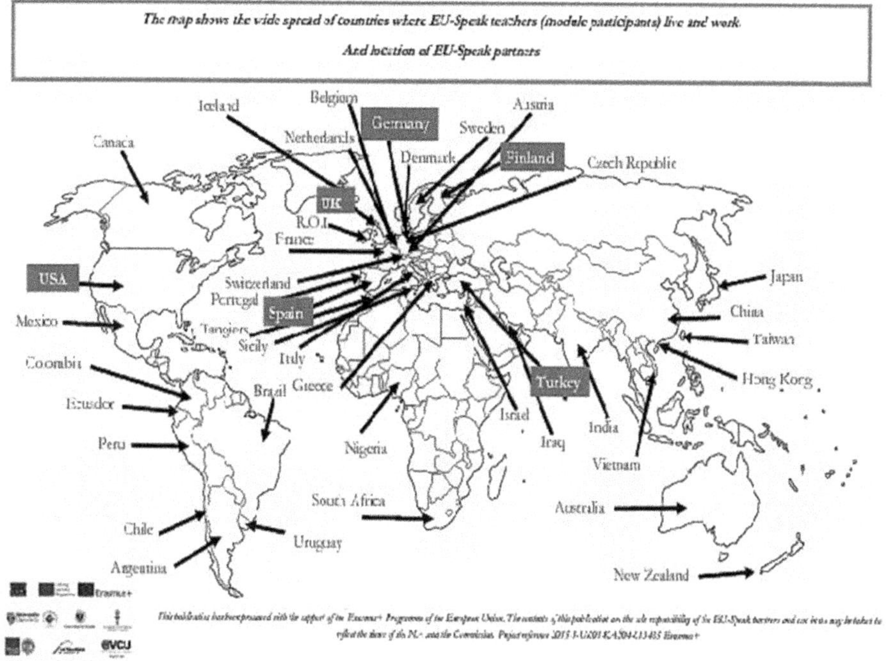

Figure 1.1 Map of EU-Speak module participants' countries

Ideas began to emerge from the 2013-2015 EU-Speak 2 project and the surveys of educators conducted, which were informed by a similar survey in the Nordic countries (Franker & Christensen, 2013). Staff working on the EU-Speak 2 project designed a questionnaire with questions in four categories: Literacy from Global, Local and Individual Perspectives; Adult Formal Learning in a Creative and Critical Learning Environment; Materials for Adult Learning and for Teaching Oral Communicative Competence; and Initial and Functional Literacy. The survey was distributed by the project partners through their local, regional and national networks and through the LESLLA user list; 308 surveys were completed by teachers, teacher trainers and program managers. Further consultation was carried out, with LESLLA experts and delegates at the LESLLA symposium in Nijmegen in 2016. This led to a distilled set of educator knowledge and skills, shown in Table 1.2.

The next step was to decide on the topics the proposed modules would cover. The project partners were guided by a second survey, the responses to which showed some misalignment between what teachers and tutors do with learners and what training they might have had that prepared them to work with these learners. While most respondents had experienced almost no specific training or professional development in working with this learner population, what they had experienced is shown in Table 1.3. Not surprisingly, if the participants had taken a professional

Table 1.2 Knowledge and skills that educators need, emerging from EU-Speak 2 surveys

Knowledge	**Current, relevant teaching materials**	**Learners' backgrounds and situations, including physical and psychological**	**Literacy skills** **Written texts that learners encounter**	**Oral language** **First language influence**
Skills	Use materials relevant to learners' lives	Use methods for active participation that draw on learners' situations and experiences	Guide learners in developing independent reading and writing skills that are relevant to their lives through multi-modal activities	Foster authentic conversation Draw on a variety of current methods to teach pronunciation, grammar, vocabulary and language usage

Table 1.3 Survey of module participants' teaching and preparation for teaching

Work with LESLLA learners	**Training or professional development focused on**
Reading	Literacy development
Writing	
Listening	
Speaking	Oral language development
Conversation	
Communication Skills	
Grammar	Assessment
Vocabulary	
	Numeracy
	Life skills
	Employability
	Health literacy
	Safety
	Materials selection/creation
	Instructional strategies
	Planning instruction

development course or module, its focus was on various aspects of survival (the five rows after assessment) and on the basics of teaching (the final three rows).

Criteria for choice of module topics to develop and offer were threefold: (1) practitioner need as revealed in the second survey; (2) expertise of the EU-Speak 3 partners; (3) additional information, which included contributions to the LESLLA symposia and subsequent publications in the LESLLA proceedings, such as Vinogradov's (2013) proposition for the knowledge base that teachers need to have, shown in Table 1.3.

2 Language and Literacy in Social Context

Minna Suni and Taina Tammelin-Laine

2.1 Introduction: The Importance of Social Context in Learning

Language and literacy do not develop in a vacuum. They are tightly interconnected with the social environments where they are used. They are developed through interacting with other people. While teachers, tutors and program directors are often among the 'significant others' for newly arrived migrants, because they mediate the language resources of the surrounding community, they are not the only people with whom migrants interact. One of the key roles of language and literacy teaching is to pave the way for and support further interactions and learning outside the classroom. Literacy development by migrant adults in a second language is a process similar to that in one's native language(s), where numerous people, in addition to the teacher, are involved and can take place during face-to-face interactions, through reading physical texts, or in the virtual world through various applications.

In this chapter, we focus on the roles of various social contexts for language and literacy development with the aim of raising the awareness of those who work with adult migrants with little or no formal education. These roles include parenting, schooling and work contexts where literacy is required and put into practice. In addition to these roles, literacy empowers individuals to play an active role in society and take on civic responsibilities. We begin by introducing different culturally bound conceptualizations of what literacy means and give examples of different types of literacy. The reader is invited to think about the roles of literacy in daily life and across the life span as well as in the history of a family and language community. The chapter also discusses research on connections between the predominant ideologies of a given society and the literacy skills of its population on the one hand, and between the literacy skills of parents and their children on the other hand.

Examples come from a context that is assumed not to be well known to those living outside the Nordic countries, the context of Finland. Using examples from the authors' own country serves to raise outsiders' awareness about one of many smaller countries in which migrant adults resettle and encourages the reader to observe similarities across contexts, starting with their own context. Features of the Finnish national curricula for literacy instruction for migrants (Finnish National Board of Education, 2012; Finnish National Agency for Education, 2019a, 2019b) are described to familiarize the reader with the ways in which literacy skills are understood in Finland. But Finland is just one example; there is well-established collaboration among professionals in the Nordic countries in supporting adult migrants' development of basic skills. The activities of the Nordic Alfa Council (Alfarådet, http://nvl.org/alfaradet), which is part of the larger Nordic network of adult education, are an example. The goal is to provide opportunities for active participation in community life and democratic processes for adult migrants with no or very short formal schooling. Finland also represents a Western welfare state with a strong positive profile in the international results of the Program for International Student Assessment (PISA) and other surveys. Yet despite these factors and the perception of some that Finland is an 'educational paradise', through the discussion below it will become clear that the same challenges confront low-educated adult migrants in Finland as elsewhere.

2.2 The Importance of Literacy in All Aspects of Life

Our world views are often egocentric: We often think of our views, beliefs and practices as neutral or even superior to those of others. When it comes to literacy, we think of our alphabet, spelling system (orthography), reading habits and literacy practices as the right ones. We can reach a deeper understanding of the literacy backgrounds of the learners with whom we work through a greater awareness of our own backgrounds. We can start by asking ourselves the following questions:

- What do we need literacy for in our daily lives?
- Why is literacy important for us in principle and in practice?
- Where do our conceptualizations about literacy come from?

Although we each have a unique learning history, life history, daily life and future plans, our conception of literacy is not created in a vacuum. Literacy is culturally mediated. We share and rely on what we have learned from others who have taught us as well as from our parents, peers and community. The dominant views and beliefs in our communities determine the roles and status of literacy in our lives and shape our identities. These views and beliefs are often so embedded in our experience that we are unaware of their origins. Many migrants' experience differs from our experience (see discussions in Gee, 1991; Golden & Lanza, 2012; Warriner, 2009). Their goals and expectations for second language literacy learning may differ from those of their teacher or even from those of their classmates. For example, some learners without first language literacy might think that reading is not for them; some might not understand the usefulness of literacy in their lives, since, so far, they have coped fine without it. Others will have strong feelings about the skills they want to develop and the ways they want to develop them.

The cultural embeddedness of literacy, along with individual perceptions of the nature and value of literacy, make it difficult for the teacher or tutor to predict how an adult migrant with limited literacy will view their future development of literacy. In post-industrialized, democratic societies, where literacy goes beyond its functional purposes to enable adults to fully and actively participate in a society, know their rights and exercise their civic responsibilities, teachers and tutors may view the main benefit of literacy as empowerment. This is a perspective that learners will not always share at the start (see, e.g. Miller & King, 2009).

2.3 Literacy in Post-industrialized Societies

We might think that the value and uses of literacy skills are similar everywhere and for everyone, but this is not the case. All uses of written text are shaped in and by their social and cultural contexts, and conceptions of literacy are rooted in social and cultural conventions, needs and values (Gee, 2000). In post-industrialized societies, literacy skills are necessary and valued, but this may not be the case in the communities and societies from which migrant adults with little formal education come. The social environment sets the criteria for what counts as sufficient literacy skills and defines what these skills are needed for and how important they are (Grabe & Stoller, 2011). Investment in literacy education varies considerably for the majority language(s) of a country, but in many countries, literacy education in minority languages may be minimal or non-existent. This presents a disadvantage for those who do not speak the majority language(s). (See Chapter 6 for a discussion of migrants' minority languages.)

Values and conventions concerning literacy and the written word have varied in what are now considered post-industrialized societies before our current era of globalization. In Europe, the roots of modern-day literacy go back 500 years to the Protestant Christian reform movement and Martin Luther, and 2017 was celebrated as the half-millennium anniversary of a reform that started in Northern Europe and led to the idea of universal literacy, not just literacy for a certain elite. At the time, the Bible was only available in Latin, and the proposal that everyone has the right to hear – and read – the Bible directly, and in their own native language, was considered radical. This led to intensive translation projects and literacy education which, in turn, resulted in rapidly rising literacy rates from the mid-1600s onwards (Gutek, 1995). The tradition of translating the Bible is still alive in the form of writing standards projects and literacy campaigns led by Christian missionary workers around the world.

Not surprisingly, those countries in which the Bible was translated into their languages (e.g. the Netherlands; Sweden, which at the time included Finland; England; and Germany) have had higher literacy rates than other countries for centuries (Graham, 1987). It was only from reforms in the second Vatican Council (1962–1965) that the Catholic Church permitted use of languages other than Latin during mass. (Visit https://ourworldindata.org/literacy to see the figures for your own country or language.) We may have grandparents or great grandparents who were not literate in their native language, and to understand where we are now and where the learners we work with are, it is helpful to seek information on the historical literacy rates and levels of education in our own countries.

In post-industrialized countries, we tend to perceive the written word as more reliable than the spoken word, a view that seems to be shared in the traditionally Protestant regions and countries in Europe but less so in Catholic parts of Europe (see, e.g. Graham, 1987). However, in many parts of the world, the spoken word is perceived as more reliable than the written word, and good oral skills are respected more than literacy skills. In non-democratic political regimes, this may result in citizens' mistrust of written texts. Moreover, printed documents are not valued if the authorities who have produced them are not regarded as trustworthy. For those in power, regardless of the type of government, citizens' access to the written word may be seen as a threat. We can see this not only in autocratic governments' attempts to control access to and use of the internet but also in democratic governments' unease regarding unmonitored popular power on social media.

A simple example of the different orientations toward written texts is the different ways that information is conveyed to people in their roles as citizens, students, patients or consumers. In many countries today, expectations of individual responsibility mean that face-to-face encounters are increasingly replaced by online services in which written language is used. The more virtual and less face-to-face that services and collaborations become, the more difficult it is to manage them without literacy. This highlights the urgent need for migrant adults to gain digital literacy skills from the start in addition to more traditional literacy. Not only second language speakers but also many others (e.g. low educated, disabled or elderly people) may need support in appropriating skills that are widely expected but have only recently become part of literacy courses.

2.4 The Role of Interaction in Second Language Development

There is much research on the development of a second or additional language as a socially embedded, interactive process regardless of culture or education. When it comes to adult migrants, oral proficiency in their new language will be gained in environments where the language is used by both native and NON-NATIVE SPEAKERS in the surrounding community. The role of language instruction might be seen simply as additional support to speed up the natural learning process that is taking place primarily outside the classroom, that of SECOND LANGUAGE LEARNING as distinguished from FOREIGN LANGUAGE LEARNING. Educators commonly distinguish 'second language learning' and 'foreign language learning'. We use the former term to describe the situation in which migrants find themselves, learning an additional language in a place where it is spoken, and the latter to refer to learning that does not take place in locations where the language is commonly spoken (e.g. Spanish learned in Finland) but rather in formal learning environments (language courses) and quite often without any regular opportunities to use the language outside the classroom, in daily life.

2.4.1 Interaction inside the classroom

A layperson's view of learning a new language may focus on memorization of new words, that one first has to memorize a considerable number of words, master the grammar and then start to use the language in social interaction. And, indeed, for older learners in foreign language classrooms, learning vocabulary and accurate grammar are commonly prioritized over oral FLUENCY and creative self-expression. Often beginners start picking up MULTI-WORD CHUNKS along with single words, which helps to build their communication repertoire, vocabulary base and linguistic repertoire, a process emphasized in the USAGE-BASED THEORY OF SECOND LANGUAGE DEVELOPMENT (Eskildsen, 2009; see Chapter 4, vocabulary, and Chapter 5, morphosyntax, in this volume, for a more extensive discussion of this topic).

Social interaction is also highlighted under the view of learning a new language as a collaborative process, which involves receiving timely support from those who already know the language. The concept of SCAFFOLDING refers to such support. In a Vygotskian, SOCIOCULTURAL THEORY of second language development, any new learning activity involves the individual's ZONE OF PROXIMAL DEVELOPMENT (Vygotsky, 1978), the area between activities that the individual is able to tackle independently and those for which the individual is supported by other, more proficient individuals and native speakers of the language, in and outside the classroom (see, e.g. Ohta, 2013). The individual's need for scaffolding for a particular activity is temporary: As soon as he or she can cope independently, there is no longer a need for support, at least at that step.

This sort of collaborative linguistic support is potentially available in any communication situation in the form of clarifications, clarification requests, repetitions and co-constructed utterances where, for example, the learner's gaps in vocabulary knowledge can be filled by the conversation partner. The Finnish example below illustrates this. Pronunciation and morphology (inflection of the Finnish verb *lukea*, 'to read', in first and second person singular) are being negotiated by a learner (NNS) and a native speaker (NS) in an extra-classroom context. The topic is whether or not the learner reads the Finnish subtitles of English-speaking TV programs (Suni, 2008: 176). In the CHILDES/CHAT-transcription below, pauses are marked by '#', interrupted turns (the other speaker interrupts the current speaker) are marked by '+...' and their uptakes (the speaker resumes speaking after the interruption) are marked by '+,' (see MacWhinney, 2000).

NS: *sinä luet niitä kuitenkin?*
you read them anyway?

NNS: *joo # now [@english] # mina # nyt*
yeah #now # I # now
mina en voi ää # luule # luul- luuse luu- +...
I can't erm # 'luule' # 'luul- luuse luu-' +...

NS: *luet.*
you read.

NNS: +, *lukea # joo*
+, to read # yeah

NNS: *lukea on lu- mina luen luen # vähän*
to read is 'lu-' I I read I read # a little

NS: *joo*
yeah

Repetitions and modifications by conversation partners such as teachers and tutors during interaction in the classroom are such natural phenomena that we hardly notice them. They are not only among the features of interaction that occurs in the classroom, but they also occur in informal learning environments, where learners may spend more time using their new language than in the classroom (Suni, 2008). The extent of this seems to be reduced for those who are more fluent and relates to power relations in a given situation (Kurhila, 2006; Lilja, 2010; Suni, 2008). Moreover, interactions may be similar regardless of the context, as illustrated by the example above. Although the interaction did not occur in a classroom, the same gap filling can be observed as in a classroom where this is prompted by tasks to consciously elicit such negotiations that lead to filling the gaps. It has been observed that more fluent learners, in particular, may not experience such overt negotiations of meaning or repair sequences in naturally occurring interactions outside the classroom.

Every teacher or tutor knows that learners, as individuals with their own learning history, level of knowledge, needs and goals do not just learn what is taught. (For elaboration on this with respect to the acquisition of morphosyntax, see Chapter 5.) Learning takes time, there are many stages on the way toward mastery, and learners often learn other things rather than what the teacher or tutor is expecting at a given time. This can mean that in the same classroom learning situation, individuals pick up different things. The concept of AFFORDANCE (van Lier, 2000) is useful for understanding what happens. People naturally seek opportunities to act, for example to learn something, and what they notice and pay attention to depends on their own orientation and current needs. What they find worthwhile becomes an affordance, a learning opportunity, for them.

Let's consider another example from Finland, this time from the classroom. After a grammar-centered lesson, one of the students came to thank the teacher, one of the chapter authors. 'Thank you so much - this was so useful!' But instead of thanking the teacher for what was focused on in the lesson, she said: 'Now I finally learned what *no niin* (here a transitional phrase, 'well') means in Finnish and what it is used for. That's the phrase you use to open a new topic when explaining something!' As teachers, we are happy with such feedback when we realize that our job is to follow the learning path of each individual student and support them in what they are currently learning rather than expecting them to learn what they are not yet ready for. It is easiest to learn what we have naturally noticed at some level and then, as a result, want to figure out. The teacher or tutor can help.

2.4.2 Interaction outside the classroom

Adult migrants are often unaware that much of their language learning is occurring or can occur outside the classroom. One of the key roles of the teacher or tutor is to provide tools for learning in the wider world and help learners to recognize the affordances that are available to them. Many learners need help with figuring out how to get involved in interactions in their new language and how to observe the linguistic and other symbols in their daily environment that they can pick up and use. Promoting interaction outside the classroom – in the wild – is a crucial part of beginners' second language learning (Lilja & Piirainen-Marsh, 2018; Wagner, 2015). Teachers and tutors can show learners how to locate and participate in real-life situations where learning opportunities exist: where to go, what to observe and how to initiate and maintain interaction.

Unfortunately, there are sometimes few opportunities for target-language interaction for migrant adults. Mothers who are home caring for their children often have few contacts in the new language, and their language and literacy class may be the primary environment in which they use it. These adults need specifically targeted support in starting to use the new language actively in their daily lives (Intke-Hernandez, 2015). This includes grassroots campaigns such as *Puhu minulle suomea*, 'Speak Finnish to me', which have arisen to raise awareness among English-speaking Finns to avoid switching from Finnish to English when speaking to migrants who know some English too.

There are also examples of good practice by international projects to promote learning outside the classroom. 'Language learning in the wild' is one of these initiatives. For example, some cafes in the countries involved in this project are committed to taking time to serve their customers in the new language, and various mobile technology apps that help to create or locate learning opportunities in daily life are being developed (Lilja & Piirainen-Marsh, 2018; Wagner, 2015).

2.4.3 Other views of adults developing language

Some researchers have suggested that, for adults, learning a new language only takes place when the learner has a genuine need for using the language (Elmeroth, 2003). However, according to Krashen (1998), having such a need is not enough. Learning a new language also requires plentiful input of the language that the learner understands (COMPREHENSIBLE INPUT), which is most likely to be comprehensible and useful if it is provided in real-life situations that the learner is familiar with. Moreover, the interactionist view of language acquisition says that the learner has to encounter language in interactional situations to receive such input (see, e.g. Gass & Varonis, 1994; Long, 1985). The classroom is often the primary and, unfortunately, sometimes the only context in which adult migrants encounter speakers of the TARGET LANGUAGE and have a chance to interact with them. However, Elmeroth (2003), a Swedish researcher, emphasizes the importance of language contact with native speakers beyond their teachers. This echoes the emphasis that Canadian researcher Norton Peirce (1995) puts on the role of contact between migrants and native speakers in the learning process. Such contact also has psychological effects: When learners have contact with native speakers of the target language, their motivation to learn the language increases, as well as their willingness to integrate into their new country. As their social exclusion begins to decrease, opportunities for interaction with native speakers expand exponentially.

Krashen's concept of input is now often replaced by the concept of 'affordance' (van Lier, 2000) to highlight the active role of the learner in noticing and utilizing relevant linguistic material available in the environment. This active role explains why people typically tend to pick up such items and expressions that they find relevant for themselves in a particular situation, as is highlighted in the example above of *no niin* 'well', which was not the teacher's emphasis in the class in which it was learned. At the same time, the concept of 'native' is also commonly challenged where no one is seen to master 'the whole language', and nativeness is not seen to define one's access to and ownership of a language anymore. Not only native speakers but also second language learners can perceive themselves as real speakers and owners of their new language (Dufva *et al.*, 2011; Ruuska, 2016).

2.5 Literacy Development in Adults

For children, literacy skills in their native language are not learned spontaneously like oral skills are. Rather, children require explicit instruction, practice and learning through experience. Reading and writing skills in one's native language can be used to acquire literacy in a second (L2) or additional language, especially when the writing system is the same and the orthographies of the languages are similar (e.g. Grabe & Stoller, 2011). However, according to Alderson (2005), in the development of L2 reading skills, a learner's oral proficiency in that language is even more important than their reading proficiency in their native language (see also Chapter 5). This stems from the fact that the oral language is what the written form is based on, in various ways (see, e.g. Linell, 2005). (See Chapter 3 for more discussion of these ideas.)

Oral L2 skills are the basis for written L2 skills: It is not possible to learn to read and write in a new language without some morphosyntactic competence and knowledge of vocabulary in the language (see Chapter 5). It is also important to recognize the purposes for which learners need reading and writing skills inside and especially outside the classroom and the level of those skills sufficient to meet those needs. As pointed out above, learners differ in reasons for gaining literacy in a new language and diverge from the expectations of teachers and tutors in post-industrialized, middle-class communities. If learners have some first language literacy, these reasons may also differ from those of their classmates (see, e.g. Grabe & Kaplan, 1996).

Another example from Finland comes from Tammelin-Laine (2014), who conducted a LONGITUDINAL STUDY of the process of learning Finnish by five migrant women (see also Tammelin-Laine & Martin, 2015). This is an important study, because the Finnish spelling system is the most regular of ROMAN ALPHABET SPELLING SYSTEMS, and children learn to read rapidly. Migrant adults can be expected to learn to read in Finnish more quickly than in the less regular spelling systems of some languages, such as Danish, English and French. Finnish, however, has a highly complex system of suffixation on nouns and verbs, and development of linguistic competence can be expected to be slower. At the beginning of data collection, the participants had no literacy skills in any language and very low oral skills in Finnish. Tammelin-Laine observed the five women in a literacy training program of approximately 10 months. Her data consist of audio recordings, field notes, oral and written tests conducted for the study and written language tests organized by the two adult education centers where she collected her data. She also compared these results with those from educated migrant learners. Tammelin-Laine's aims were to (a) describe and explore the development of learners' Finnish language skills (oral and written) during the observation period; and (b) explore the possible relationships between the development of these skills.

She found some important differences between educated and low-educated learners. For the latter, during the ten months she studied them in the program, none of them achieved FUNCTIONAL READING SKILLS, and their oral skills developed very slowly in comparison to educated learners. However, there was a relationship between the development of reading skills and oral skills: The most fluent readers had the best oral skills, particularly in RECEPTIVE VOCABULARY for nouns and PRODUCTIVE VOCABULARY for verbs, and they produced more complex INTERROGATIVE UTTERANCES. For all learners, oral skills developed the fastest, followed by reading skills and then writing skills.

2.6 The Role of Literacy in Various Aspects of Life

As pointed out above, in post-industrialized societies, various reading and writing skills among adults are taken for granted. Without these skills, it is difficult to manage everyday life and live as a full, active member of the community and the wider society. These skills are, however, not all equally necessary or highly valued in all societies of the world. The values placed on literacy skills will always define what is expected of adults (Grabe & Stoller, 2011). In this section, we describe the various arenas in the countries in which migrant adults now live where they are expected to be literate, and why.

2.6.1 Literacy as a parent

Adults are expected to be able to take care of themselves and their children in all aspects of their lives. In post-industrialized societies, as a parent or simply as an older member of the community, this includes ensuring that children have the ability to read and write. The Organization for Economic Cooperation and Development (OECD, 2000), formed by 35 countries, defines literacy skills as 'the ability to understand

and employ printed information in daily activities, at home, at work, and in the community – to achieve one's goals and to develop one's knowledge and potential' (2000: x).

Migrant adults require oral language proficiency, literacy, and numeracy in the target language to support their children's schooling. Research supports this conclusion. In a study of migrant mothers and their children in Finland, Honko (2013) found a strong positive correlation between mothers' oral skills in Finnish and children's skills during the early school years. Honko also noted the need for parents to have literacy skills to keep in touch with day care providers and schools and to write short messages, including in online interactions.

2.6.2 Literacy at work

In many countries, unemployment of migrants is two to three times higher than that of non-migrants (e.g. OECD, 2019), a rate that is certainly due to inadequate oral language and literacy skills. In the service sector, there are some typical low-skilled entry-level jobs that provide work opportunities for NEWCOMERS with limited language proficiency. Cleaning work is the most common of these so-called 3D JOBS = dirty, dangerous and demanding, as well as dead end (relevant for well-educated, literate migrants who also hold them; Strömmer, 2017). Moreover, they require more literacy skills than assumed. Cleaning involves use of tools and equipment as well as a range of cleaning agents. Equipment and cleaning agents come with printed instructions or entire user manuals, which include not only written text but also symbols, numbers, abbreviations and strategic placement of crucial information. These instructions may now be provided online and even through mobile phone applications. If we unpack the 3D, it is clear that cleaning may be dangerous for someone without literacy, and the demands are greater than we might assume (Stömmer, 2017).

These 3D jobs may also be dead end in their lack of affordances for the development of oral skills. Research by Strömmer (2017) illustrates this. Data were ETHNOGRAPHIC, collected in the cleaning sector in Finland. Her findings show the pattern found in post-industrialized countries around the world: Those who work in this sector are often isolated, and if migrants, this means their opportunities for interaction in the target language in the workplace are infrequent. This is not difficult to imagine; cleaners often work alone in empty premises, and they may be invisible to those occupying those spaces. Teachers and tutors can consider how employers can play an important role in fostering interaction and enabling language learning to take place by pairing migrant and non-migrant cleaners, offering the migrants shifts where there is customer contact, raising customer awareness of the value of positive interactions with cleaners and involving them in other ways in the work community.

Employment in the catering sector, for migrants most commonly in ethnic restaurants, is another typical entry-level job. While jobs without customer contact will not require high levels of oral proficiency in the new language, literacy skills are needed there. To begin within the European Union, all employees in cafes, restaurants, institutional kitchens, food stores and food factories must have a Hygiene Passport if they handle unpackaged or perishable foods, including milk, meat and fish. In Finland, literacy either in Finnish or in any other language used in the hygiene system is needed to pass the test, and there are easy-reading materials available for migrants with limited literacy who are preparing for the test (available in more than 20 languages: http://www03.edu.fi/oppimateriaalit/ruokaahygieenisesti/app/).

Pennycook and Otsuji (2015) have shown that in urban environments, such work communities quickly create unique multilingual practices and that the many languages spoken in the kitchen are not necessarily the same as those spoken with customers. (See also the discussion in Chapter 6 of TRANSLANGUAGING.) Moreover, literacy in not one but several languages may be needed in restaurants. Restaurant work may, therefore, offer considerably more opportunities for linguistic interaction than cleaning work, but this might not always be in the target language. There are many anecdotes about migrants to a given country learning the languages of other migrants at impressive levels.

In many countries, including the Nordic countries, so-called INTEGRATION TRAINING is provided for migrant adults. In Finland, this is provided for all unemployed migrants, typically for one year (see, e.g. Finnish National Board of Education, 2012). The focus is on knowledge of the language and surrounding society. In many countries, too, language and literacy are seen as best supported in the workplace. Strömmer's (2017) study in Finland, discussed above, and Sandwall's (2013) extensive CASE STUDY of work placements in Sweden show, however, that for certain types of work, interaction time with speakers of the new language can be limited. In Sandwall's study, this was only a few minutes per day. In the students' eyes, the 'school world' and the 'work placement world' remained as two separate, completely different worlds.

Finally, there is the agricultural sector, which relies heavily on migrant adults on both an ongoing and seasonal basis. It has a reputation as simple, physical work, where literacy has a minimal role. However, there are expectations for higher levels of literacy as soon as the tasks get more complex. One example of this is a recent attempt in Italy to support migrants with suitable backgrounds and experience in becoming entrepreneurs in agriculture (Del Percio, 2016, 2017). What created the primary barrier to entrepreneurship for them were insufficient literacy skills.

The above discussion points to the need when designing education models to pay attention to the tight interconnectedness of language and literacy instruction and work life practice. This means focusing on raising the awareness of learners of the relevant issues and uses of authentic work life experiences in the classroom, along with providing effective tutoring or mentoring practices at the workplace itself. For example, authentic recordings and documents brought by the students from their work placements could be reflected on together in the classroom.

2.7 Development of Multiliteracies

In the 21st century, literacy goes beyond reading printed text, and migrant adults must be prepared to cope with the many additional forms of what are now referred to as 'literacies'. The idea of MULTILITERACIES (e.g. Cope & Kalantzis, 2000) brings together two aspects of literacy: on the one hand, increasingly culturally diverse and multilingual communities, where there is frequent parallel use of different languages in written form (as covered in Chapter 6) and, on the other hand, new ways of communicating in technologically rich environments. The term NEW LITERACIES (Lankshear & Knobel, 2003) is also used to highlight the need to update the traditional definition of literacy that refers to how written texts are produced and how we interact with them. LINEAR TEXT is, for example, no longer the norm, with the internet and mobile technologies as the drivers of continuous evolution of new forms of communication and interaction. Linear text is often shorter and mixed with unconventional text (using abbreviations and emojis), which on websites is organized under bars and behind links, and images, sound and video elements are embedded in numerous ways and may involve multiple authors or contributors. For teachers and tutors, there is a need to guide learners in following their logic and dealing with hierarchies that differ from linearly organized printed or handwritten single-authored materials traditionally used in teaching.

Real-time communication in technologically rich environments is not only a practice of the younger generation, but families and social networks across generations and space increasingly communicate virtually (Lahikainen *et al.*, 2017), including during migration to a new country (Alencar *et al.*, 2018). Written or multimodal communication has come to be perceived as more flexible than face-to-face interaction or phone calls. Transnational relations depend on mobile technologies, and this has for a long time been, and still is, equally true for migrants (see, e.g. Alencar *et al.*, 2018; Tarnanen *et al.*, 2009). Including literacies for and through new technologies is, thus, both a realistic and a necessary part of literacy instruction.

How we write is changing as much as how we read (Brandt, 2009), and technological developments have resulted in handwriting becoming increasingly uncommon. In many countries, the proficient use of a keyboard or a touch screen is seen as a more important part of literacy skills than cursive handwriting. Therefore, this sort of handwriting is no longer taught in many schools. Printing by hand remains part of the curriculum. Such reforms have triggered public debate but have also led to considerable awareness raising. Replacing handwriting with producing texts by keyboard is a sign of a major change in the textual world. The negative consequences are intergenerational gaps in the means of written self-expression in a society. Yet, for young children, as well as for second language learners unfamiliar with the Roman alphabet, it is a relief to have one less system to figure out.

How might teachers and tutors of migrant adults deal with multiliteracies? Taking Finland as an example, the Finnish Core Curriculum for Basic Education (Finnish National Board of Education, 2014), for children's education, can be borrowed when considering how to support migrant adults. These descriptions, some of which are directly relevant to multiliteracies, are given for grades 1–2, when pupils are 7–8 years old. The curriculum also includes multi-sensory approaches, basic literacy and numeracy fluency. Use of these approaches and focus increases over time and use, production and enjoyment of age-specific texts:

- Text refers to any information expressed by using verbal, visual, auditory, numeric and kinesthetic symbol systems or their combinations.
- Multiliterate pupils can interpret, produce and evaluate different age-specific texts.
- All senses and holistic and phenomenon-based pedagogical approaches are in use.
- Pupils are encouraged to use and produce different texts, enjoy them and express themselves through them.
- Fluency in basic literacy and everyday numeracy skills develops over time.
- The development of visual literacy is supported: Pupils are guided to use visual means of self-expression and observe the visual means of influencing others in their social environment.

Approaching the textual and visual world from different angles (which includes providing space for self-expression and critical thinking) is less common among those who work with migrant adults (see, e.g. Tammelin-Laine, 2014). Given how text is used, as described above, to enable these learners to deal with multiliteracies in the 21st century, it is essential to introduce this from the very start.

2.8 Empowerment Through Critical Literacy

Functional vs. CRITICAL LITERACY has been mentioned above, and we now look at the latter in more depth. Relevant to critical literacy are the use of information technology and the presence of social media to make oneself visible and heard and to participate effectively in society (Galloway, 2017). There are numerous forums for this, and it is possible to share what one writes with a potentially infinite number of readers. There are different, and often new, practices and norms for writing in various environments and for different groups of readers, and managing these can be complicated for migrant adults. Yet from the empowerment or emancipation point of view, it is important for teachers and tutors to prepare even adults with limited literacy to recognize the existence and availability of various types of information sharing. Discussions of equality and human rights, for example, now often take place in virtual environments. Without the skills to access and participate in these forums, the migrant adult will remain at the margins of society, without a voice and without power.

Critical literacy refers to the emancipatory or transformative potential of literacy described above: Literacy enables us to understand and protect our rights (Freire & Macedo, 1987; Giroux, 1993). Critical literacy also refers to the skills to evaluate which ideas in the textual world are reliable and which are not. Attaining this level of skill is a particular challenge for young children learning to read, because they have less life experience and are cognitively less sophisticated. However, despite having little or no formal education, adults can think critically about their own lives, and their limited literacy need not be a barrier to helping them develop critical and functional literacy in parallel.

2.8.1 Promoting agency and preventing marginalization through literacy

Lack of literacy skills may be one factor in marginalization of individuals or groups. Problems with literacy are widely seen in prison populations; e.g. in the United Kingdom, a 2015 report showed that 46% of those entering the prison system had literacy skills no higher than those expected of an 11-year-old; in the general adult population in the United Kingdom, only 15% display this level of literacy skills (Creese, 2016). In the *Learning Basic Skills While Serving Time* project, implemented by Raude and Winsnes (2010), first in one Norwegian prison and then replicated in many others in that country, assignments related to low-skilled prisoners' daily work and routines (e.g. in the prison kitchen) were designed to promote numeracy and literacy development. During a four-month course, each inmate received a computer with numeracy and literacy learning programs and specific programs for text processing and numerical functions for individual use. The course resulted in a remarkable increase in their literacy and numeracy skills, developed their skills in applying for jobs, and boosted their confidence and self-esteem (Raude & Winsnes, 2010). In many countries, instruction in the majority language of the country is now provided for those inmates who are not fluent speakers of the language. This is designed to promote their wellbeing and facilitate their integration into the surrounding society when they are no longer imprisoned. For example, in Finland, Finnish as a second language instruction is available as part of the general educational program in most prisons. According to an extensive international development project, *RiUscire*, the same kinds of educational activities are being established throughout Europe (http://riuscire.org).

2.8.2 Promoting family engagement through literacy

Another example of fostering agency among migrants comes from the town of Linköping, Sweden. The *Family Learning – Learning Together* project (Länstyrelsen Östergötland, 2016) has 30 courses for migrant parents with limited literacy and their three- to ten-year-old children to collaboratively promote their development of literacy and numeracy. An important aim of the project is to lead and support the parents to recognize their role in society in supporting their children's learning and schooling. Compatriots who are already well established in Swedish society function as role models and tutors. These tutors not only typically have pedagogical experience, but they must also have a good knowledge of Swedish society and the language, and the project provides them with materials and regular training sessions by more qualified staff. Through the project, parents have become more confident within and outside the family as they have improved their basic skills. Various family reading programs have been launched in many countries, and the results are encouraging (see, e.g. Intke-Hernandéz, 2015).

2.9 International Surveys of Adult Literacy

2.9.1 Migrants in PIAAC and SAILS assessments

We now return to PISA, the international survey mentioned at the start of this chapter, to focus on its adult education counterparts. This is the extensive international Program for the International Assessment of Adult Competencies (PIAAC) survey on adult skills, also administered in Organization for Economic Cooperation and Development (OECD) countries. It uses the following definition of literacy (see http://www.oecd.org/skills/piaac/), given at the start of this chapter, which we repeat here: 'the ability to understand and employ printed information in daily activities, at home, at work and in the community – to achieve one's goals, and to develop one's knowledge and potential' (OECD, 2000: x). In the PIAAC survey conducted in 2011–2012, native-speaking Finnish adults were ranked highly in literacy, just after Japan. Two thirds of adults in Finland were rated as either 'good' or 'excellent' readers, far above the average of 50% for the rest of the OECD countries surveyed. This hides the fact that there are also adults with limited literacy in Finland: 11% of all 16- to 65-year-olds have very poor skills in literacy (Malin *et al.*, 2013; Mussett, 2015).

The International Adult Literacy Survey (IALS) and Second International Adult Literacy Survey (SIALS) were 1990s surveys upon which PIAAC has been building. IALS assessed three domains of literacy during two survey rounds (1994–1998 and 1997–2000): prose literacy, document literacy and quantitative literacy (numeracy). The survey used a scale with five performance levels, listed below. The SIALS scale acknowledges the cognitive requirements of reading activities along with the literacy demands of today's knowledge-based society and refers to the need for lifelong learning.

> *Level 1:* Mastery of basic, mechanical reading skills. The skills are sufficient for identifying pieces of information, understanding easy texts literally and dealing with simple arithmetic operations.
>
> *Level 2:* Understanding of the main content of the text and searching for, combining and comparing textual information.
>
> *Level 3:* Ability to cope with the literacy requirements of the society; interpreting textual content in context and making inferences about conditions, reasons and consequences; performing various arithmetic operations.
>
> *Levels 4–5:* Interpreting, selecting and critically evaluating different types of textual information and performing arithmetic operations in problem solving.

In the Nordic countries overall, the SIALS survey showed that all adults were above the international average, and the percentage of adults at the lowest level was very small. In Finland, the survey showed that 67% of adults had reached level 3 or higher, and 20% had reached the highest level. Even those adults whose skills were low considered their literacy skills as adequate. Length of formal education and parental educational background correlated with adults' literacy levels in all countries in which the survey was conducted. This shows what other large-scale and case studies have shown: Literacy skills are a cross-generational concern. Therefore, promotion of adult literacy plays an important role not only in the achievements of the next generation but also in inter-generational relations. This entails taking seriously literacy across generations in migrants' own languages (see Chapter 6 for a discussion of this issue). Those who fund programs for adults learning basic skills should not dismiss migrant adults with little or no formal schooling who stay home to care for their children and who may never enter the world of work and thus directly contribute to the economy of the country. Their literacy matters to their children's future.

In Finland, PIAAC results showed that adults' performance was roughly similar to the earlier SIALS survey and that general background factors such as age and parental education level were again relevant to respondents' educational choices and interest in developing literacy. As a result of migration flows over the past decade, there were more migrant participants in the PIAAC than in the SIALS, and the results showed that five years in a new country serves as a kind of boundary: Those migrants who had lived five years or more in Finland out-performed the others. However, despite Finland's remarkable overall results in these surveys, the migrant adults in Finland performed similarly to those in other countries, again emphasizing the commonalities across countries in which these migrant adults resettle. Moreover, when compared to non-migrant adults, the gap in basic or foundational skills turned out to be greater in Finland than in most other countries; 50% of first-generation migrants had a maximum of level 2 skills in literacy and numeracy (Musset, 2015: 22). In addition, only half of all adults with low skill levels were employed, and one third were inactive and not involved in an education program. Limited literacy and numeracy skills, thus, raise the risk of unemployment.

2.9.2 Young migrants in PISA surveys

Practitioners who work with migrant adults can benefit by becoming aware of findings about secondary school literacy development in their own country and beyond. As we will see below, there is a gap in literacy and numeracy skills for secondary school students, which varies between the majority language native-speaking students and those with migrant backgrounds; this is relevant to issues discussed in Chapter 6, on bilingualism and multilingualism. There are also differences across countries, which likely reflect the provisions for education of secondary school migrants and also the languages that these pupils speak in a given country.

As noted earlier in this chapter, the Program for International Student Assessment (PISA) is a triennial OECD survey that compares the numeracy and literacy skills and knowledge of 15-year-olds in 70 countries. While Finland has been ranked at the top since 2001, does this apply to migrant students? PISA reveals that secondary school migrant students who share a common country of origin and, therefore, many cultural similarities, perform very differently across the countries in which they resettle. There is strong evidence that the education systems differ sufficiently across countries to account for these differences. Intriguingly, the difference in performance between migrant students and non-migrant students of similar socio-economic status is smaller in countries with large migrant populations where migrant students are as diverse in socio-economic status as other students (e.g. Australia, Canada and the United States). In countries such as Finland, with a relatively small proportion of migrant students and with larger variation in the socio-economic status among migrants than among native-born students, there are much larger differences in PISA performance (OECD, 2013). In Finland, the survey showed that first- and second-generation migrant secondary school students lagged about two years behind their non-migrant peers, with a greater proportion of first-generation students not reaching the minimum level of mathematical proficiency. Those who had arrived in their early school years or had migrated from countries geographically closer to Finland (and thus with similar educational systems) performed better than others. Proficiency in the language of instruction (either Finnish or Swedish in Finland) was found to be a key factor. The study also suggests that migrant students need support for both their first language and the language of instruction in school, as both are fundamental for their learning (Harju-Luukkainen *et al.*, 2014; see also Chapter 6).

In the Finnish education system, a one-year preparatory instruction with a focus on Finnish (or Swedish) as a second language is mostly available for migrant students entering preschool (age six) or basic education (grades 1–9). This is followed by regular second language classes and a gradual transition to mainstream Finnish (or Swedish) language classes during the later school years. Optional mother tongue instruction is available in any language (for two hours per week, given a minimum group size of four students) if the municipality is committed to providing such instruction and able to hire a competent teacher. A state subsidy is available for arranging such instruction.

It is noteworthy that across the countries surveyed with PISA, in comparison to their non-migrant peers, students with migrant backgrounds had more positive attitudes toward school, a stronger sense of belonging to school and a more positive perception of teacher–student relations. These positive findings do not mean that performance gaps are bridged. What most of the low-performing migrant secondary school students (65% in the first generation and 57% in the second generation) lack at home are books. In PISA and some other international surveys, the number of books (in any language) available at home is used as an indicator of cultural capital, the valuing of literary in homes. In low-performing groups, it is thus common to find that there are few if any books in the home. Those migrant students who performed well typically had lots of books (over 200) at home, as did the high-performing non-migrant students (Harju-Luukkainen *et al.*, 2014). There is, however, compelling evidence that the community-level availability of books can compensate for absence of books in the home if students can be encouraged to develop the habit of reading for pleasure (Neuman & Celano, 2001; Sonnenschein & Schmidt, 2000). It is also to be noted that the increasing preference for online reading will make the number of printed books a less reliable factor in the future: People may read a lot without having books at home.

2.10 Literacy Education for Migrant Adults: The Case of Finland

We end this chapter with a snapshot of how migrant adults are educationally provided for in the country which has been our focus. Since the late 1980s, immigration flows have brought an increasing number of migrants with limited education and literacy to Finland who are beyond the age of compulsory schooling. In response, literacy programs have been developed to meet their needs. Finland has been actively seeking to learn from good educational practices developed in countries with longer histories of migration, but linguistic and other differences have meant that pedagogical practices have been adapted. In 2012, a national curriculum for literacy education for adult IMMIGRANTS was launched by the Finnish National Board of Education (2012: 27, currently being revised). It lists the following types of literacy when setting goals for basic literacy education: mechanical literacy, basic reading skills, textual skills and image literacy. In addition to reading and writing, this covers oral language skills and numeracy. The curriculum states that after training for approximately ten months, the student should be able to

- combine sounds/letters into SYLLABLES and words; break a familiar word into syllables and sounds/letters; make use of syllable division to read a new word (mechanical literacy);
- read a short text in addition to individual words and sentences (basic reading skills);
- identify specific information in a simple text, provided that they can reread it as required (textual skills);
- understand from a picture what it represents and refers to in reality (visual literacy).

For a number of years, most of the adults who need basic education in Finland have had a migrant background, and the goal of the reforms implemented in 2017–2018 has been to make the instructional path for migrant adults more flexible and relevant by combining literacy training with courses of integration training for Adult Basic Education (ABE). In the updated curriculum for ABE (Finnish National Agency for Education, 2019b), the duration of the literacy phase (comparable to grades 1–2, where the pupils are seven to eight years old) is approximately six months. However, since this phase includes courses on other topics, such as mathematics, the environment, natural history and student counselling and working life skills, the total length of actual literacy training is only three months. After the literacy phase, students are expected to have sufficient skills and knowledge to continue in classes leading to an ABE (comparable with grades 3–6). If they cannot reach the goals set in the curriculum, their learning path may continue at other places (e.g. voluntary organizations/non-governmental organizations, NGOs).

The literacy phase is designed especially for young adults who have realistic opportunities to graduate from an ABE program and need it for further studies; e.g. vocational studies. Instead of ABE, some learners will be guided to literacy training organized by adult education centers, folk high schools, summer universities or study centers (i.e. institutions organizing what is referred to as LIBERAL ADULT EDUCATION). There are no guidelines for the duration or extent of this kind of training, but the contents are expected to be based on curriculum guidelines issued in 2017 by the Finnish National Agency for Education. This type of literacy training is designed primarily for stay-at-home parents, migrants with special needs and others who cannot study full time because of a variety of reasons (Finnish National Agency for Education, 2019a).

2.11 Conclusion

In this chapter, we have discussed the roles of various social contexts for language and literacy development and the value of literacy in different societies and historical periods. Literacy development has been introduced as a socially driven, empowering process through which adult migrants can play an active role in their daily life in the new society and take on civic responsibilities.

To learn oral and written skills in a new language, migrant adults need opportunities to engage in interactional situations both inside and outside the classroom. In addition, the development of literacy skills requires time and effort from adults who are expected to learn oral and written skills at the same time, often with limited study skills and experiences with formal learning. In modern adult literacy education, it is important to introduce the idea of multiliteracies from the start and for the teacher or tutor and ultimately the learner to see literacy as a multimodal, versatile set of skills and not only as reading and writing on paper, as it has been understood in the past. To meet the literacy needs of adults living in the modern information society, the teacher or tutor has to give them the tools to cope with non-linear texts and visual and numerical information and to be able to move smoothly between spoken and written modalities and registers.

When adult literacy skills are supported, the whole family benefits. Literacy skills have an impact on each generation through better self-esteem and wider opportunities for further studies, employment and civic involvement, and they thus promote both individual and collective well-being.

3 Reading from a Psycholinguistic Perspective

Marcin Sosiński

3.1 Introduction

Investigation into the mental processes that adult migrants with little or no formal education follow during reading development remains limited, but there is a growing body of relevant work, which is discussed in this chapter. The discussion addresses reading, along with its teaching, from a PSYCHOLINGUISTIC point of view, covering the skills and knowledge associated with reading and how they are represented in the reader's mind. From a pedagogical point of view, Smyser (2016) broadly discriminates between SOCIAL-FOCUSED APPROACHES and SKILLS-FOCUSED APPROACHES. The former connects learning to students' experiences (as discussed in Chapter 2), and the latter focuses on the mechanical development of skills, including how they link to what is known as PHONOLOGICAL AWARENESS, and on pedagogical approaches to learning to read words and longer texts.

The large body of literature on reading reveals that attention is largely focused on children and on educated, literate learners of second and additional languages. Adults who are learning to read for the first time in their lives in a new language, which they are also learning to speak, are outside the realm of mainstream research. While research on adult migrants is increasing, the starting point has been studies of children and educated second language learners, whose theoretical basis allows us to draw some conclusions that can be applied to migrant adults.

Experts emphasize that reading is a complex phenomenon that combines different types of knowledge and skills (Grabe & Stoller, 2002; Hudson, 2007; Koda, 2005). Here, we pinpoint linguistic knowledge, lexical knowledge and phonological awareness as being important. In this sense, adult learners whose oral language acquisition may be at a low level are different from young children learning to read in the language they have been acquiring, but they also are similar to them, since they also have developed certain aspects of phonological awareness in their first language (Young-Scholten, 2015). The similarity with children is also observed in these learners' lower degree of metalinguistic reflection on language and in similar stages of reading development (Kurvers, 2007, 2015). Of relevance here is a study by Young-Scholten and Strom (2006), which concludes that there is no critical period in learning to read, even though it is a slower process for migrant adults with little or no formal schooling. (See also Condelli *et al.*, 2003; Filimban, 2019; Kurvers, 2007; Tammelin-Laine & Martin, 2015; Young-Scholten & Naeb, 2010).

This chapter is divided into the following sections: the reader's task; how writing systems and scripts vary and what this means for learners; how phonological and phonemic awareness underpin the ability to read; what we know from the research on early reading; teaching early reading to adults; and approaches tailored to boosting readers' fluency as they read for pleasure and develop text comprehension.

3.2 The Reader's Task

In the *Cambridge Dictionary*, reading is defined as 'the skill or activity of getting information from books'. Underlying this definition are independent but interrelated skills; for example, knowledge of the language, of the alphabet and of vocabulary, as well as the cultural and social contexts for learning to read including, importantly for LESLLA learners, the contexts of their own lives, as discussed in Chapter 2. Skills can be classified into **LOWER-LEVEL** or bottom-up skills (relating to the recognition of letters/**GRAPHEMES**) and **HIGHER-LEVEL** or **TOP-DOWN** skills (relating to the meanings of words in a text; Grabe, 2009; and the characteristics of written discourse, for example recognition of the aim of a text; Grabe & Stoller, 2002; Hudson, 2007). New readers have to develop and automatize the lower-level skills in order to apply the higher-level skills to be able to comprehend sentences and longer texts.

3.2.1 Lower-level skills

DECODING, also referred to as **WORD RECOGNITION**, takes place when the written (graphical) form of a word is recognized by the reader. The reader's success at decoding depends on phonological awareness, the reader's awareness that words are made up of sound units and of syllables and that syllables consist of sub-parts called **ONSETS** (the start of the syllable) and **RIMES** (the end of the syllable). In learning to read in languages that use the Roman alphabet, such as English and Spanish, word recognition also involves awareness of an even smaller subpart of words, **PHONEMES**. Phonemes are the smallest linguistic unit of meaning in terms of the characteristics of individual vowel and consonants. Linguists use a simple test to determine whether a consonant or vowel is a phoneme or whether it just demonstrates a speaker's varying pronunciation, influenced by other consonants or vowels. This test involves creating a **MINIMAL PAIR** by changing a single aspect of a consonant or vowel in one of the words in the pair to see whether it results in a different meaning. For example, in English, we know that /t/ and /d/ are *phonemes*, because the variation in vibration of our vowel cords, known as **VOICING**, distinguishes words that are otherwise exactly the same: 'tip' and 'dip'. However, when it comes to /t/, its pronunciation varies based on its phonological environment, and the surrounding vowels and consonants. These are variations that do not change word meaning. For example, when /t/ begins a word, we release a burst of air, as in 'tip'. When /t/ is followed by another consonant, there is no aspiration, as in 'trip' or 'twin'. However, in some languages (e.g. Korean; Thai) release of a burst of air changes the meaning of the word. For English speakers, even though our ears acoustically detect these different pronunciations of a /t/ at the start of a word, our minds process the phoneme at a more abstract level in terms of whether it distinguishes meaning. That phoneme is represented in spelling as <t> using this bracketing.

An individual's awareness of words, syllables, onsets, rimes and phonemes is referred to as phonological awareness, which is strongly connected to a beginning reader's ability to grasp the ALPHABETIC PRINCIPLE, the idea that a single letter (a grapheme) or a sequence of letters (a DIGRAPH or TRIGRAPH) corresponds to one phoneme.

3.2.2 Models of decoding

How exactly does decoding occur? What happens in the reader's mind? Four main models have been proposed. Under the PHONOLOGICAL ROUTE MODEL OF READING, (e.g. Katz & Frost, 1992), the reader analyses sequences of graphemes into the graphemes or grapheme combinations corresponding to a single phoneme. Next, the reader accesses the PHONOLOGY of the word by applying what is known as GRAPHEME-PHONEME CONVERSION, or correspondence, to assemble phonemes into a complete phonological representation of that word. That is, the reader decodes the word (Gillon, 2017).

The DUAL ROUTE MODEL (e.g. Coltheart, 1978; Ehri, 1992) recognizes that the spelling systems, or orthographies, of English and some other languages (e.g. Danish and French) contain irregularities. These are known as OPAQUE ORTHOGRAPHIES. The reader follows the phonological route for sounding out regularly spelled words and a VISUAL ROUTE by associating the ORTHOGRAPHIC REPRESENTATION of a word stored in memory as a whole with its meaning. This means that irregularly spelled words are learned by rote as SIGHT WORDS. Once the individual can read rapidly, the process for reading known words is largely visual and regularly spelled words are processed similarly to irregularly spelled words. Under the dual route model, learning to read is a longer process for languages such as English. One study of reading development showed that after one year of instruction, 98% of children learning to read in German, with its much more TRANSPARENT ORTHOGRAPHY, were accurate; while only 34% of children learning to read in English were (Seymour *et al.*, 2003).

Under the ANALOGY MODEL, the phonology of both regularly and irregularly spelled words is accessed through patterns stored in the reader's memory (Glushko, 1979; Marcel, 1980). For example, the reader recognizes a word he or she cannot yet read, such as <bake>, by making an analogy with a word that he or she can read, such as <cake>. This model may be more useful for readers who are more advanced and have developed MORPHOLOGICAL AWARENESS, the awareness that words include more than one unit of meaning, such as prefixes and suffixes, such as <prebake> and <baker> (Marsh *et al.*, 1981).

The CONNECTIONIST MODEL aims to explain the gradual formation of simple and complex representations through the repeated interaction of orthography, phonology and meaning during learning. Computer modeling is used to account for difficulties in processing and learning new words, particularly when these words do not fit patterns already learned (Seidenberg & McClelland, 1989).

3.2.3 Higher-level skills

The next step after individual words can be recognized/decoded is the processing of longer texts; for example, phrases, clauses, sentences and paragraphs. This requires drawing on syntax, the position of words in discourse and on the world knowledge of the reader. For example, when proficient readers read the sentence below and come across the word <cake>, reading it automatically evokes the concept of something that humans eat and enjoy.

> 'That piece of cake is being eaten by Mary'

Word order (syntax) along with our experience with and knowledge of the world mean that even if we cannot read and understand some of words or parts of words (e.g. in the sentence above <that piece of> and <being>), we would not jump to the conclusion that the sentence means 'The cake is eating Mary'.

For experienced readers, bottom-up word recognition is an effortless and subconscious process. Word recognition occurs rapidly, at four or five words per second, and results from continuous practice over a long period of time. When words are automatically recognized, the information retained for several seconds in WORKING MEMORY is not overloaded by painstaking decoding, and attention can be devoted to the entire sentence, to syntax, higher-level processing. If lower-level processing is too slow, this creates a bottleneck that impedes higher-level processing. The automation of lower-level processes is time consuming, and how long it takes depends on how regular the orthography is in the language. It also depends on the extent of the learner's vocabulary. (See Chapter 4 on vocabulary for discussion of the role of vocabulary knowledge in reading.)

Higher-level skills (Grabe, 2009; Grabe & Stoller, 2002: 25–30), which move readers beyond decoding, are those that result in comprehension of a text. These are sophisticated skills that are more available to the reader's conscious control than components of phonological awareness might be. When decoding becomes automatic, the reader is able to deploy the strategies listed below. Even first-time, beginning readers can use strategies such as the first three below and, with practice, will be able to use the last five, to start to be able to read critically:

(1) Noticing how written text differs from spoken text.
(2) Determining the aim of the text.
(3) Predicting the content of the text.
(4) Distinguishing main ideas from secondary ones.

(5) Identifying relationships between ideas.
(6) Interpreting the text.
(7) Figuring out the structure of a text.
(8) Recognizing how certain linguistic elements, such as pronouns and adverbs of time, explicitly connect text (known as COHESION).

3.2.4 More on bottom-up and top-down approaches to reading

Let's look more closely at these two different starting points in reading. As we have seen above, in a BOTTOM-UP APPROACH, the reader builds meaning step by step, from small units (words or smaller) to phrases, clauses, sentences, paragraphs and the whole text. In a top-down approach, the reader starts with expectations about the whole text and then checks those expectations with increasingly smaller units. Since skilled readers engage in both bottom-up and top-down processing, many specialists prefer to talk about an interactive approach to reading (Bernhardt, 2011; Kintsch, 1998; Lee, 1997; Nassaji, 2002; Stanovich, 1980). The integration of these processes is influenced by four factors: (1) the learner's linguistic competence; (2) similarity of the L1 LEXICON to the L2 lexicon; (3) transparency of the L2 spelling system; and (4) the learner's level of literacy in their home and other languages (Koda, 2005). We discuss these in turn, leaving the last two points for the next sections on writing systems and scripts, spelling systems, and how phonological and phonemic awareness underpin early reading.

(1) Linguistic competence

When monolingual children start learning to read, usually around ages four and five, they do so in a language in which they have acquired linguistic competence (syntax, morphology, phonology, vocabulary). The child's vocabulary, already substantial by this age, will continue to expand throughout the lifespan. Second language learners with no home or other language literacy skills are in the same position as young children except for one crucial difference: Their linguistic competence in the language in which they are learning to read is at a lower level and in some cases may be minimal when they start to learn to read. Literate, educated beginning learners of a new language can transfer their reading skills, and if the language uses the same writing system, they can start recognizing COGNATES and borrowed words to bootstrap their reading. For comprehension beyond words, a THRESHOLD LEVEL applies, and sufficient linguistic competence is required. (See in Chapter 2, discussion of the variable contributions of L2 linguistic competence and L1 literacy skills.)

Why would a non-literate beginning second language learner have little linguistic competence in a language when they start to learn to read in that language, the target language? There are various reasons for this. First, they may not work with speakers of the target language, and even if they do, there may be little interaction (see discussion in Chapter 2). Second, their family life, and extra-family socializing, may take place entirely in their home language. Lack of target language input slows down their acquisition of linguistic competence and, in turn, slows down development of literacy in their new language.

(2) Similar lexicons

Recognizing words common in the L1 and L2 when starting to read is helpful in reading, as it reduces working memory load and allows the reader to focus on other processes. The opportunity to recognize such words is connected to whether the L1 and L2 writing systems are similar. For example, although unrelated languages such as English and Swahili share no cognates, because both are written using the Roman alphabet, words borrowed from English may be recognized by new readers.

3.3 How Writing Systems and Scripts Vary and What This Means for Learners

For new readers of a language, some literacy in a home or other language and the use of the same alphabet for both languages facilitate their literacy development in the target language. Spelling varies in terms of regularity (shallow or transparent) or irregularity (deep or opaque). Regularity refers to a 1:1 relationship between graphemes and phonemes. As noted in Chapter 2, Finnish is at the transparent end of the spectrum, because the letters (graphemes) correspond to the sounds (phonemes). The orthography of English (and Danish and French) is opaque; although there are regularities, the relationship between some graphemes (and digraphs and trigraphs) and phonemes can be non-existent. This creates challenges for beginning readers, as we have pointed out above. We return to this further below. If the learner's writing system does not use the Roman alphabet and the target language does, this can also create challenges.

3.3.1 Writing systems and the history of writing

The invention of the Roman alphabet was late in the 6000-year history of writing, a brief period when compared to spoken language, which by traditional estimates has a 50,000-year history (Klein, 2000; Sampson, 1985) but now is considered by many as much older, maybe even as old as *homo sapiens* (roughly 250,000 years: Botha & Knight, 2009; Mellars *et al.*, 2007). Moreover, the origin of literacy is POLYCENTRIC, i.e. it emerged independently in different places, the most important of which were Mesoamerica, China and the Middle East, and seems to have emerged in response to the need for keeping track of trading exchanges in increasingly large and urban societies. In the old PROTO-WRITING systems, written PICTOGRAPHS represented meaning and were used for only a few SEMANTIC fields (names, accounts, calendars). Well-known examples are Egyptian hieroglyphics and Aztec writing.

Writing systems have evolved from these early systems. An early innovation was use of the REBUS PRINCIPLE, where two pictographs are combined to create new meanings. These early systems also began to draw on oral language and to use symbols to represent the spoken word. For the Aztecs, for example, such symbols were mainly used for place names, such as *Tochtepecan,* which uses the pictograms for 'rabbit' and 'mountain' to indicate how the place name is pronounced.

In thinking about the history of writing systems, there are two perspectives: EVOLUTIONIST and TYPOLOGICAL (DeFrancis, 1996; Gelb, 1963; Peres Rodrigues, 1999; Sampson, 1985; Stubbs, 1987). The evolutionist perspective holds that a writing system aims to be efficient and that alphabetic writing is most efficient. As an ideal system, it has spread widely. However, the reason for its spread likely has more to do with European imperialism and missionary work than with its efficiency. The typological perspective focuses simply on classifying systems and the linguistic units they represent. These include LOGOGRAPHIC and SYLLABARY SYSTEMS, similar to the older systems described above, both of which emerged early and in different places. An example of the former is Chinese HSING SHENG writing. Each character has two parts: a root that provides information about the meaning and a phonetic component that informs pronunciation. A character such as the first one below means 'horse'. This character is used as a root in a large WORD FAMILY, which includes words of which the original character is a part:

(1) Chinese writing

mǎ 'horse' *jià* 'drive/driver' *lúo* 'mule'

In *syllabaries*, each grapheme represents a syllable. Modern examples are the two KANA syllabaries used in Japanese: HIRAGANA, used for example for particles and verb endings; and KATAKANA, used for foreign words. This works well in a language such as Japanese because its syllables are simple, consisting of a single consonant and single vowel; there are no CONSONANT CLUSTERS. Moreover, the only consonant that a word can end in is a nasal, which is the only single phoneme which has its own grapheme. In Figures 3.1 and 3.2 below, the Roman alphabet versions, with spaces between the kana for clarity, show what the *kana* represent. (Note that <ch> in English is a digraph that represents a single consonant; it is not a consonant cluster.)

car	ku ru ma	くるま
good luck	ta chi yo mi	たちよみ

Figure 3.1 Hiragana script

email	me ru	メル
cake	ke ki	ケキ

Figure 3.2 Katakana script

When writing systems represent spoken language rather than concepts, the need arises in some languages to represent both consonants and vowels. The current Roman alphabet is a slightly modified version of its original, whose origins can be traced to a single occurrence, the Phoenician alphabet. When the Greeks adopted the Phoenician alphabet, they added graphemes to represent consonants and vowels separately due to the existence of consonant clusters, such as /kr/ as in the Greek-based word referring to time, <chronological>.

There are also writing systems that have features of a syllabary and an alphabet. These are efficient writing systems for languages that contain few consonant clusters. The term for this is ABUGIDA (from the Ge'ez language) or ALPHASYLLABARY. These include scripts in South Asia and Southeast Asia, Ethiopic, Canadian Aboriginal scripts, Arabic and Hebrew. An abugida varies in how and whether it represents vowels separately. In Arabic, graphemes represent long vowels, but optional diacritics above and below consonants represent short vowels. These diacritics are used (i) when there is a need to know the precise form of the word (for example in the Quran, where a vowel can change the meaning of a whole word) and (ii) when the readers are not 100% skilled: children/foreigners.

Writing systems also vary in the direction in which they are written and read; Arabic is written using a right-to-left writing system. In Arabic, the word *kataba* 'he wrote' consists of a three-letter root, and is read from right to left: 'k', 't' and 'b'. The short vowel 'a' can be added, as shown by diacritics in the form of the slanted lines shown in (3). The dots above and below in the example in (2) are not diacritics but are part of the consonant graphemes for /t/ and /b/.

(2) The three-letter root: 'k' 't' 'b'

كتب

(3) kataba 'he wrote'

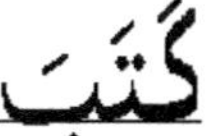

Another abugida is the DEVANAGARI SCRIPT used in South Asia to write Hindi, Nepali and Kashmiri, for example. In *Devanagari*, there is a basic grapheme, which represents the syllable and its expansion in combination with vowels.

3.3.2 The learning task

The advantage to the learner of a logographic system is that it does not require sophisticated phonological awareness. However, this system demands from the reader considerable effort to memorize thousands of individual LOGOGRAMS. Syllabaries and abugidas, however, require awareness of syllables as linguistic units. Researchers have confirmed that this is a relatively simple level of awareness to master (see, e.g. Goswami

& Bryant, 1990) and, as we will see below, this awareness is apparent in children and non-literate adults before they learn to read. With a language such as English or German, which has plentiful consonant clusters, learning an alphabet with 30 or so graphemes that represent phonemes is much easier than learning a syllabary with hundreds, if not thousands, of graphemes. The efficiency of the Roman alphabet does not translate into an easy task for the beginning reader. As we discuss in more depth in the next section, awareness of larger phonological units, such as words, syllables, onsets and rimes, develops naturally without schooling; but awareness of phonemes does not. Rather, it requires an effortful process of learning to read, in most cases, through schooling. This probably explains why the alphabet did not emerge independently in various places around the world, unlike syllabaric and logographic writing systems.

3.4 How Phonological Awareness and Phonemic Awareness Underpin the Ability to Read

Phonological awareness is the explicit, conscious knowledge of the sound structure of spoken language. This awareness enables the analysis and manipulation of language for a range of activities. For example, poets (whether they are literate or not) use their phonological awareness to find just the right word to convey experience through sound and all readers use this awareness in various ways. Full phonological awareness includes phonemic awareness and is essential for the successful development reading in an alphabetic writing system. This awareness, particularly for first-time readers such as children and migrant adults without literacy in any language, requires having acquired the phonology of the language in which they are learning to read. That is, this and awareness in other domains of language piggybacks on their linguistic competence (Gombert, 1992). However, logographic and syllabaric systems do not require phonemic awareness, and research suggests that readers who only use such systems possess only the awareness they require to read in that system (Ben-Dror *et al.*, 1995; Read *et al.*, 1986). This has implications for learners with some literacy; if the writing system in which they are literate is not an alphabetic system, they will not have developed phonemic awareness.

For beginning readers, both children and adults, the phonological awareness which emerges without formal schooling (e.g. of words, syllables and their subparts – onset and rime) allows them to see how spoken and written language relate before they learn to read (Goswami & Bryant, 1990). But, as we have said above, phonemic awareness develops only with learning to read in an alphabetic script.

To be able to read in any of the orthographies in the Roman alphabet, the reader has to grasp the alphabetic principle: that a grapheme represents a phoneme; that two and three graphemes can also represent a phoneme, as in the phoneme /f/ in the digraph <ph> in <photo> and as in the phoneme /ʃ/ in the trigraph <sch> in <schilling>. The alphabetic principle and phonemic awareness are the basis of word recognition, and there are two views, that phonemic awareness develops before reading and then underpins word recognition, or phonemic awareness develops as the result of learning to recognize words. We take no position on this here. One thing is clear: Phonemic awareness and reading in an alphabetic script go hand in hand.

word level	syllable level	onset-rime level	skeletal level	segmental level
'closet'	klo	onset: kl	consonant	features of each phoneme, for instance, /k/ is a voiceless, velar, stop consonant
			consonant	
		rime: o	vowel	
	set	onset: s	consonant	
			vowel	
		rime: et	consonant	

Figure 3.3 Classic model of the syllable (Hidalgo Navarro & Quilis Merin, 2012: 245–247)

The classic model of the syllable in Figure 3.3 above shows the relationship between units of spoken language and in the English word <closet>.

In studies of children, phonological awareness with respect to the syllable is seen as a continuum, with three degrees of difficulty (Anthony & Lonigan, 2004):

(1) Inter-syllabic awareness: awareness that words have a syllabic structure.
(2) Intra-syllabic awareness: awareness that a syllable has an onset and rime.
(3) Phonemic awareness: awareness that syllable onsets and rimes can be further broken down, that they consist of individual consonants and vowels.

When learning to read in languages with transparent orthographies, such as Finnish and Spanish, phonemic awareness, and in turn word recognition, develop more rapidly than in a language with an opaque orthography, such as English. Phonemic awareness does not have to be developed anew for alphabet-literate L2 readers, but non-literate adults start from the same position as a young child, albeit with far less linguistic competence in the phonology of the language in which they are learning to read. If they are literate but in a non-alphabetic writing system, the picture is more complicated. Let's now look at what research reveals about the connection between phonological awareness and early reading.

3.5 Research on Early Reading

In this section we delve more deeply into the relationship between phonological awareness and literacy. The starting point is the research conducted on children, but the results are meaningful for the adult migrants that are the focus of this book. At the end of this section, we focus on these adult learners.

3.5.1 Print awareness

Print awareness is relevant and includes being able to recognize the functions and uses of print, the letters of the alphabet (in an alphabetic writing system) and the meanings of high-frequency words. Ecalle *et al.* (2008) find that letter knowledge is one a predictor of literacy achievement in children who are pre-readers in their L1. Letter knowledge takes into account both letter-name and letter-sound/

grapheme-phoneme knowledge, suggesting a relationship between knowing the name of a letter, knowing the sound it represents, and literacy skills. While alphabet knowledge is important, this knowledge alone is not sufficient for reading. Print awareness and oral language proficiency are closely linked (Pettitt & Tarone, 2015; Young-Scholten & Strom, 2006). Grabe (2009) argues that oral language knowledge and skills are critical for literacy learning, and Tarone *et al.* (2009) argue for its importance with adults with limited literacy in their first language. That is, print awareness skills and oral language skills are connected.

3.5.2 Phonological awareness in children

Research has shown that phonological awareness is the best predictor of successful reading and spelling in a language such as English, with a Roman alphabet orthography. Children with weak phonological awareness display challenges with reading (Brady & Shankweiler, 1991; Goswami & Bryant, 1990; Stanovich, 1992). A study by Anthony *et al.* (2002) looked at children's phonological awareness and found that it develops at different rates and along the lines of the degrees of difficulty presented in the previous section. In a study of word awareness, Karmiloff-Smith *et al.* (1996) found that on a word awareness task, three-year-olds had poor performance, four-year-olds scored 74–77% and five-year-olds, 95–97%. Syllable awareness is evident around ages three or four, and onset and rime awareness by ages four to five. But children demonstrate awareness of the smallest phonological unit, the phoneme, when they are actively learning to read, as noted above and this is independent of age (Goswami & Bryant, 1990). This is nicely shown in an earlier, seminal study by Liberman *et al.* (1974), who gave three age-based groups of children a syllable tapping task and a phoneme tapping task. The four-year-olds scored 46% on syllable tapping, but 0% on phoneme tapping. The five-year-olds scored 48% on syllable tapping and 17% on phoneme tapping. The six-year-olds, who had been learning to read for almost a year, scored 90% on syllable tapping and 70% on phoneme tapping. A later study by Treiman and Zukowski (1991), using different tasks (same-different judgements) for onset-rime awareness showed steady progress on this aspect of phonological awareness: the four-year-olds scored 56%; the five-year-olds, 74%; and the six-year-olds, 100%. What is interesting is that while word, syllable, rime and onset awareness are present at quite a young age and before reading, they improve with age and the phonemic awareness required for reading in an alphabetic script emerges during early reading in this script. We now focus on the awareness of the smallest phonological unit.

3.5.3 Phonemic awareness in adults

The relevance of this research to non-literate adult migrants is that because phonemic awareness does not emerge naturally as the child grows, it should be possible for individuals to develop phonemic awareness after childhood. Thus, while we only learn to read once (Saville-Troike, 1991) and can then transfer these skills, that once can be later in life. That this is possible is further strengthened by two additional lines of research, on educated readers who have learned to read in a system such as logographic Chinese or abugida Hebrew, whose graphemes do not represent short vowels. In one study, Chinese readers who had also been exposed to the Pinyin alphabet in primary school were significantly better at detecting phonemes than those without such exposure (Read *et al.*, 1986). In another study, English readers were better than Hebrew readers at detecting phonemes (Ben-Dror *et al.*, 1995). The other line of research has looked at those who learn to read in their native language later in life. Morais *et al.* (1979, 1988) studied native speakers of Portuguese learning to read for the first time as adults and found that they followed patterns similar to children: Before being taught to read, they had developed the various aspects of phonological awareness except for phonemic awareness, which developed as they were trained in phonemic awareness or learned to read in Portuguese.

3.5.4 Non-literate migrant adults' phonological awareness

In comparison to the considerable attention that children and even late-reading native speakers have received, there is a very modest body of research on adults learning to read for the first time in an additional language. Two of the earliest studies focused on adults who were first taught to read in their home languages: in Haitian Kreyòl (Burtoff, 1985) and in Hmong (Robson, 1982). These pioneering studies confirm Saville-Troike's (1991) statement that we only learn to read once, showing that, later in life, individuals can develop phonemic awareness and word recognition/decoding skills and then transfer this awareness and these skills to use in reading in another language with an alphabetic orthography. In recent years there also has been an effort to describe how adult migrant non-readers develop aspects of phonological awareness and other related knowledge before and while they become literate.

The LESLLA organization (Literacy Education and Second Language Learning for Adults; www.leslla.org), mentioned in the Introduction to this volume, has been prominent in promoting such research. Since its inception in 2005, the organization has published its symposium proceedings and on its website makes these available along with symposium presentations and student papers, all of which report on studies exclusively on adults learning to read for the first time in a range of languages in different countries. These studies include action research in the classroom, case studies of a few learners and large-scale studies of hundreds of learners, and they include qualitative, quantitative and mixed-methods research. Studies by, for example, Young-Scholten and Strom (2006), Young-Scholten and Naeb (2010), Tammelin-Laine and Martin (2015) and Kurvers (2007, 2015) of adult migrants learning to read for the first time in their new language (English, Finnish and Dutch, respectively) underscore the relationship between linguistic competence, reading, and phonological awareness. Kurvers (2007) compared children and adult learners and found that they pass through the same phases in the process of developing word recognition; for example, the stages/phases of reading development proposed in models by Frith (1985) and Ehri (1992), described here. Frith (1985) offers three stages of reading development:

(1) The LOGOGRAPHIC STAGE, with recognition of logos, brands and signs by visual shape and memorized sight words.
(2) The ALPHABETIC STAGE, when the *emerging reader* starts to detect systematic associations between sound and spelling and gradually becomes able to attack unfamiliar words.
(3) The ORTHOGRAPHIC STAGE, when alphabetic processing becomes automatic and morphological awareness embellishes proficient reading.

Ehri (1992) expands these stages to four phases of reading development, which overlap: PRE-ALPHABETIC, PARTIAL ALPHABETIC, FULL ALPHABETIC and CONSOLIDATED ALPHABETIC. At the pre-alphabetic phase, the learner is unable to detect the difference between (in English) <pepsi> and <xepsi> due to their similar visual shapes (Masonheimer *et al.*, 1984). At the partial alphabetic phase, when the learner starts to make grapheme-phoneme correspondences to decode words, he or she may *glance* at an unfamiliar word and *guess,* but the guess will be based on a familiar word and possibly be incorrect. The difference between the full alphabetic phase and the consolidated alphabetic phrase is gradual: at the latter phase, the grapheme-phoneme associations that the reader has mastered are automatically applied to multisyllabic words and unfamiliar words.

At the intermediate stage/phase in both Frith's and Ehri's models, the learner shows sensitivity to and enjoyment of alliteration, rhyme and repetition, awareness of conventions of the orthography in their environment, and understanding of sorting into categories by sound, shape and function.

3.6 Teaching Early Reading to Adults

In this section, we briefly cover the application to teaching of the ideas presented in previous sections. First, we suggest how we can place students in different groups, depending on their degree of literacy-related skills development. Second, we propose some ideas to teach reading with a focus on learners who are beginners in Roman-alphabet-based literacy and who, therefore, need to develop phonemic awareness.

3.6.1 Placement of learners

Basic language skills support for adult migrants is underfunded in some countries, and this often results in reliance on volunteers and one-to-one tutoring. For those who work with groups rather than individual learners, it is important to consider creating sub-groups with different literacy profiles. Here we adopt a learner profile classification used in Finland (see Chapter 2 this volume). The starting points are the learners' skills at three levels. Under text skills, comprehension of discourse is also included. At this level, linguistic competence, particularly that of syntax and morphology, plays an essential role, unlike at the other two levels. To place learners in a sub-group, the teacher checks whether they have the following skills:

- **Mechanical literacy:** Can combine sounds/letters into syllables and words; break a familiar word into syllables and sounds/letters; make use of syllable division to read a new word.
- **Basic reading skills:** Can read a short text going beyond individual words and sentences.
- **Text skills:** Can identify specific information in a simple text, with rereading as needed.

To assign levels, the teacher could:

- Interview the learners to find out how much formal schooling they have participated in and what their level of literacy is in their home language(s).
- Conduct an objective test in which the learners have to demonstrate the skills above, with a word list, sentences and a paragraph.

In theory, one could create nine groups of learners, where each cell in Table 3.1 represents a group according to the literacy level and linguistic competence that they demonstrate.

Table 3.1 Classification of learners based on literacy level and linguistic competence

	Basic linguistic competence	**Intermediate linguistic competence**	**Advanced linguistic competence**
Beginning literacy	Mechanical literacy and word recognition + basic linguistic competence	Mechanical literacy and word recognition + intermediate linguistic competence	Mechanical literacy and word recognition + advanced linguistic competence
Basic literacy	Basic level of text reading skills + basic linguistic competence	Basic level of text reading skills + intermediate linguistic competence	Basic level of text reading skills + advanced linguistic competence
Developing literacy	Higher-level text skills + basic linguistic competence	Higher-level text skills + intermediate linguistic competence	Higher-level text skills + advanced linguistic competence

What are the options in teaching reading? In the teaching of reading to children in an alphabetic script, there long have been two main approaches: the SYNTHETIC APPROACH and the ANALYTICAL APPROACH. The synthetic approach is mechanical and bottom up: The reader starts with smaller units and combines them into larger units. Graphemes are combined to form syllables, and syllables are combined to form words. The analytical approach is a more recent innovation, less mechanical and top down. The reader starts with the larger units and divides them into smaller ones. Words are divided into syllables, and syllables are divided into graphemes. These approaches are not equivalent options from a pedagogical point of view. Where learning must be meaningful from the beginning, this is more feasible in the analytical approach than in the synthetic approach. In the synthetic approach, it can be the case that before considering elements with meaning, time is first spent on learning phonemes and graphemes in isolation.

Among options for supporting migrant adults in developing word recognition and decoding skills is the use of software. The Digital Literacy Instructor (DigLin, http://diglin.eu) is a recent example. The software starts out with 300 words to build decoding for adults who are complete beginners in a new language. It was developed and tested from 2013 to 2015 by a project consortium led by researchers at Radboud University in the Netherlands (see Cucchiarini *et al.*, 2015b for a description of the project). The software supports individualized learning and continues to be developed as independent learning of words, phrases and sentences for use on a PC, tablet or smart-phone, in British English, Dutch, Finnish, German and Spanish. Because DigLin does not assume pre-existing (home language) literacy of participants, it can be used by literate adults to learn new words, pronunciation and grapheme-phoneme correspondences for the language being learned.

Each item that the DigLin user attempts elicits immediate feedback in each of its exercise types (see Table 3.2). It is a flexible system that enables individual learners to develop their own strategies. The teacher or tutor can track the user's behaviour via log files automatically created by a user's keystrokes and mouse movements. Malessa and Filimban (2017) discuss what those who work with English and with Finnish learners have gained from looking at learners' log files. Filimban (2019) describes a more extensive study of a group of learners of English and their progress in reading as a result of using the DigLin software.

Finally, although phonemic awareness is essential for developing reading skills, when it comes to opaque English and its irregularly spelled words, because such words are among the most common vocabulary in the language, they are introduced early. One of the best-known lists of sight words was created by Dolch (1948) and, with changes, it has been used in teaching reading to children since then. An example of such irregularities is that the initial <th> in <the> and in <think> is pronounced differently as is the <oo> in <look> and <boot>. These may be treated as sight words, as if they were unanalysable units, much like Chinese characters and children indeed start to recognize such words by sight without having developed phonemic awareness, and the

Table 3.2 The Digital Literacy Instructor software and example exercise types

Exercise type	Aim
Listen to words	Written word + meaning via photographs
Listen and drag the letters	Grapheme-phoneme correspondences
Listen and drag words	Grapheme-phoneme correspondences
Listen to letters + drag words	Grapheme-phoneme correspondences
Listen and type words	Automatization of decoding
Reading aloud	Automatic Speech Recognition: evaluation of oral production

(van de Craats & Young-Scholten, 2015)

same applies to migrant adults, who by learning to read them can then concentrate on mastering the regular patterns which involve phonemic awareness as well as moving on to develop awareness of the morphological building blocks of English.

3.6.2 The generative word method

Among the various possibilities in early reading pedagogy is an analytic method called GENERATIVE WORD OF GENERATIVE THEME. Generative word refers to the idea that new readers generate the words that they then work with. In his *Pedagogy of the Oppressed* (1970/1993), Paulo Freire introduced this with non-literate adult native speakers of Portuguese and Spanish in South America. While it depends on an adult-level lexicon, it is nonetheless feasible to adapt this method for use with adult migrants with limited vocabularies. Steps are demonstrated in videos from the Mexican Institute of Adult Education that can be found at the links in the Appendix, where photographs have been included from a literacy class held in Spain. Exercises are introduced in the context of topics important to adults and for critical literacy (e.g. health and the environmental protection), and AUTHENTIC TEXTS and REALIA are used (forms, receipts, leaflets, advertisements) for practical relevance. A task then brings everything together in the form of a composition (e.g. as a poster), where students reflect on the text's functions, its objective, where the text belongs and so on. The process connects learning with life outside the classroom.

While interacting with these texts and realia and creating a composition, students learn and use new words, following these five steps.

(1) Talk with someone else about the word and its meaning.
(2) Break down the word into syllables and syllable strings.
(3) Put the word back together and possibly create a new word, using prefixes and suffixes.
(4) Use the word in writing.
(5) Integrate the word into meaningful texts and create new texts.

Between the second and the fifth step, there is opportunity for the teacher or tutor to carry out additional activities for phonological awareness, particularly those relating to phoneme-grapheme correspondences. For example, in order to create new words, learners need to become aware of DERIVATIONAL MORPHOLOGY, that prefixes and suffixes can change the meaning and word class of words as in the verb <teach> and the noun <teacher>.

3.6.3 The language experience approach

The LANGUAGE EXPERIENCE APPROACH (LEA) is another instructional approach that takes advantage of students' life experiences as the context for beginning reading instruction (Crandall & Peyton, 1993; Nessel & Dixon, 2008; Taylor, 1992;

Vinogradov, 2008, 2010; see also discussion in Chapter 7). It is an example of a social-focused approach based on the classification presented in Smyser (2016), which distinguishes such approaches from skills-focused approaches. It can involve group activities, such as shopping trips and other visits to places relevant to learners (e.g. a bus station, a farmers' market), looking at a sequence of images, or watching a film. After the shared group activity, a learning unit follows three steps, which revolve around the activity:

(1) Create the text: Learners give oral accounts, using pictures and other non-text supporting materials; the teacher/tutor prompts with questions.
(2) An account of the shared activity is written by the teacher/tutor, who tries to make few changes in the learners' oral account.
(3) The learners engage in activities using the text, such as independent and paired or whole-group reading; copying paragraphs or the whole text; sequencing parts of the text; and focusing on phonological awareness (e.g. of words, syllables and phonemes).

LEA can be used at various learner proficiency levels and to develop a range of skills, from syllabification and decoding to summarizing, schematizing and drafting texts. The advantage of this approach is that it starts and ends with the learners' skills, experiences and interests.

3.7 Gaining Fluency and Moving to Comprehension: Reading for Pleasure

Once the new reader is able to automatically recognize words (bottom up) and has developed basic strategies to apply experience and world knowledge to predict what a text says (top down) and linguistic competence has developed to a suitable level (see Chapter 5 on vocabulary and Chapter 6 on morphosyntax), working on reading comprehension is the next step. What activities and materials best support the development of reading comprehension?

To answer this question, it is worth considering why we, as fully literate adults, read. In post-industrialized societies, we read for a range of purposes. We read to check ingredients on food labels and dosage on medicine bottles. We read signs and timetables and maps to navigate our way through life. We read newspapers and magazines for news and gossip. We interact textually on social media (see Chapter 2 for a discussion). Many of us also read for pleasure. Pleasure reading is different from other types of reading. It often has no utilitarian or social purpose (unless we are part of a reading group). In fact, if we read fiction, rather than relate to daily life, it transports us. We read tales of imaginary characters in settings and situations that we never encounter in our daily lives. Short stories and books open doors to worlds that we never directly experience. For the vast majority of those who have enjoyed the Harry Potter series, the English boarding school setting is a culture apart from their experience. In many cases, we would not want to experience these worlds; consider the highly popular crime genre. Story telling is universal (see, e.g. Labov & Waletsky, 1997), and the human themes in narratives are universal. In the treatment of these themes by skilled authors, we develop empathy for those who are unlike ourselves. Not all of us read fiction, but everyone should have the chance to do so, including migrant adults who are starting to go beyond word recognition.

The term EXTENSIVE READING is often used to refer to pleasure reading to distinguish it from the sort of reading we do in school or university classes (Cassany *et al.*, 1998). Extensive reading aims for a global understanding or gist of the text while its counterpart, INTENSIVE READING, involves reading texts with the aim of complete and detailed comprehension of the text. If learners are still improving their reading, the texts will be short, and if they involve intensive reading, they will include focus on specific skills.

Extensive reading is as important as intensive reading for building reading comprehension, and there is growing evidence that it is indispensable in doing so. For decades, numerous studies and surveys of both native speaking and second language readers report impressive benefits of extensive reading (e.g. Bamford & Day, 2004; Elley & Mangubhai, 1983) and this includes the PISA studies discussed in Chapter 2. Studies have found that extensive reading is a better predictor of reading success than socio-economic status or number of books in the home (Neuman & Celano, 2001; Sonnenschein & Schmidt, 2000). Stephen Krashen, a vocal expert in promoting what he instead calls FREE, VOLUNTARY READING, has long claimed that in a second language, the amount of reading that an individual engages in strongly correlates with performance on a range of reading and writing tests and also with the less conscious acquisition of syntax, morphology and vocabulary that he promotes in his ideas about comprehensible input (Krashen, 1982, 1985, 1989, 1993, 2004). With respect to vocabulary, researchers argue that readers should know at least 95% of the words that appear in the text they are reading (see Chapter 4).

With respect to learners' level of syntax and morphology, the Simply Cracking Good Stories project (www.simplystories.org) is based on providing new adult readers with books whose text is at suitably levels (see Chapter 5 on morphosyntax). Even if learners know the meanings of 100% of the nouns, verbs, adjectives and prepositions in a text, if the morphosyntax is above their current level, they will have difficulty comprehending the text. Simply Cracking Good Stories is in line with the tradition in beginning reading, both for young children learning to read and for those learning to read in a foreign language, of providing what are called graded or leveled readers, texts that have been simplified for various levels and in various ways. While the idea of extensive reading means that the reader can choose when, where and what to read, Rodrigo *et al.* (2007) found that readers overwhelmingly preferred general fiction. It turns out that reading stories – narrative texts – increases learners' intake of the linguistic aspects of the text (Lee, 2009).

Extensive reading in general, and reading of fiction in particular, has the potential to transport the reader to different times and places. It is, therefore, no surprise that it correlates with an increased sense of well-being (Djikic *et al.*, 2009; Mar &

Oatley, 2008). Because extensive reading is individualized, it promotes autonomy and ultimately boosts independence and self-confidence. For adults in particular, extensive reading establishes a foundation for critical literacy and active citizenship by drawing on readers' experiences and expectations and encouraging reflection and perspective taking (Auerbach & Wallerstein, 2005; Cooke & Simpson, 2008; Duncan, 2014; Freire, 1970/1993; Graff, 1993; Schellekens, 2007; Spiegel & Sunderland, 2006).

3.7.1 Extensive reading with LESLLA learners

Earlier in this chapter we note that considerable practice is required for the automatic word recognition that accompanies higher levels of reading comprehension. If reading material is at the right level and engages the reader, it can provide the missing link in providing the extra-curricular practice that is required for comprehension of texts. A handful of studies of migrant adults in the United States and the United Kingdom show the same benefits of extensive reading for more proficient learners (Laymon, 2013; Rodrigo *et al.*, 2007; Williamson, 2013; Yaden *et al.*, 2003), but only Laymon's study looked at the lowest level learners. These studies found gains in learners' L2 reading skills, L2 linguistic competence, critical thinking, literacy practices, community engagement and motivation to read more. Use of extensive reading with migrant adults depends on meeting two basic criteria: (1) books are available at the right level of difficulty, including the right length (Crossley *et al.*, 2012; Hill, 2008); and (2) there are interesting books that engage the reader, without which 'very little is possible' (Williams, 1986: 42). The practice of extensive reading with these is not widespread, and this may because these two criteria are difficult to meet. Moreover, extensive reading is at odds with the dominant approach to reading imposed on many if not most adult immigrant basic skills classes, where the emphasis is on learners' immediate, functional literacy needs (Williamson, 2013). This is unfortunate, because narrative texts provide another way for learners to draw on their life experience and real-world knowledge. Extensive reading, particularly when the learners select what they read, also addresses the problem of the decontextualization of language and of cognitively unchallenging and demotivating materials.

Compared to books for children, teenagers and adult native speakers, there are far fewer engaging and linguistically accessible books for adult migrants just starting to read in a new language; that is, the two criteria are difficult to meet, as stated above. Rodrigo *et al.* (2007) used a 6:1 ratio, where for every student in their study, there were six books at their level. To set up an extensive reading program for a class of 15 learners would, therefore, require 90 simple books of potential interest to the reader. How does one know what might interest a new reader if that person does not yet read for pleasure? This is a matter of finding out what, in general, interests the learner, including the television shows and films they enjoy. Creating a library for extensive reading is only a first step but one that can involve the learners, thereby raising their awareness of the function of books that can be read for pleasure.

Whether there are topics to avoid in creating a library, depending on the learner population, the key to the success of extensive reading is the freedom that the reader has to decide what to read. Both children and adults are drawn to the adventurous and the dangerous. Dubin and Olshtain (1977) note our attraction to taboo topics, and in *Bad Books in Easy English*, Murphy (1987) defends the reader's freedom to choose such books. Migrant adults' lives are complicated in various ways, and the teacher or tutor is best placed to treat the issues that might arise sensitively. The teacher's or tutor's aim is to instill the habit of reading for pleasure and for a program to work, time needs to be set aside during teaching sessions for silent reading, and learners need to be able to borrow books to take home and read whenever and wherever they like. Consider these seven criteria when creating a classroom library for the lowest level learners. These are just suggestions; in the end, learners' preferences and their ability to tackle a given book will be the most important criteria.

(1) Short, not more than 300 words.
(2) Interesting narratives.
(3) Fiction and non-fiction.
(4) Different fiction genres.
(5) Different types of materials, including newspapers and magazines.
(6) Linguistically accessible.
(7) Books with images to support the text.

For criterion 6, 'linguistically accessible', keep in mind, for example, the idea of a threshold level, that the reader should have achieved a sufficient level of linguistic competence to be able to comprehend a text without difficulty. With respect to criterion 7, Rodrigo *et al.* (2007) discovered that images positively influence the reader's experience with a book, from the point at which they choose which book to read to their enhanced interpretation and enjoyment of the text through the images that accompany it. Images can contextualize the narrative to allow a simpler text that does not include the details of setting or characters. This allows the reader to focus on the story itself.

3.7.2 Examples of reading materials

Since 2010, the EU-Speak project partners at the University of Granada and Newcastle University have been involving creative writers at Newcastle in writing short fiction books that meet the relevant criteria (see Simply Cracking Good Stories above), and students at Granada have been writing books in Spanish: http://wpd.ugr.es/~sosinski/ (see Young-Scholten *et al.*, 2015b).

Another option for beginning readers are artists' wordless picture books, also known as silent books. They are not specifically intended for those without literacy, and they can be both age neutral and culture neutral. They can be the first step toward encouraging learners to read for pleasure. Two well-known books are Shaun Tan's *The Arrival* and Marla Frazee's *The Farmer and the Clown*.

3.8 Conclusion

In this chapter, we describe key aspects of learning and teaching beginning reading. We reflect, from a theoretical point of view, on the components of reading skills, including phonological awareness, that underpin reading. We present the idea of lower-level and higher-level strategies and note the need to automate lower-level processing. There appears to be no critical period to learn to read, a parallel can be drawn between migrant adults and children who are native speakers of the language they are reading, in both the nature of reading and its development over time.

On the practical side, we briefly describe two instructional approaches to teaching reading: the generative word method and the Language Experience Approach, along with newly developed software for decoding. Finally, we address the topic of extensive reading.

We hope that this is only a starting point for wider reflection and, above all, for a practical application of the ideas introduced in this chapter. The necessary simplification of the contents of the chapter might be a stimulus for research, for example, about the phonological systems of learners' languages, their levels of phonological awareness, teaching methods useful in a particular context, available materials and suitable division of learners into levels.

Appendix: Links to Activities (Activities are in Spanish)

1. Diálogo sobre la palabra y su significado
   (Discussion of a word and its meaning)
   https://www.youtube.com/watch?v=14JQSq2SgPM
2. Separación de la palabra en sílabas y presentación de familias silábicas
   (Separation of a word into syllables and presentation of syllable families)
   https://www.youtube.com/watch?v=Fod5uqUX5G0
3. Formación de otras palabras
   (Formation of other words)
   https://www.youtube.com/watch?v=1YhcECWmJLo
4. Integración de elementos funcionales del lenguaje escrito
   (Integration of functional elements in writing)
   https://www.youtube.com/watch?v=rDTs7V5aXTo
5. Integración y producción de textos significativos
   (Integration and production of meaningful texts)
   https://www.youtube.com/watch?v=QMYE6JGVMLA
6. Asignación y revisión de tareas
   (Assignment and revision of homework)
   https://www.youtube.com/watch?v=KznV09wJvLo
7. Reflexión y evaluación del avance
   (Reflection on and evaluation of the learning progress)
   https://www.youtube.com/watch?v=0kif04vZFUI

4 Vocabulary

Andreas Rohde, Kerstin Chlubek, Pia Holtappels, Kim-Sarah Schick and Johanna Schnuch

4.1 Introduction

Knowledge of the vocabulary of the language in which one is learning to speak, understand and read is critical. Wilkins (1972: 111–112) points out that 'without grammar very little can be conveyed; without words nothing can be conveyed'. Along the same lines, Lewis (1993: 89) says that 'lexis is the core or heart of language'. Grabe (2009) argues that when it comes to reading in a second language, vocabulary knowledge is one of the strongest predictors of success. This chapter provides insights into how we learn words in a language we are learning, along with practical instructional strategies for supporting migrant adults in learning words. After we address the basics of what a word is, how words are linked, what the human word store or lexicon involves and the importance of being able to access many words and meanings of words quickly, we look at our ability to learn words and how we systematically make sense of the world around us by naming objects. In Section 4.6 we describe ways that words can be taught to adult migrants and the strategies that adult migrants with limited reading and writing skills can apply to learn and permanently retain words.

4.2 Words and Word Knowledge

4.2.1 What's in a word?

When people think about word knowledge, they are usually thinking about the number of words that a person knows. What we often neglect is the complex knowledge associated with really knowing a word. This becomes clear when we consider any word we know; for example, the word 'dog'. As we start thinking about what we know about this word, we soon realize that we know quite a lot and that to represent what a noun such as *dog* means, there are a vast number of bubbles in our mind map.

What usually comes to mind first are the semantic aspects of a word, other words related in some way to the meaning of 'dog'. We may think of different CO-HYPONYMS (words on the same level that are subordinates to 'dog'); i.e. breeds of dogs such as Labrador, poodle, German shepherd or Chihuahua. We know that 'dog' is the

HYPERNYM (superordinate), since all of these breeds fall under the category of dog. We can also name different body parts of the dog, like tail or paw. We may think of our own dog (personal association) and its name or associate feelings and memories with a dog (e.g. fear, love).

In addition to our semantic associations with the word 'dog', we also have phonological knowledge of this word, knowledge about its sound structure. We know how to pronounce 'dog', that its first sound is the same as in the word 'duck', and that 'dog' has one syllable. Then there is our ORTHOGRAPHIC KNOWLEDGE; we know how to link the phoneme /d/ with <d> and so on. Our SYNTACTIC KNOWLEDGE tells us that 'dog' is a noun and that in the sentence 'I love my dog', it is a direct object. Our MORPHOLOGICAL KNOWLEDGE enables us to add a suffix to the word to create an adjective, as in 'This blanket has a doggy smell'.

These five aspects – semantics, phonology, orthography, syntax and morphology – are not everything we might possibly know about the word. There are many other things we may add to our detailed knowledge about a word, which include PRAGMATIC KNOWLEDGE (for example, that calling someone a dog can be an insult in certain contexts or cultures); and real-world knowledge, that some pure-bred dogs have genetic deficiencies or that poodles are not used as police dogs. The extent to which our knowledge of a word involves further details is partially individual.

When asked which meaning aspects a word contains, we usually come up with one or more of the following, as shown in Figure 4.1, the example of the word 'bird'. As their proficiency increases, migrant adults' knowledge of a word will increase accordingly.

Second language speakers usually know fewer meanings of a word, but even most native speakers of a language do not know all of the possible meanings. Second

Encyclopaedic knowledge:
A bird is an animal. It has two wings and can fly. Most birds can sing. They lay eggs, etc.

TAXONOMIC KNOWLEDGE:
Eagles, sparrows and blackbirds are birds. Birds are not amphibians or mammals, but they belong to the category of *sauropsida*, which in turn, is a subcategory of animals.

Common collocations:
Killing two birds with one stone. Birds of a feather flock together. Free as a bird.

Morphological knowledge:
Bird – birds – birdy

Syntactic knowledge:
I see a bird.
Birds can fly.
* The shape of this painting looks bird. (Ungrammatical because bird isn't an adjective or adverb.)

Personal experience/connotations:
I still remember once being attacked by a dove near the cathedral. Therefore, I am afraid of birds. I am even terrified, especially after watching Hitchcock's classic film 'The Birds'.

Pronunciation/spelling:
[bɜːd] <bird>

Figure 4.1 Meaning aspects of a word

language speakers, however, may know that 'blue' and 'black' refer to colors but not the shades of these colors or other uses of the words (e.g. that red, white and blue refer to the US flag or that All Blacks refers to the New Zealand rugby team). We learn new words and expand meanings and uses of words we know throughout the lifespan, and experience with the language results in this learning.

Research suggests that detailed knowledge about a word, also called a LEXICAL ENTRY, can be divided into two parts: the LEMMA and the LEXEME. The lemma contains all of the semantic and syntactic information about a word; and the lexeme, all the phonological and morphological information. Under this view of a word, the lemma and the lexeme are stored separately in the mind, but they are connected by so called LEXICAL POINTERS (Levelt, 1989), as shown in Figure 4.2.

Evidence that Levelt's model is psychologically valid comes from the TIP OF THE TONGUE PHENOMENON and slips of the tongue (Levelt, 1989) as well as from studies of patients with APHASIA, a language disorder caused, for example, by a stroke that affects the ability to produce or to understand language. Here, we often find patients who are able to recall the word but cannot remember its meaning or, the other way around, who know exactly what they intend to say in terms of meaning but cannot produce the relevant word (Steiner, 2003).

The tip of the tongue phenomenon refers to word retrieval problems we have all experienced. Think about speaking a foreign language when you are on a trip abroad. You want to say something, it's on the tip of your tongue, you are sure you know the word you are searching for, you would definitely recognize it if somebody else said it, and maybe you even know the initial sound or the number of syllables that it contains. Because the meaning of the word is available – you have access to the lemma – but not the word form, the lexeme, this serves as evidence for the separate storage model in Figure 4.2. An example of a slip of the tongue would be someone saying ring instead of sing, which can happen with two phonologically related lexemes.

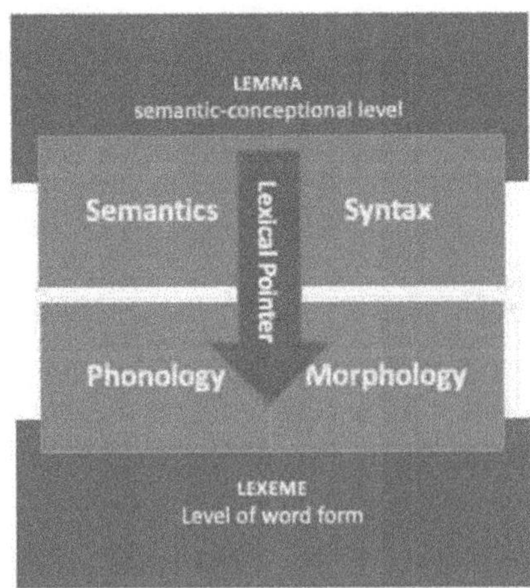

Figure 4.2 Model of the mental lexicon (based on Levelt, 1989: 182)

4.2.2 Breadth and depth of vocabulary knowledge

Breadth and depth are two important dimensions of vocabulary knowledge (Ma, 2009). **Breadth of word knowledge** refers to how many words we have stored in our **mental lexicon**; for example, in addition to the word 'dog', we might know 'hound', 'mutt', 'canine'. **Depth of word knowledge** (Anderson & Freebody, 1981) refers to how much we know about the word; e.g. the breeds of dogs mentioned above (Labrador, poodle, German shepherd, Chihuahua) and knowing about dogs; e.g. that a dog is a four-legged animal that can bark. The more bubbles our mind map of 'dog' has, the deeper our understanding is of this word. The mind map of a migrant adult whose proficiency level is still that of a beginner is not likely to contain many bubbles. But as proficiency grows and there is increasing experience in specialist areas (e.g. for work, for supporting children's education; see Chapter 2) bubbles will multiply.

The distinction of breadth and depth of vocabulary knowledge is addressed by the following two questions that researchers continue to ponder and that are relevant to teachers:

- When can we say that someone has breadth of word knowledge? Does knowing a word count if someone simply recognizes it as sounding familiar but cannot remember its meaning?
- When can we say that someone knows a word in depth? There are no commonly accepted norms of when knowledge is deep or not. It appears to be a matter of different degrees of knowledge for each word. (See, e.g. Nation, 1990, 2001, for a discussion of the 'learning burden' of a new word.)

Regardless of the challenges with applying breadth and depth to a given speaker's mental lexicon, these notions are worth thinking about in understanding a migrant adult's mental lexicon, particularly when it comes to knowing that the more we know a word in depth, the faster we can access it when we need to use it.

4.2.3 How word knowledge is structured and stored in the mind

The adult native speaker's knowledge of words in a language is not only vast and detailed, it is also highly structured in the mind. If there were no such structure, we would not be able to account for how rapidly speakers normally access words during listening, speaking, reading, and writing (Aitchison, 2012). The activation of a word is the activation of various links that lead to the one word we are looking for at that time. The idea of a network also means that the breadth and depth of vocabulary knowledge depend on each other. The more words we know, the more connections we can make between different words. For example, we can make connections between the word 'bark' and 'Labrador'; 'dachshund' and 'hot dog'; or 'dog' with words it rhymes with, such as 'smog'. The more connections, or paths, we have, the more rapidly a word is activated when we need it. Having deep knowledge of a word, with a complex network of meaning built around the word, eases the process of retrieving the word (Glück, 1999, 2007).

The retrieval of words from our mental lexicon depends on the number of times we have had to access the word (Glück, 2007). When it comes to applications to language teaching, the more often we give learners opportunities to hear, see (in print) and produce a word, the more successful they will be in using the word both in and outside the classroom. The speed with which a word is accessed also matters. Research suggests that learners who have accessed a word very quickly several times are more successful in retrieving it later (Glück, 2003). Hence, classroom activities that encourage migrant adult learners to quickly access and produce words they have just learned will ease the process outside the classroom.

4.2.4 Word fields

How are words linked to each other? There are a number of different types of LEXICAL RELATIONS. One word may simultaneously participate in a number of lexical relations, and this demonstrates that the mental lexicon is a network, rather than a list of words, as in a dictionary. An important organizational principle is LEXICAL FIELD or WORD FIELD. This refers to a group of words that belongs to a particular activity or area of knowledge, such as words used in cooking or in a particular field of endeavor such as by doctors, musicians, farmers or secretaries. Related here are specialized words, like *lexicon* in linguistics or *gigabyte* in computing. Figure 4.3 gives an example of the different meanings of the word *blanket*. The first meaning is a relatively common one, and the second is a highly specialized meaning:

blanket[1] verb.	To cover as with a *blanket;* the snow blanketed the town.
blanket[2] verb.	*Sailing*. To block another vessel's wind by sailing close to it on the windward side (the side of the boat that is facing the wind).
ledger[1] noun.	*Bookkeeping*. The main book in which a company's financial records are kept.
ledger[2] noun.	*Angling*. A trace that holds the bait above the bottom in fishing.

Figure 4.3 Different meanings of a word (Saeed, 2016: 60)

4.2.5 Hierarchy: SUPERORDINATE and SUBORDINATE WORDS

In a lexical field, words can often be ordered in a TAXONOMY, a hierarchical order.

In the example in Figure 4.4, 'tool' is the hypernym that contains all of the words on the lower levels; both 'saw' and 'jigsaw' are HYPONYMS, of tool; 'fretsaw', 'chainsaw' and 'jigsaw' are co-hyponyms. Some authors (e.g. Calderón & Soto, 2017; Oxford, 1990; Wangru, 2016) argue that in second language teaching, one should give learners opportunities to learn and use words in lexical fields, as part of an overall theme, as the theme (in this case 'tool') holds the words together and, therefore, provides clues to their meanings.

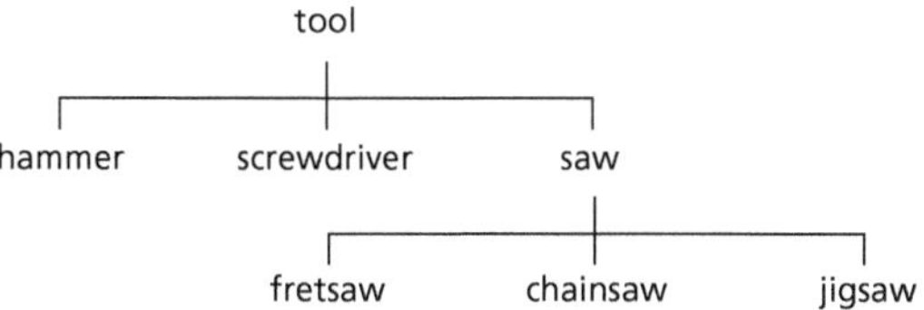

Figure 4.4 Example of a taxonomy of a word (Saeed, 2016: 65)

4.2.6 Sameness and oppositeness: Synonyms and antonyms

Words may also be related to each other in two major ways. SYNONYMS are words that have the same or very similar meanings: these can be words that differ in terms of regional VARIETY or register:

couch/sofa boy/lad autumn/fall toilet/lavatory

ANTONYMS are words, quite often adjectives, that are opposite in meaning:

big-small high-low hot-cold beautiful-ugly dead-alive
true-false female-male full-empty

(Saeed, 2016, separates these types of opposite meanings into gradable and complementary antonymy.)

Gradable antonymy: big-small high-low hot-cold beautiful-ugly
Complementary antonymy: dead-alive true-false female-male

4.2.7 Different languages, different vocabularies

Although migrant adults might not yet be in a position to use text-only dictionaries, we briefly comment on them here, with a description of how dictionaries can be used later in the chapter. A dictionary may give the impression that each word in a language neatly corresponds to a single word in another language. This is not the case. Each language and its culture carve up the world differently. In German, for example, the word *Himmel* translates into English as both 'sky' and 'heaven'. That is, one word in German translates to two different concepts in English. Things become more complex when we look at abstract words, such as 'liberty' or 'home', *Freiheit* and *Heimat* in German. It takes experience with the language to discover to what extent these words cover the same or different ground in each language. Table 4.1 shows how words represent different concepts in four European languages.

Table 4.1 Words used to express concepts in four different languages (Nirenberg & Raskin, 2004: 151)

English concept	**Tree**	**Wood (as stuff)**	**Firewood**	**Small forest**	**Large forest**
Language					
Spanish	árbol	madera	leña	bosque	selva
French	arbre	bois			forêt
German	Baum		Holz		Wald
Danish			trae		skov

4.3 Learning Words: Fast Mapping

We now turn to what researchers know about how words are learned from infancy throughout the lifespan. Considering how young children learn words allows us to expand our thinking about how migrant adults learn words when they have limited or no literacy and thus limited ability to learn words from dictionaries or from context during reading, and they have few of the metalinguistic word LEARNING STRATEGIES that educated second language learners can use.

Implicit and EXPLICIT LEARNING are thought to work in a complementary fashion (Haudeck, 2008). A child or an adult may learn words when they are told explicitly by an interlocutor what a word means and told to remember both the word form and its meaning. Explicit learning is described in more detail in Section 4.5 of this chapter. Words are also learned implicitly when the process is incidental – it does not involve being instructed or consciously noticing. In fact, since we learn numerous words from infancy onwards, throughout our lives, it would require unrealistically many cognitive and time resources if we only learned words explicitly. Children who learn new words seem to apply certain principles that guide, facilitate, and accelerate the process and enable them to build up a large lexicon in a remarkably short period of time.

Here we describe IMPLICIT LEARNING of words and the process known as FAST MAPPING. Fast mapping is what we all have done since we were babies and what we continue to do when we quickly link a word we hear to a meaning (although that meaning may turn out to be incomplete). A meaning is mapped onto a linguistic form, a word. It is then, of course, important for the language learner to remember the new word and retain its meanings. In order for this to happen, the learner needs to be exposed to this new word again and again. This strengthens the learner's memory and also allows her/him to specify and extend word meanings (Carey, 1978).

4.3.1 Components of the fast mapping process

The 'fast' in fast mapping refers to the learner's ability to connect a word quickly with a meaning after little exposure, in some cases after hearing the word just once. How does this work? In the research literature, fast mapping has the following three characteristics. These are described in more detail in Section 4.4.

- The speed of the mapping process.
- The incomplete nature of the process; at first, the learner's meaning is not complete.
- The implicit nature of naming. All language learners grasp aspects of the meaning of a new word without any explicit act by an interlocutor of pointing or and naming; learners are able to infer meaning on the basis of attention, EYE GAZE, or interpretation of the interlocutor's intention (Tiefenthal, 2009).

In both first and second language acquisition, research shows that nouns are more easily fast mapped than verbs or adjectives. Nouns that are fast mapped often refer to permanent real-life objects that are visually clear. The meaning of a verb refers to what is being done. The fast-mapped verb form has to be retained in memory, which is a challenge for the learner if an action lasts a very short time (e.g. singing, running, breaking something). Adjectives refer to a single characteristic of a noun, which must be discerned from other characteristics (Clark, 1993; Tiefenthal, 2009).

4.3.2 Prerequisites for fast mapping

In order for the learner to know what a word they have just heard or read refers to, specific components or meanings of the word must be salient. Research offers various suggestions regarding how often a word has to be heard or seen before it becomes part of the mental lexicon. For example, Thornbury (2002) argues that a word must be heard or read five to 16 times to be learned by adolescent foreign language learners in a classroom, who have the benefit of being literate. Calderón and Slakk (2019) argue that a learner must hear and produce a word a minimum of 12 times before it begins to become part of a learner's long-term memory and can be retrieved for effective use.

A prerequisite for learning words is the learner's previous knowledge. In the case of children, the more words from a particular semantic field that the child has already acquired, the more reliably the child can hook a new word onto words already in their mental lexicon (e.g. in the color example above, in Section 4.2.1). The physical environment in which words are learned is another prerequisite, which particularly applies in second language acquisition since, unlike for babies, a low-anxiety language learning situation is not guaranteed. The learner has to feel comfortable and relaxed, and there must not be too much information given at once (Tiefenthal, 2009). For this reason, it can be more challenging for the teacher to think about how to introduce new words implicitly instead of drawing explicit connections between a label and an object ('Look, this is a …'). The implicit teaching of words requires the learner to infer the meanings of new words; e.g. in an utterance such as 'Look at this picture in the magazine', learners have to infer that 'magazine' refers to the object the teacher is holding in his/her hand, if they do not already know the word and, for non-literate adult migrants, have no concept of the word. The model by Hirsh-Pasek *et al.* (2000), shown below in Figure 4.5, developed with young children in mind, includes the most important prerequisites or cues for successful naming and fast mapping. The figure places the migrant adult, the LESLLA learner, instead of the child at the center.

Imagine a situation in which a migrant adult is shown a street map of Newcastle upon Tyne (England) and is told, 'We are going to meet at the intersection of Grainger and Nelson Street'. Let's assume that the learner knows the names of these two streets, understands the future use of 'going to', has acquired the definite and indefinite ARTICLES 'a' and 'the', and knows the verb 'meet' but has never heard the word 'intersection' before. How can the six cues in the figure help him/her identify (and then store) the meaning and word form 'intersection'? This can be done in the following ways:

(1) PERCEPTUAL SALIENCE: Ideally, the two streets are clearly labelled and visible on the map.
(2) Grammar: 'Intersection' is preceded by a definite article, so it must be a noun.

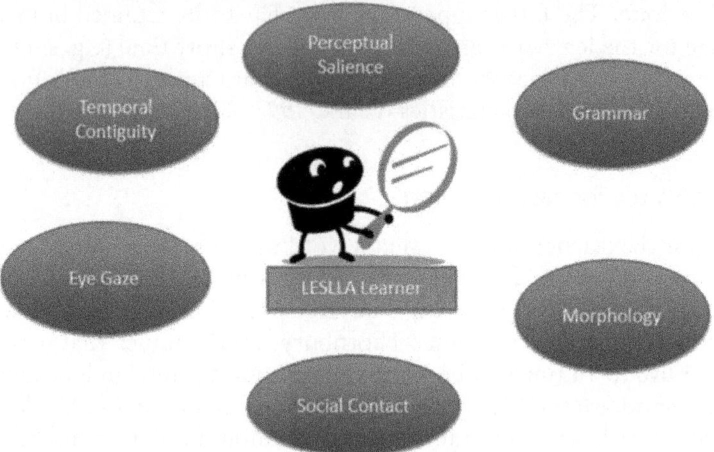

Figure 4.5 Cues for successful naming and fast mapping (based on Hirsh-Pasek *et al.*, 2000: 136)

(3) Morphology*:* 'Inter' is perhaps known from 'international', so the learner may know that it has the meaning of 'between'.
(4) Social contact*:* The teacher/speaker uses a pointing gesture or he/she outlines the intersection on the map with his/her fingers.
(5) Eye gaze*:* Social contact is closely linked to the speaker's eye gaze, which may guide the learner to the object referred to.
(6) TEMPORAL CONTIGUITY: Naming the intersection on the map usually coincides with pointing to it.

A similar process can be followed, with use of the six cues, when the learner is encountering the word in print, possibly in a text about the community and the sentence, 'The fire station is at the intersection of Grainger Street and Nelson Street'. The teacher or tutor can model the use of these six cues in working with migrant adults, for example, while reading a text aloud to them.

4.3.3 Fast mapping experiments in child L2 acquisition

Most of the research on fast mapping has been carried out with children. As we have already noted, young children without literacy are highly skilled fast mappers, and fast mapping is a process that is available across the lifespan in the effortless learning of new words. We can, therefore, apply findings from studies of children to migrant adults.

Rohde and Tiefenthal (2002) carried out a number of experiments with three- to six-year-old German children acquiring English as a second language in a bilingual kindergarten class. One of these experiments involved a new toy animal, a toy moose with a blue cap, and a word created for the study ('swop') for the toy. This was introduced in an interactive session in English in which the children heard the label 'swop' 10 times. 24 hours later, the children were shown seven objects, including the new toy, the swop. Twelve out of the 27 children were able to identify the toy moose when asked 'Which one is a swop?' after hearing the word 10 times in the interactive session with the toy. However, eight of the children failed to correctly name the swop in a subsequent test; they were not able to produce the label. A second experiment involved 15 monolingual German children who heard a different word created for the study, 'glop', 10 times for the toy moose. These children showed better recall than the bilingual school children. All 15 were later able to identify the toy, and nine were also able to correctly name the toy moose as 'glop' in a subsequent test two hours later.

Rohde and Tiefenthal asked themselves why the monolingual children were better able than the bilingual children to remember the novel name after hearing it 10 times and then after a 24-hour delay. They speculated that fast mapping in a second language may be less effective than in a first language, because it is more difficult to use some of the cues. Not unexpectedly, this relates to the second language learner's level of linguistic competence. For example, novel words may not be as salient when learners have not yet acquired the phonology of the new language. The second language situation, therefore, requires more effort from the learner in following utterances and applying all possible cues. In a monolingual context, however, a new word such as 'glop' will more easily stick out as being unfamiliar.

Rohde and Tiefenthal then conducted eight follow-up experiments with bilingual and monolingual German children to investigate the influence of various factors on the success of fast mapping. These factors included word class (not only nouns, as in most child language studies); the medium of introduction (a game, a song, a video film); the temporal delay between the introduction of the new words and testing them; the amount of new words introduced; the FREQUENCY of labelling a new object; and the sex, age and the size of children's vocabularies in the lexical field relevant to the new word. The results led to eight conclusions, some of which have been mentioned above:

(1) Word class is an influential factor: Nouns are better learned than verbs, and verbs are better learned than adjectives, thus supporting the understanding of the primacy of nouns in fast mapping (Gentner & Boroditsky, 2001).
(2) The ability to fast map is not affected by different contexts in which the word is introduced. Even if the children in an experiment are not given the opportunity to ask questions about a word's meaning, as in one video experiment, they are able to infer the target-like meaning and learn it.
(3) The level of attention and concentration involved in a particular task is important. When a play context was too exciting, the children did not remember any new vocabulary.
(4) Children did better when new vocabulary was introduced to them individually rather than in a group situation.
(5) Children did better when the new word was used more frequently.

(6) Children were far more successful in comprehending/recognizing the meanings of new words than they were in producing them. New words may be understood after a delay of 24 hours, but very few of the children were able to produce the words as well.
(7) The amount of time that elapsed, however, did not make a significant difference. Children performed the same regardless of whether they were tested after 24 hours or a week after the introduction of a new word.
(8) The monolingual German children performed better than the bilingual children in every task. Due to the dominance of German for the bilingual children, fast mapping was consistently more successful in a German context than in English, where more attention was required by the children to understand instructions, for example.

The implications of these conclusions for migrant adults' recognition of the meaning of new words they hear – including outside the classroom – are that they will be able to infer meaning from context if demands on their attention are not excessive; if they are alone and interacting with one other person; and if they hear the word frequently, particularly if it is a noun. Teachers and tutors can encourage learners to fast map by considering the information presented in this section and experimenting with new ideas, such as those described in Section 4.6, perhaps even by conducting action research, such as the studies with children described here. Given that there is no research on fast mapping by migrant adults, there is considerable scope for exploring exciting new avenues of word learning for adults who are often held back by having small vocabularies.

4.4 How We Learn the Meaning(s) of Words

We now turn to two basic questions, one of which we have answered above: What exactly is it that enables us to learn and retain words? The discussion above of fast mapping shows that we are equipped with the ability to encode, store, retain, and subsequently recall information, and that for humans, this includes word forms and what they relate to in the real world (their meanings). Our memory enables us to store and retain word shapes. However, this says nothing about how words relate to our reality, so we still need to address a second question: How do we figure out the meaning(s) of words? To address this question, we discuss two views: LEXICAL PRINCIPLES and Theory-of-Mind.

4.4.1 Lexical principles

Words are linked to our world by the SYMBOLIC FUNCTION that we humans develop between two and four years of age. This function gives us the insight that a word, a sign, or an icon refers to something in the world: a specific object, a particular action, or a quality. We can refer to children's development of this as the NAMING INSIGHT (Golinkoff & Hirsh-Pasek, 2000). This ability is shared (at least to some extent) by other species, such as apes and dogs (Kaminski *et al.*, 2004). If a child knows that a word has the power of reference, we still need to ask what exactly a given word refers to. The word 'ball' refers to a ball or balls in general. But that doesn't answer the question, since we have to explain how the child knows that the word 'ball' refers to the ball in its entirety and how the child knows the word does not refer to some quality of 'ball', such as its shape, color or texture, or the trajectory of a ball, or the ball and its owner. According to the Lexical Principles view, from a young age, humans follow principles derived from three assumptions (listed below). There is no reason to think that migrant adults would not also automatically follow these principles in their word learning. When one thinks about teachers' and tutors' interactions with migrant adult learners, their guesses will also be based on these assumptions.

THE WHOLE OBJECT ASSUMPTION: For very young children between about one and three years of age, words refer to objects in their entirety and not to their parts or substances (Markman, 1989; Rohde, 2005).

THE TAXONOMIC ASSUMPTION: Words refer to objects of like kind. When the child learns the word *dog* for the family dog, he/she will assume that other objects identified as dogs can also be referred to as *dog*. This is an important point if we consider that children, upon perceiving differences between two dogs, could conclude that a new second exemplar should require a different word. Children do, in fact, on occasion, UNDEREXTEND the meaning of a word when they only refer to the family dog as *dog* and deny that other dogs can be called dogs. They OVEREXTEND the meaning of a word when they use the word *dog* to refer to all four-legged animals (Markman, 1989; Rohde, 2005).

THE MUTUAL EXCLUSIVITY ASSUMPTION: Children between one and three years of age prefer one label per object; for example, the child might deny that a dog can also be called a dachshund or an animal (Hansen & Markman, 2009; Markman, 1989; Rohde, 2005).

These three assumptions serve to limit a child's or other learner's assumptions and facilitate the word learning process by constraining guesses about what a form might refer to in the real world. They also account for the ability of children to build a large mental lexicon so quickly.

4.4.2 The whole object and taxonomic assumptions

The taxonomic assumption (and, indirectly, the whole object assumption) has been tested in experiments in which the researcher asks children to match a target object (e.g. a car) with another object from a set of three, containing another car, a traffic light, and a book as a DISTRACTOR (adapted from Markman & Hutchinson, 1984). While it would be difficult to conduct this sort of experiment with lower-level migrant adults due to vocabularies that are usually limited, it is worth thinking about applying a modified version of this experiment as a task or game with learners but using real new words rather than nonsense words. Examples of words used in this task are shown in Table 4.2.

Table 4.2 Taxonomic vs. thematic choices in a selection task (Rohde, 2005: 178)

Standard object	Taxonomic choice	Thematic choice	Distractor
car	van	traffic light	book
pair of shoes	pair of pumps	naked feet	piano
German shepherd	beagle	doghouse	pen
armchair	highchair	boy sitting	flower

These tests suggest that a new word (e.g. a car, named with a made-up word such as 'flane') in instructions to children, 'This is a "flane". Can you find another "flane"?', tends to prompt the children to select the taxonomically related item (the second car). However, when no new word is offered, as in, 'See this? Can you find another one like this?', children, particularly those below the age of four, picked the thematically related traffic light. There was always a distractor word included in the experimental setup to make sure that the children had the choice of selecting neither the taxonomic nor the thematic choice. The results from this sort of experiment show that words function as invitations to form categories in our mental lexicons. When objects were not labelled by words, younger children – including bilingual kindergarten children aged three to six – focused more on thematic relations (Rohde, 2005).

4.4.3 The mutual exclusivity assumption: Disambiguation

When children assume mutual exclusivity (the preference for one word to name each object), this does not mean that they cannot learn a second word for an object, as noted above. Research shows, however, that children clearly prefer to identify one word with one object (this will differ for bilingual children). Migrant adults may resist learning a new word for an object or concept for which they already have a word, and this assumption explains why.

Experimental designs to test the mutual exclusivity assumption include simple disambiguation tasks. In these tasks, children show the ability to disambiguate a potentially ambiguous situation when they decide that an unfamiliar word refers to an unknown or novel object. This involves the researcher showing the child four objects, three of which are familiar and one which is unfamiliar, referred to by a new word, for example, 'flane'. Children apply the new word to the unfamiliar object rather than assuming that the new word is an alternative word for one of the familiar objects (Davidson *et al.*, 1997; Mervis & Bertrand, 1994). Interestingly, similar experiments have been carried out with border collies, arguably the most intelligent breed of dogs, demonstrating that at least some dogs apply the mutual exclusivity principle (Kaminski *et al.*, 2004). We address this issue again below.

So far, we have discussed the receptive side of word learning. Researchers have not yet experimentally investigated whether these lexical principles are also at work in word production. Second language studies, for example, of German children who acquired English in the United States NATURALISTICALLY (without instruction) indicate that they abide by these principles in word production. In this longitudinal study, the children's first 700 to 1,000 words did not display hierarchical taxonomies but rather words for objects all at the BASIC LEVEL OF CONCEPTUALIZATION ('dog', 'fish', 'car'; Rohde, 2005: 153). Although no research we know of has been conducted on migrant adults' developing vocabularies, it is very likely that the results would be the same. Moreover, the children did not learn words for parts of objects but used words for objects in their entirety (apart from words for body parts). In line with mutual exclusivity, they did not learn words that could be identified as synonyms of other words they had learned (Rohde, 2005; Rohde & Tiefenthal, 2002).

What are the implications of this research for migrant adults? The focus on vocabulary learning with these learners is often on what is required for survival. As should be clear by this point, it is crucial to consider what we know about how the human mind deals with learning new words from infancy and across the lifespan, i.e. into adulthood. Some of this discussion has made explicit what we take for granted, that we assume a new word refers to an entire object. But when we consider the principle of mutual exclusivity for second language learners, we might assume that they are prepared to learn synonyms, since they are already doing something similar when they learn words in a new language for objects for which they already have words in their first language. Yet exclusivity, that two different words cannot be used for the same concept or object, still applies within the new language, as shown by Rohde and Tiefenthal (2002).

4.4.4 The social-pragmatic approach combined with the theory-of-mind view

Some researchers take another approach and attribute word learning entirely to what happens in the child's social environment and how the child interprets the thoughts and intensions of others (see also Chapter 2 on language acquisition and social context). According to this view, language is one way that adults encourage children to attend to certain phenomena in a shared social situation, and they limit the possible referents for a word (Tomasello, 2001). Those who take this approach give the child a role in the process through assuming that the child is able to take another person's perspective. What is known as THEORY OF MIND solves the word learning problem: in a situation where the child sees a familiar object (e.g. a banana) and a novel object (a whisk) and the researcher asks the child to 'point to the "fendle"' (using an unfamiliar made-up word), the child's task is to interpret the speaker's intention instead of assuming that words are mutually exclusive, as discussed above. The reasoning is as follows (Bloom, 2000).

> I know that this is called 'banana'.
>
> If the speaker meant to refer to the banana, she would have asked me to show her the banana.

But she didn't; she used a strange word, 'fendle'.

So, she must intend to refer to something other than the banana.

A plausible candidate is the unknown object [the whisk].

'Fendle' must refer to the unknown object [whisk].

It is certainly true that lexical principles cannot work in a vacuum. Word learning is a socio-cultural process, and children's language acquisition is influenced by the ability to interpret other people's communicative intentions, as will be the case for migrant adults as well (see Chapter 2 on language learning from a social context perspective). With respect to PRAGMATICS, the ability to interpret others' intentions allows us to understand that the intention behind utterances such as 'the door is open' or 'it's cold in here' could be requests to shut the door or to shut the window, respectively. But this approach only shifts the question of why children prefer to name whole objects and suggests that the above account explains more than the social account does. If the young child assumes that an adult wants to establish joint attention by pointing to a car and the adult exclaims, 'Look, there is a car', the question arises why the adult only refers to whole objects when interacting with the child. Perhaps the adult is convinced that the young child will not understand utterances like 'Look, see the dent in the car?'. Why would the adult think that the child does not understand 'dent' at the age of two or three? The answer is because the adult believes – without conscious reflection – that the child perceives objects as wholes and naturally prefers to use words for whole objects. Woodward (2000) summarizes the need for an integrated approach to word learning with children, which is also relevant to word learning of migrant adults:

> There is no silver bullet for word learning. No single factor can account for the word-learning success of young children. It is much more likely that each act of learning reflects the interaction of multiple constraints. (Woodward, 2000: 79)

4.5 Language Learning Strategies

As noted in Sections 4.2 and 4.3, there are two ways of learning new words: explicit and implicit learning. When it comes to implicit word learning, in addition to what has been discussed in the previous section, certain aspects of our word knowledge, such as COLLOCATIONS and their phonologic forms, are learned mostly incidentally in a native language and in a second language. In foreign and second language classrooms a lot of implicit vocabulary learning takes place. Here we discuss the strategies that learners use to notice and focus on a new word in order to learn its meaning. Their use has been one of the most important topics in the study of vocabulary learning (Calderón & Soto, 2017; Nation, 1990, 2001), and teachers and

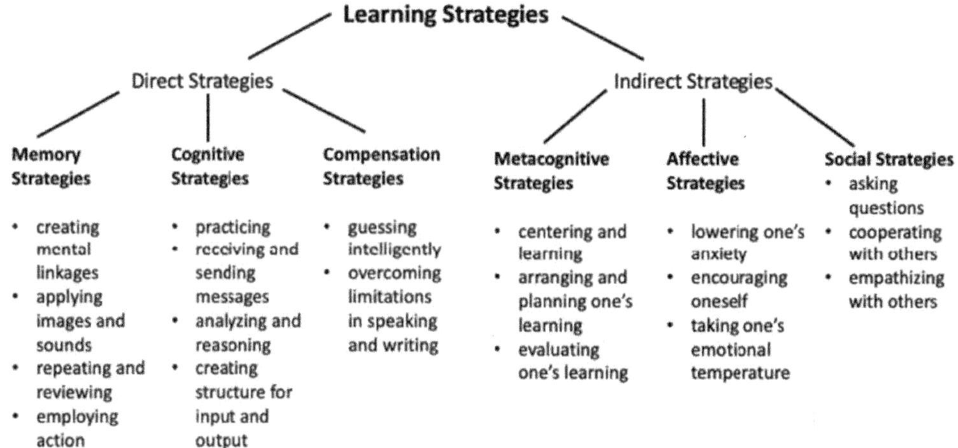

Figure 4.6 Direct and indirect learning strategies (based on Oxford, 1990: 17)

tutors may already be familiar with them based on experience as a second or foreign language learner and in working with educated older learners. Oxford categorizes these as shown in Figure 4.6 above, and defines them as:

> operations employed by the learner to aid the acquisition, storage, retrieval, and use of information … [and] specific actions taken by the learner to make learning easier, faster, more enjoyable, more self-directed, more effective, and more transferrable to new situations. (Oxford, 1990: 8)

Researchers have conceptualized language learning strategies to include not only the cognitive and intellectual but also the affective and social sides of learning, which are discussed in Chapter 2. As we go through these strategies, it is important to consider to what extent beginning-level adult migrants, with limited literacy, have developed the skills that underpin the strategies. If most strategies are currently unavailable to them, it is worth keeping in mind that they will be eventually, as they increasingly have control of their own learning.

Direct language learning strategies require teachers, tutors and learners to engage in mental processing. Indirect strategies focus on ways to support the learning process on a more general level, providing a supportive context for learning. Some of these are strategies that learners use without prompting, and some are strategies that teachers and tutors can support learners in developing. Cognitive strategies support comprehension and production of language, and memory strategies help to store and retrieve newly gained information. Compensation strategies make up for missing knowledge and comprehension gaps; for example, in the use of contextual clues or gestures to infer the meaning of a new word in an utterance or text. Metacognitive strategies help to monitor cognitive processes for focusing on, planning, and evaluating our own learning. AFFECTIVE STRATEGIES are responsible for building and maintaining self-confidence. Social strategies enable us to engage in conversations and interactions, orally and with written texts, and foster SOCIOLINGUISTIC COMPETENCE as well as CULTURAL AWARENESS (Oxford, 1990: 16ff.).

'Research continues to prove that strategies help learners take control of their learning and become more proficient' (Oxford, 1990: 22). Strategies are, at least to a certain extent, explicit, and thus learnable. Oxford (1990: 12) also notes that initially explicit learning can, after a certain amount of practice, become automatic. How migrant adults with varying levels of prior education use such strategies is presented in work on learner interactions (for example Pettitt & Tarone (2015) and Bigelow & King (2016) and how teachers and tutors might support migrant adults' development of strategies can be seen in work on learner portfolios in the Netherlands (see, e.g. Nuwenhoud, 2015); see also Chapter 2 and presentations and proceedings on the LESLLA website, www.leslla.org).

Research also indicates that the use of those strategies depends on a range of factors, such as the learner's level of METALINGUISTIC AWARENESS, the level of language proficiency, the specific demands of a task, expectations of the teacher, age, gender, nationality, general learning behaviour, personality traits, motivation and learning goals (Nuwenhoud, 2015; Oxford, 1990; see also Mißler, 1999). This suggests that the greatest challenges in using these strategies will be for older non-literate adults with weak metalinguistic awareness and lower levels of linguistic competence. Training learners to use learning strategies and providing plentiful opportunities for them to practice them should be an essential part of vocabulary teaching. It will also help them become more aware of and evaluate their strategy use and gain autonomy to enhance their own learning processes as they monitor and control their learning (Knapp-Potthoff, 1997; Zahedi & Abdi, 2012).

4.5.1 Word learning strategies

Zahedi and Abdi (2012: 2273) call for teachers to assist learners in developing word learning strategies, noting that, 'It has been suggested that teaching vocabulary should not only consist of teaching specific words but also aim at equipping learners with strategies necessary to expand their vocabulary knowledge'. Why should learners use word learning strategies if vocabulary learning can proceed implicitly, as in fast mapping? According to the DEPTH OF PROCESSING HYPOTHESIS (Craik & Lockhard, 1972), the storage of vocabulary items depends on cognitive engagement, the 'depth to which the stimulus is analyzed' (Craik & Lockhard, 1972: 2274). Under this hypothesis, shallow processing (e.g. the analysis of just visual or acoustic properties of a word) engages working memory. SEMANTIC PROCESSING, analysing the meaning of an item and relating it to previous knowledge, is the 'deep' processing that leads to storage in the learner's long-term memory (Craik & Lockhard, 1972). Examples of strategies that support deep processing are SEMANTIC MAPPING, which includes strategies such as grouping words, using imagery, associating and elaborating. While

Craik and Lockhard do not consider non-literate migrant adults, they argue that semantic mapping 'can be introduced to learners at any level of proficiency [...]. It has the effect of bringing relationships in a text to consciousness for the purpose of deepening the understanding of a text and creating associative networks for words' (Craik & Lockhard, 1972: 2274). A description of the application of semantic mapping is given in Section 4.6.3.

4.5.2 Learning strategies and multilingual learners

As we have pointed out above, learning new words implicitly through incidental exposure requires multiple exposures to the word. Because adult migrants usually receive considerably less language input than children (see Chapter 2), the use of explicit learning gains in importance (Haudeck, 2008). However, we know that migrant adults, particularly those with little or no formal education, are much less equipped to develop strategies than the educated learners to which the strategies shown in Figure 4.6 are intended to apply. This means that teachers and tutors will need to provide different types of support in helping them develop the strategies that will enable them to take more control of their learning process.

Some migrant adults have grown up bi- and even multilingually or have naturalistically acquired another language (such as Swahili in a refugee camp in Kenya), and research shows that these learners are more successful than their monolingual peers due to the enhanced metalinguistic awareness conferred by growing up with more than one language (see Chapter 6). Besides use of communicative strategies, the readiness to make guesses and take risks, and the application of hypothesis testing are strategies that may be enhanced in learners used to using more than one language, and this increases the probability of success when using strategies to learn new words (Mißler, 1999).

If the learner wants a new word to become a permanent entry in his or her mental lexicon, he or she can consciously connect it to words already known. The greater the breadth of vocabulary, i.e. the more extensive this existing knowledge is, the more points of reference there will be to more efficiently learn new words (Haudeck, 2008).

4.5.3 Inductive inferencing and intercomprehension

Previous language knowledge and skills are especially helpful when guessing the meanings of new words. Intelligent guessing or (inductive) INFERENCING fall under compensation strategies in Figure 4.6. When guessing the meaning of a new word, the learner can draw on different kinds of knowledge: IMPLICIT KNOWLEDGE about the target language, knowledge from languages known, general metalinguistic knowledge and world knowledge and contextual information that accompanies the word (Mißler, 1999).

INTERCOMPREHENSION originally referred to the ability of speakers of languages belonging to the same LANGUAGE FAMILY (for example Slavic, Romance or Germanic) to have some understanding of each other when speaking or reading without actually knowing the language. Intercomprehension identifies specific resources that multilingual learners might use to infer the meaning of a word in the target language. The claim is that learners have some knowledge in various categories at their disposal to exploit, and that teachers and tutors can help them use this knowledge to understand new words (European Commission, 2012: 9).

According to Doyé (2004), learners can use categories to make inferences on the basis of the languages they know. While some of these refer to written text and will not initially be available to migrant adults with little or no formal education, others are a useful encapsulation of the knowledge and experience they possess as adults, which they will be able to apply to comprehension of written texts as they continue to develop their literacy.

General world/encyclopaedic knowledge, cultural and socio-cultural knowledge, include what is listed below; some of these are covered in Chapters 2, 3 and 5.

Knowledge about the situation that a *spoken or written* text is embedded in:

(1) Behavioural knowledge (ability to recognize and interpret culture-specific behaviour, non-verbal signs).
(2) Pragmatic knowledge (knowing the purpose that a *written* text serves).
(3) Graphic knowledge (writing systems).
(4) Phonological knowledge (sound system).
(5) Grammatical knowledge (grammatical structures, syntax, and morphology).
(6) Lexical knowledge (international – *borrowed* – vocabulary as well as related vocabulary from related languages (cognates).

(European Commission, 2012: 9; text in italics has been added by the authors)

With respect to migrant learners in post-industrialized countries, the ability to strategically draw on related languages pertains to those who may have been exposed to English, French or Portuguese in their home countries, particularly in sub-Saharan Africa, but who are in the process of learning another language from the same family. Let's say a learner knows English but has resettled in a country where one of the languages shown in Table 4.3 is spoken. Möller (2014) lists the following cognates that could be helpful when being exposed to new words in one of these languages:

Table 4.3 Cognates in North and West Germanic languages (Möller, 2014: 28)

Swedish	Norwegian	Danish	Icelandic	English	Dutch	German
ja	ja	ja	já	yes	ja	ja
nej	nei	nej	nei	no	nee(n)	nein
dag	dag	dag	dagur	day	dag	Tag
natt	natt	nat	nòtt	night	nacht	Nacht
här	her	her	hér	here	hier	hier

Once learners have acquired a certain level of linguistic competence and have begun to develop awareness of the derivational morphology involved in the creation of a range of words through the addition of prefixes and suffixes, this helps considerably in figuring out the meaning of new words. If the learner knows an adjective such as ‘happy’, learning its antonym ‘unhappy’ is straightforward with knowledge that the prefix *un-* means not. If the learner knows a verb such as ‘drive’, knowledge of the suffix –er can help in learning the word for someone who performs this action, e.g. as a ‘bus driver’.

4.6 Implications for Teaching Vocabulary

We have noted that a certain amount of word learning will take place implicitly, outside the classroom. What about word learning in the classroom? In addition to the points made above, what should be considered? Older, experienced language learners who decide to take a language class will expect their teachers to explicitly present them with language, and this may also be true of adult migrants. Therefore, teaching words is an important part of every language learning programme. But which words should be taught? How can new words be introduced? How can learners be supported in deepening their word knowledge?

4.6.1 Which words to teach

How many words a second language learner needs to know depends on the situations in which he or she will use the language. While starting a new job requires knowledge of vocabulary specific to that job (see below), a second language learner also needs to be equipped with a core vocabulary of words that are frequently used in daily interactions with native speakers, the survival vocabulary with which teachers and tutors who work with migrant adults are familiar.

One criterion for choice of words to teach is frequency of use of the word in the language. Most adult native speakers of English have a core vocabulary of around 2000 words (Thornbury, 2002). The most frequent words in any language are function words (words, as well as prefixes and suffixes, that express a grammatical relationship with other words in a text such as ‘but’, ‘the’, ‘that’ as well as suffixes such as past tense –ed and plural –s.) These are not the nouns, verbs, and adjectives whose learning we have focused on in this chapter. Chapter 5 is devoted to such words in its coverage of the acquisition of morphosyntax. (For a list of the categories of function words and of the words in each category, see https://www.thoughtco.com/function-word-grammar-1690876.) There are now CORPORA of the most frequent words used in both spoken situations (e.g. radio broadcasts) and written texts (newspapers, novels) in various languages, and these can easily be found online. Because these lists are often based on contexts not relevant to adult migrant learners, the teacher or tutor will need to carefully consider their usefulness.

Migrant adults will also need less frequently used words for work, and helping learners with these can be a challenge when the meaning of a word cannot easily be described or paraphrased. For example, perhaps a learner has just gotten a job as a tailor, and the word 'thread' is important. To describe or paraphrase it, words such as 'sew', 'needle', 'wire', 'fiber' or 'strand' could be used, but these are not high-frequency words, and the learner might not know them (Gairns & Redman, 2004). Here picture dictionaries are indispensable.

In relation to the survival vocabulary mentioned in the first paragraph in this section are words that reflect the learners' needs in terms of their cultural and religious backgrounds and their interests outside of class. While these might well lie outside core frequency lists and the concepts may even be unfamiliar to teachers and tutors (Gairns & Redman, 2004), including them guarantees relevance and increases learners' motivation. Use of approaches such as the Language Experience Approach (see Chapters 3 and 7) is one way to explore the words important to individual learners.

This observation leads to the next category of words a learner needs to know in order to interact orally, read, and write effectively. These are words relating to work and include the highly specialized words found on job applications. (See Chapter 2 for more on migrant adults and work.) The learner's need for and understanding of the relevance of such words can increase motivation to learn them and override the observed tendency to start with basic-level words (i.e. words that are often used in daily life, e.g. house, go, nice) discussed above.

Last but not least, there are words used in the classroom by teachers (e.g. book, pen, listen). Although these might not be high on frequency lists, their regular use in the classroom, orally and in written texts, means that they will be considered when deciding on words that learners need to know from the very start (Gairns & Redman, 2004).

4.6.2 Introducing new words

Dealing with the explicit learning of words entails deciding how to present them. There are a number of decisions to make:

(1) How many words should the teacher or tutor aim to introduce?
(2) What should be introduced first, meaning or form?
(3) Is the aim recognition or production of words or both?
(4) Which means of presentation should be chosen?

The number of words introduced during a given session depends on factors such as the difficulty of the words and the learners' current language levels. Teachers and tutors will also consider how easily the meanings of words can be explained or even demonstrated. They will also want to decide whether learners should recognize the new words being presented or also produce them. This will depend on the learners' needs, the particular word, and the learner's literacy level, if learning words in written text is involved (Thornbury, 2002). How words are presented also depends on the morphosyntax of the language (see Chapter 5). A study of migrant women in Finland, discussed in Chapter 2, found that after many months, they had learned only a few words. The authors attribute this to the extensive inflectional marking in Finnish (Tammelin-Laine & Martin, 2015).

The traditional way of presenting vocabulary in the classroom or in one-to-one tutoring is to start with the form, saying the word a few times and having the learners repeat it each time. If the word is something like 'jacket', the teacher or tutor will simultaneously include meaning by pointing to his/her jacket, and having learners point to their own and others' jackets. They might then use pair or small group work, during which learners use the new word 'jacket' with words such as 'wear' and in sentences such as 'I wear a jacket in the winter'. Meaning can also be the starting point and can create a need to learn a given word as well as to see whether any of the learners already know that word. The teacher or tutor can show the learners the object (or provide a photograph of it) and then introduce its form. Researchers argue that by presenting the **MEANING FIRST**, learners develop a need to know the form and memorize it more easily (Thornbury, 2002).

Calderón and Soto (2017) and Calderón and Sinclair-Slakk (2018) offer a tried-and-true seven-step process for pre-teaching words before learners use them for oral interaction and/or reading, which is adapted slightly here. Note that if the teaching situation involves learners who speak a number of different languages (and the teacher or tutor does not speak them), translation is not feasible (Thornbury, 2002).

(1) The teacher or tutor says the word (or phrase) and asks learners to repeat it three times, with correction if required. (This helps learners with pronunciation and avoids learners learning a mispronounced form of the word.)
(2) The teacher or tutor uses the word in a clear and relevant context; e.g. 'I am wearing a jacket today, because it is cold outside'.
(3) The teacher or tutor gives a dictionary definition of the word in language at the learners' level; e.g. 'a piece of clothing you wear when it is cold outside. It usually has long sleeves and a zipper. You wear it in addition to a pullover'. There are various reasons for not having learners consult a dictionary initially. Even if they are able to do so, it takes too long, and they can easily select the wrong meaning, which can cause confusion. Learners should also not be asked to guess the meaning of the word for reasons of efficiency. This takes too long, and guesses can be wrong. (See below for discussion of use of dictionaries with migrant adults with limited literacy.)
(4) The teacher or tutor provides a **LEARNER-FRIENDLY DEFINITION**, as some dictionary definitions are much more difficult than the word itself; e.g. 'I wear my jacket to stay warm'.
(5) The teacher or tutor highlights linguistic aspects of the word, its word class (noun, verb, etc.), how it is used in a sentence, its spelling and perhaps one or more prefixes and suffixes that can be added to change its meaning.
(6) Learners engage in a teacher-/tutor-provided sentence frame and use the word in the sentence; e.g. 'Ali is wearing a red jacket'. If in a classroom, the learners

can practice using the word in pairs, in sentences, speaking back and forth, using the sentence frame; e.g. changing the name of the person wearing a red jacket or changing the color of the jacket. While learners use the word, the teacher checks to see how they are doing.

(7) The teacher or tutor creates ideas for learners to practice using the word before they come to class again for reinforcement over time, so it enters their long-term memory. This can be in conversation with those with whom they speak the target language, or, in the example of jacket, they can find advertisements in newspapers or online.

The teacher can then use various means, e.g. oral or written exit passes, for learners to say or write the word in a sentence before they leave class. The words should then be reviewed in the following lessons to ensure that they are learned.

There are various options to illustrate or demonstrate the meanings of words (Thornbury, 2002). For nouns, teachers and tutors, as well as learners, can refer to or bring real-life objects (realia) to class. For many nouns and verbs and other word classes, such as adjectives and adverbs, teachers and tutors use **FLASH CARDS** with photographs or pictures, which they may have drawn or gotten from the internet. Facial expressions, gestures and miming are particularly useful. Some words, however, cannot be illustrated easily, so other options should be considered, including providing dictionary definitions, as described above in the third of the seven steps. The fastest and easiest way to find definitions of words is using monolingual dictionaries. Nevertheless, the use of dictionary definitions is not unproblematic, and it may be only the teacher or tutor who uses the dictionary to find definitions and even then does not read out the full definition, until learners have advanced in their reading abilities and in their linguistic competence/oral proficiency. In some cases, too little information is given or the meaning is paraphrased in a way that allows wrong interpretations of the word. Consider, for example, the word *erode*. The traditional definition of the word in a monolingual dictionary might include the phrase *eating out*, based on which one student created the sentence 'My family erodes a lot' (Graves *et al.*, 2013: 28). To avoid such problems and misunderstandings, it makes more sense to provide students with learner-friendly definitions (see step four above) and provide a clear and relevant context for use of the word (Graves *et al.*, 2013). Adult migrants with limited literacy find picture or photo dictionaries useful, although the teacher or tutor must keep in mind that some of those published (e.g. by Longman) contain themes that are not immediately relevant to migrant adults' lives, such as taking trips abroad and staying in hotels. Furthermore, abstract concepts that cannot be depicted are less likely to be included in such dictionaries.

4.6.3 Supporting learners in achieving depth of word knowledge

When presenting new words to migrant adult learners, the teacher or tutor can consider breadth and depth of word meaning, as discussed above. It is not only important that learners know many words but also that they know different aspects of words. They will know the meaning of the word, its form and its spelling, and, with time, they should discover related words, words' connotations, synonyms and new contexts in which the word is used. Depth of knowledge for a given word depends on learners' needs. The following methods, adapted from Graves *et al.* (2013), can help support learners in achieving vocabulary depth.

4.6.3.1 Semantic mapping

Semantic mapping can be used to deepen word knowledge and also support comprehension of topics that learners are currently dealing with. A simple example is 'family'. The teacher or tutor writes a word for that central concept (family) in the middle of a board or on a large sheet of paper and the learners, working in pairs or small groups, write as many words as they know related to that word around it (mother, father, sister, brother). The teacher or tutor helps them expand to words such as mother-in-law.

4.6.3.2 Venn diagrams

VENN DIAGRAMS represent different sets of word meanings (shown in overlapping circles) and their differences and similarities. In vocabulary learning, these diagrams are useful in working with words that are hard to differentiate, which share most but not all meanings or contexts of use. This activity has the potential to engage migrant adult learners in critical thinking concerning word meaning and to raise their language awareness. Working with the diagrams provides a way for learners to grasp the subtleties of word meaning. To do so, learners take two words that are hard to differentiate, draw two minimally overlapping circles, and write what the two words share in the overlapping part of the circles. Features that only belong to one of the words are written in the outside part of the circle, not in the overlapping part (see Figure 4.7). As this sort of activity may pose a challenge for beginning-level migrant

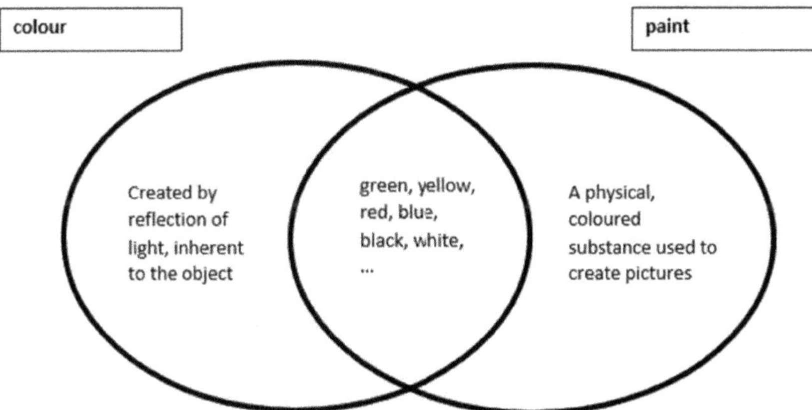

Figure 4.7 Example of a Venn diagram (based on Graves *et al.*, 2013)

adults, the starting point could be the learner's native language. The language used in the example here is beyond that of beginning-level migrant adults but provides an illustration of what is possible.

4.6.3.3 Four squares

Four squares is a simple technique to deepen the knowledge of single lexical items. It does not need much preparation. Learners start by folding a blank piece of paper into four parts. In the upper left quadrant, they write a word, e.g. the adjective 'furry'. Then they write things that are furry in the upper right quadrant and things that are not furry in the lower right quadrant. Learners may need to be guided to use suitable examples of the word and to be encouraged to discuss problematic examples. More advanced learners might write a sentence using the word or try to come up with their own simple definition of the word and write it in the lower left quadrant, as shown in Figure 4.8.

(*Word learners want to deepen their knowledge of*) **furry**	**cats** **rabbits** **dogs**	(*things that are furry*)
(*Own simple definition of the word*) **Things that have hair and feel very soft are furry.**	**snakes** **fish** **stones**	(*things that are not furry*)

Figure 4.8 Example of the Four Square method (based on Graves *et al.*, 2013)

4.6.4 Teaching word parts

Word parts – MORPHEMES – are useful in helping learners work out the meanings of new words (Graves *et al.*, 2013). DERIVATIONAL AFFIXES (prefixes and suffixes) change the class of a word and, sometimes, its meaning. If the learner knows the basic form of the word, the WORD STEM, knowing certain prefixes and suffixes can expand their vocabulary considerably. This is discussed briefly above, with 'drive' and 'driver', and 'happy' and 'unhappy' as examples. Awareness of derivational morphology can result in learners noticing patterns in sets of words they are learning. For example, if a class session is focused on jobs, learners can be led to notice that many of these words end in *–er;* e.g. teacher, gardener, cleaner, hairdresser, taxi driver. The ability to discern prefixes and suffixes in words relates to morphological awareness – one factor that will help with visual word recognition as their reading develops (Maag, 2007).

4.6.5 Using context to learn word meanings

The contexts in which new words are used can be provided by either listening texts or reading texts. Listening texts can be used first. Once the learner is moving beyond reading of single words and starting to read short sentences, written text becomes relevant. If the topic and the context are clear and familiar to the learners, they may already know many of the words and can guess the meaning of new words. The advantage of using a text for building vocabulary is that when words are learned in a given context, there is information about the use of the word, such as its grammatical function and specific connotations (McCarter & Jakes, 2009). Hearing or seeing a word in context, particularly when reading, enables the learner to achieve greater vocabulary depth (Koda, 2005; Nation, 1990, 2001). This also increases the learner's ability to use the word (McCarter & Jakes, 2009). Note, however, that the learner needs to know between 95% and 99% of the words in a written text to learn new ones from context as well as to read for pleasure (Koda, 2005; Nation, 1990, 2001). The teacher or tutor can prepare or arrange listening or written texts to reduce the number of new words to optimize the learner's chances of guessing new words from context. Then questions can be posed to small groups of learners, visuals included to heighten motivation, and learners' own experiences and viewpoints can be discussed (McCarter & Jakes, 2009).

Another way to use context for introducing words is to create LEXICAL SETS, groups of words that are related in meaning, as shown above in the discussion of semantic mapping and word families. Learners have the opportunity to connect new words with words they already know, or with familiar areas of knowledge and personal experience. For the classroom, it may be useful to choose lexical sets for topics that are likely to be relevant to all of the learners (e.g. 'health'). A way to work with the lexical set 'location' could be to download a map of the city and ask them to describe to a partner where they live or shop or where their children attend school. In this way, learners become familiar with, and use, specific words related to 'location' (McCarter & Jakes, 2009).

4.6.6 Learning about language register

In word use, we distinguish between FORMAL and INFORMAL REGISTER. Even though it might be very challenging for many learners to use different registers and accommodate their language to formal settings, teachers and tutors should consider teaching register, as adult migrant learners will be faced with situations in which they are confronted with a more formal register; e.g. applications, conversations with work superiors, job interviews.

To help them, learners can be asked to match formal and informal words and expressions with the same meaning but used for different registers and then indicate which is formal and which is informal (McCarter & Jakes, 2009). This can be done orally or in writing. Some example pairs would be: May I please vs. I would prefer; drink vs. beverage; whole vs. entire; need vs. require; buy vs. purchase or help vs. assist.

4.6.7 Vocabulary knowledge and reading

As noted in Chapter 3, vocabulary knowledge is fundamental in reading comprehension (Koda, 2005), and all of the aspects of word knowledge presented in this chapter are important for the learner to move beyond decoding to reading comprehension (Grabe, 2009). There are several perspectives on how word knowledge and reading comprehension are related. One perspective is that vocabulary knowledge comes first and enables the reader to comprehend a text. Research shows that vocabulary knowledge is one of the strongest predictors of second language reading ability (Grabe, 2009). The other is that through extensive reading, vocabulary knowledge considerably expands through incidental exposure (Koda, 2005; see also discussion in Chapter 3). Research also shows that learning vocabulary is a by-product of reading (Koda, 2005). This and the above discussion of learning from context underscore the relevance to migrant adults of learning words in both oral and written contexts. This learning could be supported by, e.g. the teacher asking questions that activate different types of knowledge relating to context (e.g. linguistic knowledge that learners have already gained, knowledge from previously LEARNED LANGUAGES) and explicitly training learners to make informed guesses about new words they encounter. Teachers and tutors may, for example, ask about the word class (consider the word 'family': Is it a noun? Is it a verb?) or other words that the word in question is connected to (e.g. mother, father, sister, brother, etc.) (Aebersold & Field, 2003).

4.7 Conclusion

In this chapter, a wide range of issues related to vocabulary learning are discussed. The vast majority of the research referred to focuses on young children and educated second language learners. This is because there is very little research on the vocabulary development of migrant adults with little or no formal schooling. It is also because this research can usually be directly applied to migrant adults, because the processes discussed, such as (fast) mapping of meanings onto word forms, is an ability that humans are endowed with from birth and does not disappear with age. Upon entering school, young children already have thousands of words in their mental lexicons. They can use many of these productively and understand the rest (the number of words reported in the research differs drastically, depending whether one counts individual words or families of words). Learning the vocabulary of a second or third language raises specific issues. General word learning ability is still intact, but words in a new language are not simply equivalents to the words already known in one's first language, and they may cover different semantic ground. Words enter language-specific collocations and idioms to such an extent that one can claim (e.g. Hausmann, 1993) that not only does the vocabulary differ across languages, what it represents also differs, implicating world views and cultural values. Hausmann's view should not discourage the teacher and tutor. There is no critical period beyond which the learning of vocabulary by adults fundamentally changes, and with the right motivation, appropriate learning strategies, and use of targeted teaching techniques and methods designed for migrant adult learners with little or no formal schooling, amassing a sizable vocabulary is feasible.

5 Acquisition and Assessment of Morphosyntax

Martha Young-Scholten and Rola Naeb

5.1 Introduction

In the introduction to this volume, the editors clarify the relevance of this chapter for those who work with adults starting their acquisition of a new language without the support of literacy. In addition to the obvious role of morphosyntax in building learners' oral proficiency, morphosyntax is closely tied to reading comprehension. The learner can decode individual words without competence in the morphosyntax of a language, but such competence is required to understand sentences.

The editors also make the point that much of the research described in this volume was not carried out on migrant adults with little or no education or native language literacy. It is worth restating there that this is because there is very little such research. While this also holds for research on the L2 acquisition of morphosyntax, not only has there been slightly more such research in this realm but there is also a strong tradition of research on migrant adults dating back to the 1970s on which to draw.

Let's begin by taking a brief look at the widely used Common European Framework (CEF) of Reference for Languages and its CAN-DO STATEMENTS, shown in Table 5.1. The six CEF levels (and scales, which have adopted similar descriptors) are of interest to second language acquisition (SLA) researchers, practitioners, and learners who want to track how use of a second language develops over time, from the bottom of the scale, A1, to the top, C2. For over a decade, there have been calls to add a level below A1 to represent beginning-level non-literate migrant adults' language use (see Minuz & Borri, 2016).

Can-do statements are insufficient if we want to know how the morphosyntax of a new language is represented in the learner's mind. In this chapter, we therefore focus on the language learner's morphosyntax, exploring what underlies the can-do statements at these levels. This exploration reveals the hidden dynamic interplay between the learner's mind and the input received, whether it is in the classroom or outside the classroom. We refer to the MENTAL REPRESENTATION OF LANGUAGE as linguistic competence. When we produce language, we place words in a certain order in a sentence, and we understand and produce a range of words and parts of words

Table 5.1 Common reference levels: Global Scale (Council of Europe, 2001)

Proficient user	C2	• Can understand with ease virtually everything heard or read. • Can summarize information from different spoken and written sources, reconstructing arguments and accounts in a coherent presentation. • Can express him/herself spontaneously, very fluently and precisely, differentiating finer shades of meaning even in more complex situations.
	C1	• Can understand a wide range of demanding, longer texts, and recognize implicit meaning. • Can express him/herself fluently and spontaneously without much obvious searching for expressions. • Can use language flexibly and effectively for social, academic and professional purposes. • Can produce clear, well-structured, detailed text on complex subjects, showing controlled use of organizational patterns, connectors and cohesive devices.
Independent user	B2	• Can understand the main ideas of complex text on both concrete and abstract topics, including technical discussions in his/her field of specialization. • Can interact with a degree of fluency and spontaneity that makes regular interaction with native speakers quite possible without strain for either party. • Can produce clear, detailed text on a wide range of subjects and explain a viewpoint on a topical issue giving the advantages and disadvantages of various options.
	B1	• Can understand the main points of clear standard input on familiar matters regularly encountered in work, school, leisure, etc. • Can deal with most situations likely to arise whilst travelling in an area where the language is spoken. • Can produce simple connected text on topics which are familiar or of personal interest. • Can describe experiences and events, dreams, hopes & ambitions and briefly give reasons and explanations for opinions and plans.
Basic user	A2	• Can understand sentences and frequently used expressions related to areas of most immediate relevance (e.g. very basic personal and family information, shopping, local geography, employment). • Can communicate in simple and routine tasks requiring a simple and direct exchange of information on familiar and routine matters. • Can describe in simple terms aspects of his/her background, immediate environment and matters in areas of immediate need.
	A1	• Can understand and use familiar everyday expressions and very basic phrases aimed at the satisfaction of needs of a concrete type. • Can introduce him/herself and others and can ask and answer questions about personal details such as where he/she lives, people he/she knows and things he/she has. • Can interact in a simple way provided the other person talks slowly and clearly and is prepared to help.

(morphemes) with little or no semantic content that represent certain functions – morphosyntax. This competence consists of rules and forms that a native speaker of a language subconsciously knows and automatically uses (Chomsky, 1957).

In looking at morphosyntax, this chapter addresses a question that has long been asked: Why don't learners always learn what they are taught? (Allwright, 1984). The flip side of this is a question asked less frequently: How do learners learn what is not explicitly taught? This chapter considers both of these questions to reach a nuanced understanding of adult L2 learners' journey from lower to higher levels of competence in morphosyntax. The chapter also takes seriously the idea that teachers and tutors can have great expectations for their students. This was expressed by Lightbown (1985), who pointed out how important it is to understand learners' internal acquisition processes.

When considering a language learner's journey toward linguistic competence, it is useful to think of two dimensions; the learner's perspective and the linguist's or teacher's/tutor's perspective, as shown in Figure 5.1.

easy	....	difficult
simple	....	complex

Figure 5.1 Ease and difficulty of acquisition of components of a language

Does what is easy for the learner to acquire in a given language parallel what we consider to be the simplest? A relevant example is subject-verb agreement and third person singular –s in English. In the sentence 'Mary loves John', the function of –s is to show that the verb 'loves' agrees with the subject, 'Mary'. The morphosyntax involved is the simple attachment of the morpheme –s to the verb. However, researchers have found that children and second language learners take a long time to acquire third person singular in English. Why is this? We answer this question further below.

Knowing what distinguishes a phenomenon that is easy vs. difficult for the learner is an ongoing challenge for the linguist. The distinction could entail what is referred to as LANGUAGE PROCESSING, how individuals construct mental representations when they listen to or read language. Importantly, the study of processing includes what individuals do when they misperceive language input. It is safe to say that input that is beyond a learner's current proficiency will be ignored. The internal changes that occur in language learners' mental representations during acquisition mean that at certain points they will 'recognize evidence in their surroundings that they were blind to before' (Phillips & Ehrenhofter, 2015: 438; for an overview of how such ideas are relevant to second language teaching, see Marinis & Cunnings, 2018).

We can add a third dimension to the easy-difficult and simple-complex dimensions in Figure 5.1 above: importance in communication. The communicative importance of third person singular –s is low in English. If a child, non-native speaker or speaker of a variety that omits third person singular –s fails to produce it, the listener has no problem understanding not only that it's Mary who loves John or if Mary is replaced by a pronoun as in 'She really does love John', that 'she' refers to Mary. Subject-verb agreement is, however, communicatively essential in PRO-DROP LANGUAGES where subject pronouns can be omitted. For example, in Finnish, Italian, Spanish and Turkish, a suffix on the verb indicates the verb's agreement with the subject of that verb. The suffix –o in Spanish enables the listener to identify the non-expressed or EMPTY SUBJECT as first person singular in a sentence such as *No tengo dinero* 'I have no money'. The subject pronoun in Spanish is *yo* 'I' and it could precede *no*, but only if the pronoun is stressed to, for example, express a contrast between I and another possible subject. It's I who have no money, not someone else.

Keep these three dimensions in mind to think about the implications for teaching of the research presented in this chapter.

5.2 Child Language Acquisition

The GENERATIVE VIEW OF LANGUAGE promoted by Noam Chomsky since the 1950s sees humans as innately predisposed to acquire language. For generative linguists, language – particularly syntax – is seen as separate from GENERAL COGNITION. When linguists study language acquisition, they are interested in exploring how linguistic competence comes to be represented in the language learner's mind. Chomsky put forward the idea that humans possess a UNIVERSAL GRAMMAR, which accounts for similarities and certain differences across languages and also guides children's acquisition of language (e.g. Chomsky, 1981). Universal Grammar (UG) is also applied to explain the highly systematic steps that children have been observed to take in their journey toward adult linguistic competence when their mental representations are non-adult versions of the language they are learning.

Under a GENERATIVE APPROACH to child language acquisition, researchers ask how all children (even those who are cognitively impaired) acquire the complex syntax and functional morphology of their speech community after only three or four years, before they have mastered the cognitive challenges of similar sophistication. Researchers point out that caregivers are inconsistent in their correction of children's non-adult language, and caregivers and others such as siblings and friends provide imperfect input; for example, their speech may contain false starts and even random mistakes. More important than these two observations is that the input is not labelled. When the child receives acoustic input, she/he has no idea where one word ends and the next word begins or what the function of words is once the SPEECH STREAM is segmented.

Alternative theories of language and of its acquisition by children include Halliday's FUNCTIONAL GRAMMAR (1994), Goldberg's (2007) CONSTRUCTION GRAMMAR, and Tomasello's (2003) and O'Grady's (2005, 2018) usage-based, EMERGENTIST THEORY of acquisition. These place considerably more emphasis on the role of language input than does the generative approach. Some SLA researchers also assume a greater role for input and for GENERAL COGNITIVE MECHANISMS. One line of research focuses on how L2 learners respond to the explicit teaching of language and to various types of feedback that indicate that their L2 production is not target-like. Early contributors to this idea are Schmidt (1990) with his NOTICING HYPOTHESIS and Ellis (1990, 2001); Robinson and Ellis (2008); VanPatten *et al.* (2004). Written specifically from this perspective, Tarone and Bigelow (2005) apply these ideas to their analysis of adult migrants' oral language in relation to their level of literacy. A related line of research has focused on the role of interaction with native and non-native-speaking interlocutors during language learning (e.g. Gass & Madden, 1985; Long, 1996; see Chapter 2 for a discussion of interaction in SLA).

Support for the idea of innately driven child language acquisition that characterizes the generative approach to language has come from researchers pursuing the NATURE VS. NURTURE DEBATE from different angles., In their ground-breaking study, Newport *et al.* (1977) wanted to see whether there was a link between the presumably simpler way in which the mothers spoke to their daughters and their daughters' MORPHOSYNTACTIC DEVELOPMENT over six months. Newport *et al.* concluded that the language mothers use with young children is, in fact, not syntactically simple at all. In addition, they did not find any strong links between the mother's language and the child's production. Researchers such as Crain (1993) have conducted imaginative experiments that show that the child is able to develop certain aspects of complex syntax when there is no direct evidence for these aspects in the input they receive. This ongoing line of inquiry addresses the question posed above: why and how learners acquire what is not taught? Such 'poverty of the stimulus' research closely considers what is not evident at all in the input in relation to what learners acquire, and attributes this to the role of our innate Universal Grammar; for more recent work in SLA, see Schwartz and Sprouse (2013). There are also intriguing studies of unfortunate children who received only rudimentary input and then created a more sophisticated system for the language they were using. One example comes from work on younger and older deaf individuals in Nicaragua before and just as they were brought together for vocational training (see Senghas & Coppola, 2001). For an overview of these ideas in child language acquisition, see Pinker's (1994) now classic *The Language Instinct: How the Mind Creates Language.*

5.3 Second Language Acquisition Research

Humans have learned each other's languages for millennia, and the effect of a learner's native language, their first language or L1, on the learning of a new or second language has long been observed (see, e.g. Thomas, 2013, on the history of the study of SLA). L1 influence is easy to observe in phonology, the sound system of a language. It is not difficult to identify an L2 speaker's native language by their pronunciation, but it is difficult to identify a speaker's native language by their L2 morphosyntax.

The theoretical foundation for the study of L1 influence dates back to Lado (1957) in which observations about L1 influence were formalized in the CONTRASTIVE ANALYSIS HYPOTHESIS (CAH). The hypothesis involves two simple equations, shown in Figure 5.2.

If there are rules or forms that differ in one's L1 and the L2 being learned, we can predict that the learner will make errors in the L2. When the L1 and L2 are similar, the learner will effortlessly acquire these rules or forms in the L2. Ever since Lado put forward the CAH, teachers have observed, and researchers have discovered, that the situation is more complicated. Since the 1960s, the quest to explain the errors that L2 learners do and do not make has led to a worldwide explosion of research

L1 – L2 differences = L2 difficulties
L1 – L2 similarities = L2 facilitation

Figure 5.2 Contrastive Analysis Hypothesis, Lado (1957)

in Chomskyan/generative-linguistics-based SLA. This quest entails investigating how learners represent in their minds various L2 linguistic phenomena at given points during acquisition. Researchers use the term INTERLANGUAGE (Selinker, 1972) to refer to the evolving system that the learner subconsciously creates in his or her mind.

5.3.1 The role of age in second language acquisition

The ingredients that contribute to a learner's interlanguage are the learner's L1, the language input the learner receives, and Universal Grammar. There has long been a consensus that both younger and older L2 learners' acquisition of morphosyntax is as systematic as children's L1 acquisition, and that older learners also demonstrate sensitivity to aspects of the L2 that they could not have figured out from the input alone (see, e.g. Schwartz & Sprouse, 2013). The majority of generative SLA researchers now hold the view that UG guides acquisition across the lifespan. (For what is now the position held only by a minority – that general cognitive mechanisms, not linguistic mechanisms, drive L2 acquisition – see the seminal publications by Bley-Vroman, 1989; Clahsen & Muyksen, 1989.) For researchers who hold this view, studies which reveal the operation of UG provide evidence against the well-known critical period, the idea that there is heightened sensitivity to language input until around puberty and after this period, language acquisition is no longer possible (Lenneberg, 1967). There was a flurry of new research activity on the critical period starting in the 1970s, when the wild child 'Genie' was discovered as a young adolescent in southern California without any language. It emerged that this was due to her extreme deprivation.

Genie's case and other cases researchers have considered support the existence of a critical period for first language acquisition (see Curtiss, 1977; Fromkin *et al.*, 1974), particularly for morphosyntax. But whether and how the critical period applies to L2 acquisition continues to be debated. It is easy to observe (and many studies have done so) that younger learners typically attain native-speaker proficiency in their L2, while older learners rarely do. Early on, some researchers argued for multiple critical periods (Seliger, 1978) while others rejected the idea of a critical period outright preferring to use the term SENSITIVE PERIOD and to link older learners' lack of success in reaching higher levels of proficiency to external factors (Bialystok & Hakuta, 1999; Krashen, 1973). Mounting evidence that older learners demonstrate access to UG continues to point to such factors. For a comprehensive discussion of the age factor in all domains of language learning, see Herschensohn (2007).

Newer evidence is emerging from NEUROLINGUISTIC INVESTIGATION, suggesting that proficiency is responsible for the different neurological patterns detected rather than study participants' age of initial exposure. For example, Pliatsikas *et al.* (2014) found that, despite exposure after puberty, highly proficient L2 learners processed regular past tense inflection similarly to native English speakers. A longitudinal study in this line of investigation indicates that type of exposure plays a role, where adult L2 learners who had received language input outside the classroom showed evidence of certain changes in the brain when compared to classroom-only learners (Faretta-Stutenberg & Morgan-Short, 2018).

Farett-Stutenberg and Morgan-Short's study relates to a difference between younger and older L2 learners: pre-school children do not have a sophisticated ability to reflect on their own learning processes. Children slowly become aware of their own language as they acquire linguistic competence. (See Gombert, 1992, for a description of all aspects of children's development of metalinguistic awareness.) Adults, regardless of their level of literacy or amount of formal education, are more cognitively sophisticated than pre-schoolers. This includes their ability to think about their acquisition processes in various ways to enable them to recognize when they are being corrected and try to respond appropriately. By adolescence and even late childhood, educated individuals are able to consciously learn a second language. Krashen's (1985) **ACQUISITION-LEARNING DISTINCTION** and Schwartz's (1993) **LINGUISTIC COMPETENCE-LEARNED LINGUISTIC KNOWLEDGE DISTINCTION** refer to the additional means by which older L2 learners can accumulate knowledge of a new language. This distinction is also reflected in two types of knowledge that cognitive psychologists distinguish: **DECLARATIVE KNOWLEDGE**, what is consciously learned and consciously applied, and **PROCEDURAL KNOWLEDGE**, what is subconsciously learned and automatically applied (Ullman, 2001; Paradis, 2009). We return to this topic further below.

5.3.2 Children's acquisition of morphosyntax

There is an extremely rich line of research on acquisition of morphosyntax dating back to the 1970s which includes migrant adults. The story begins with children and with the studies of children acquiring English, which dominated the early research. Not long after Chomsky put forward his ideas, child language experts began to search for evidence of the universality of human language in the patterns that young children exhibit during their development of language. Two seminal studies described here are Brown's (1973) longitudinal study and de Villiers and de Villiers' (1973) **CROSS-SECTIONAL STUDY**. In the United Kingdom, similar work was carried out by Crystal *et al.* (1976) who sought to discover procedures for analysing the morphosyntax of children suspected of **ATYPICAL DEVELOPMENT**.

Brown examined the acquisition of a number of aspects of language, including 14 grammatical morphemes in English, which were initially absent in the earliest oral production of three intelligible and talkative monolingual children who had started combining words into sentences. The children (identified by the memorable pseudonyms they were given) produced language during sessions over several years: Eve from age 1;6 to 2;3, Adam from age 2;3 to 3;6 and Sarah from age 2;3 to 4;0. Eve was more advanced than the other two (she started combining words when she was one-and-a-half years old), and this is a useful reminder that not only older L2 learners but also child L1 learners acquire language at different rates.

Brown's methodology was simple: The researcher engaged each individual child in play several times a month, and the sessions were audio recorded and subsequently transcribed. In determining acquisition of a morpheme, Brown applied the notion of SUPPLIANCE IN OBLIGATORY CONTEXT (another way of referring to what we might call errors). For example, the child might say: 'Daddy counting toe'. The singular auxiliary 'is' is obligatory, but the child does not produce it; the plural –s is obligatory, but the child does supply it. Using this methodology, Brown concluded that a child had acquired a morpheme when she or he almost always used it (he set this at 90%) over three data collection sessions in a row.

De Villiers and de Villiers reported on their study of 21 monolingual children learning English whose ages spanned those at which the children in Brown's study were showing the morphemes were absent (16 months) and supplied (40 months). Again, the researcher played with individual children to collect hundreds of utterances from each of them. Analysis of the data, of these utterances, then focused on a subset of 8 of the 14 morphemes and applied the same technique of suppliance in obligatory context to arrive at a percentage indicating MORPHEME ACCURACY.

These 24 unrelated, unacquainted children growing up in different environments followed the same, common route of development (see Figure 5.3). Brown refers to this as a PHENOMENON OF SUBSTANTIAL GENERALITY (Brown, 1973: 277). That is, this was is evidence of children's innate predisposition for learning language and is a developmental order which can be applied to all children everywhere acquiring English.

Brown; de Villiers & de Villiers **L1 children**	**Dulay & Burt** **L2 children**	**Bailey, Madden & Krashen** **L2 adults**
(1) plural *-s*	(1) plural *-s*	(1) progressive *-ing*
(2) progressive *-ing*	(2) progressive *-ing*	(2) contractible copula
(3) irregular past	(3) contractible copula	(3) plural *-s*
(4) articles	(4) contractible auxiliary	(4) articles
(5) contractible copula	(5) articles	(5) contractible aux
(6) possessive *-s*	(6) irregular past	(6) irregular past
(7) third person singular *-s*	(7) third singular *-s*	(7) third singular *-s*
(8) contractible auxiliary	(8) possessive *-s*	(8) possessive *-s*

Figure 5.3 Morpheme order for L1 and L2 acquisition of English

5.3.3 Acquisition of morphosyntax in a second language

Just as with young children's non-adult utterances, the utterances L2 adult learners produce have provided evidence of use of linguistic mechanisms rather than general cognitive mechanisms to acquire morphosyntax. Before the 1970s studies of children, Corder (1967) had already put forward the idea that L2 learners' errors are systematic, and Selinker (1972) had offered the term 'interlanguage' to L2 learners' linguistic systems. Empirical evidence for interlanguage came later, from several cross-sectional studies. The first two were carried out by Dulay and Burt (1973, 1974) with

151 Spanish-speaking 5- to 8-year-olds and of 60 Spanish-speaking and 55 Chinese-speaking 6- to 8-year-olds. The study by Bailey *et al.* (1974) added adults and expanded the L1s: 73 from 12 different L1 backgrounds. The children and adults were living in the United States and acquiring English. Unlike the studies of young children, the methodology used in these studies did not involve play sessions but instead asked the learners to orally describe pictures. Data analysis was then similar to that used by de Villiers and de Villiers for scoring morpheme accuracy. Statistical analyses of the data from all three studies indicated a common morpheme accuracy order across L2 learners, regardless of their age of initial exposure or their native language background. These similarities can also be seen by taking a look at the accuracy orders across the three learner groups – L1 children, L2 children, and L2 adults – for the three nominal morphemes (plural, articles, possessive) separately and the five verbal morphemes (progressive, **IRREGULAR PAST**, copula, third person singular, auxiliary).

However, there were statistically significant differences between the young children – the L1 learners – and the younger and older L2 learners, and researchers pondered why this might have been the case. They also questioned what was responsible for the L2 order found. Most recently, Goldschneider and de Keyser (2001) proposed an explanation for the L2 order that has to do with the greater perceptual **SALIENCE** of the earlier acquired morphemes. There was also criticism of use of a data collection methodology that was not strictly comparable for the younger L1 and L2 learners and the older L2 learners and of the data analysis. Criticisms of data analysis included researchers' use of suppliance in obligatory contexts. Wagner-Gough (1978), in her longitudinal study of a young boy, 'Homer' learning English as an L2, observed that while he supplied –ing in obligatory contexts, he also supplied –ing in contexts where it was not correct, using verbs with –ing to refer to completed events in the past, as in the use of 'going' in 'Mark and Fred going' to mean 'Mark and Fred went'. For Homer, the function of –ing was not yet the same as for native English speakers. This suggests that one cannot simply look at what the learner does not supply in obligatory contexts, at errors, in assessing interlanguage. Rather, the researcher needs to also look at where the learner does not make errors and whether the function of a given morpheme is that of a native speaker.

Researchers have continued to look for microscopically detectable patterns in the acquisition of this set of English morphemes by conducting both longitudinal and cross-sectional studies (e.g. Bliss, 2006; Cox, 2005; Haznedar, 1997; Kahoul *et al.*, 2018; Klein *et al.*, 2004; Lardiere, 2003). An ongoing topic is what the researcher can conclude when the learner varies in their use of a given morpheme. Questions asked are whether that morpheme and the syntax it represents have been acquired and what the influence of phonology is when the learner's production of a morpheme does or does not result in a consonant cluster not allowed in their L1 phonology as in 'goes' vs. 'likes'. In early studies, data were usually from various types of production, usually oral, but sometimes written (e.g. free compositions). And over the years, researchers have increasingly turned to conducting experimental studies and exploring what learners comprehend or perceive. They have looked at the L1 and L2 acquisition of many, many more languages than English.

From the 1970s onwards, some of the most important major studies of L2 morphosyntax have been of migrants. The study by Bailey *et al.* (1974) was of such adults in the United States, and it was mirrored by contemporaneous and subsequent studies on L2 English as well as on the L2 acquisition of European languages. The methods used to collect data in these studies have included techniques such as oral interviews and conversations with the researcher as well as oral retelling of silent films. One of the best-known studies of adult migrants acquiring a language other than English is the cross-sectional and longitudinal ZISA **STUDY** (*Zweitspracherwerb italienischer, portuguesischer und spanischer Arbeiter* 'Second language acquisition of Italian, Portuguese and Spanish Workers'). It set out to look at adult **GUEST WORKERS** in Germany who were receiving no instruction but were instead acquiring their L2 naturalistically in the workplace and the community. The ZISA study was preceded by a similar study, the cross-sectional-only Heidelberger Pidgin study described in publications in German such as Becker *et al.* (1977); for a summary of key points in English, see Vainikka and Young-Scholten (2011). This study set out to determine if migrant workers in Germany were creating the sort of **PIDGIN** that laborers from different language backgrounds without a common language for communication have created in various parts of the world; see e.g. Roberge (2011). The researchers found that these workers were not creating a pidgin. In the process of carrying out this study, the researchers instead revealed how learners' rates of acquisition were connected to certain social factors, including amount of schooling in their native language The ZISA study is better known worldwide because of two publications in English which sparked heated debate about the mechanisms responsible for the systematic patterns exhibited by the learners studied: Clahsen and Muysken (1986, 1989). The multi-language and multi-country ESF study (European Science Foundation), with publications also in English, was another ground-breaking study of adult migrants' L2 acquisition, which included an expanded set of target languages: Dutch, English, French, German and Swedish (see, e.g. Klein & Perdue, 1997). The study involved 40 Arabic, Finnish, Italian, Spanish and Turkish speakers learning another language, with a study design in which two speakers of an L1 were learning two different L2s; there were two Turkish learners of German and Dutch, two Italian learners of German and English, two Arabic-speaking learners of Dutch and French and so on. The data from these studies, listed in Table 5.2, and a range of data from other L1 and L2 acquisition studies can be found at http://talkbank.org/access/SLABank.

Table 5.2 Earlier studies of migrant adults learning an L2

Study	L1 → L2	Description
Heidelberger Pidgin 1970s	Spanish → German	Cross-sectional: 48 learners
ZISA 1980s	Spanish, Portuguese, Italian → German	Cross-sectional: 45 learners Longitudinal 2 years: 12 learners
ESF 1990s	Five L1s → Five L2s	Longitudinal 2½ years: 40 learners
LEXLERN 1990s	Korean & Turkish → German	Cross-sectional: 17 learners

Studies from the 1970s onwards on the L2 acquisition of morphosyntax by adults have, in Hawkins' (2001) assessment, converged on the conclusion that there are common stages of development that are largely independent of (1) the learner's first language; (2) the learner's age at initial exposure to the L2; (3) the type of exposure (naturalistic vs. classroom); and (4) the learner's educational background. These conclusions have important pedagogical implications for migrant adults with little or no formal education. After first considering in depth the idea of common stages, the next section then examines evidence for Hawkins' conclusions.

5.4 Stages in the L2 Acquisition of Morphosyntax

The idea of developmental stage can be readily observed in babies learning to walk. Once the baby can sit up, she or he starts to mobilize her/himself by crawling or possibly sitting while using her/his legs for pulling around. Next is standing, then tentative teetering and toddling, and finally fluid walking. Babies might skip a stage, but they do not reverse the order of stages; they do not walk before they crawl. In the study of first and second language acquisition, researchers engage in the same sort of observation by looking at the LINGUISTIC PROPERTIES of the learner's system at a given point in time (Gregg, 1996). A description of linguistic properties at various successive points in time is expressed as a series of stages that reveal the developmental route or path the learner takes toward the end state of acquisition.

Child language researcher Ingram (1989) has proposed several criteria to apply when observing a behaviour that changes over time. To consider a behaviour to unfold in stages, the first one must logically precede the second, and the second the third, and so on. Imagine an L2 learner without previous exposure to English who is enrolled in classes for 15 hours per week. The researcher visits the learner every two weeks, shows them the same silent film, and then asks them what happened. (Watching the same silent film might seem to run the risk of learner boredom; however, this allows the researcher to better track development when obligatory contexts and expected lexical items are the same each time.) Stages are identified by stabilization; that is, the learner's behaviour – here their oral production of language – is consistent over a certain period of time.

(1) The learner's initial, stable behaviour: For the first three months of L2 exposure, the learner produces bare verbs in obligatory contexts for past tense.
(2) The learner's behaviour shows variation: In months four and five, the learner produces TARGET-LIKE irregular past tense verbs, but many verbs that should mark tense are still bare forms.
(3) The learner's behaviour shows a new variation: The learner continues to use irregular verbs and starts to produce regular forms with –ed. The learner also attaches the –ed suffix to some irregular verbs; i.e. the learner overgeneralizes the past tense rule.

The stages proposed in L2 acquisition for a given linguistic phenomenon are based on what researchers have observed in learners' oral production, and – less often – on their written production. Evidence for a stage can come from learners' production of NON-TARGET-LIKE word forms or non-target syntax, but evidence can also come from what is absent in a learner's production. Consider data from the study of Jorge (Hilles, 1986; based on Cazden *et al.*'s 1975 study) of six Spanish immigrants to the United States, where the researcher and Jorge were playing various games. In the first example, Jorge omits the pronominal subjects 'they' and 'she'. Several months later, Jorge uses the subject pronoun 'it'.

1. **Researcher:** What does she look like?
   Jorge: The *pelo* black and the eyes is, I don't know what colour, and is fat.
2. **Jorge:** It doesn't even spin.

Use of 'it' (both referential, as in (2) to refer to the dial in a board game, and particularly NON-REFERENTIAL as in 'it seems…') is an important step in both first and second language acquisition, and looking at learners' production of pronominal subjects has long been a fruitful way of tracking development.

Question formation is a useful indicator of development in languages such as English, because it involves functional morphemes and requires a different word order than DECLARATIVES. In English, the subject ('S' in Table 5.3) and the auxiliary verb or copula or modal verb ('V' in the table) are inverted, while the position of the object ('O') does not change. In the 1970s, researchers found that L2 learners, regardless of their L1, followed common stages in their acquisition of questions in English. Even the final stage is not yet native-like.

Table 5.3 Acquisition of question formation in English

Stage	Word order	Description	Examples
1	Single words	Rising intonation	Spinach?
2	SVO	Rising intonation	You like spinach?
3	Wh-SVO Do-SVO	Initial wh-words 'Do' initial in yes/no Qs	What you like? **Do** you like spinach?
4	Aux-SV Wh-cop-S	Auxiliaries before subjects in yes/no Qs Copula before subjects	Have he seen it? Where **is** he? **Is** he at work?
5	Wh-aux-S	Auxiliaries before subjects but also in embedded wh-Qs	Where **is** he working? Do you know where **is** he working?

In one of the studies of the acquisition of languages other than English referred to above, the ZISA study, researchers looked at learners' acquisition of word order, along with their acquisition of functional morphology. Analysis of the data pointed to five stages common to the Italian-, Portuguese- and Spanish-speaking learners of L2 German, shown in Table 5.4 (Clahsen *et al.*, 1983; Clahsen & Muysken, 1986; 1989, who added Turkish). Under their account, acquisition begins with the CANONICAL WORD ORDER in German declarative clauses – SVO – and they claimed that learners are guided by general cognitive mechanisms rather than by their L1 or by linguistic mechanisms, by UG. Pienemann (1998, 2003) took this analysis and expanded the

Table 5.4 ZISA-study stages in adult L2 German (Vainikka & Young-Scholten, 2011: 168)

(1) SVO order	*Die Kinder spielen mim ball.* 'The children play with the ball'.
(2) Adverb preposing	*Da Kinder spielen.* target: *Da spielen Kinder.* 'There children play'.
(3) Verb separation	*Alle Kinder muss die Pause machen.* target: *müssen* 'All children must take a break'.
(4) Inversion	*Dann hat sie wieder die Knocht gebringt.* target: *gebracht* 'Then she brought the bone again'.
(5) Verb-end	*Er sagte, dass er nach hause kommt.* 'He said that he'll come home'.

ideas into his PROCESSABILITY THEORY, which views these stages as the result of the operation of linguistic mechanisms but not as a result of Universal Grammar.

Clahsen and Muysken's conclusion that these stages do not show adult L2 learners' access to UG quickly triggered heated debate at the international level (e.g. Du Plessis *et al.*, 1987; Schwartz & Tomaselli, 1990; Vainikka & Young-Scholten, 1994).

As noted above, the majority of generative SLA researchers now hold the view that UG continues to guide L2 acquisition across the lifespan, and they continue to search for evidence thereof in a range of L1–L2 combinations. Schwartz and Sprouse (2013) is but one example of a study that shows unequivocal post-puberty UG access.

Relevant to migrant adults with little or no education or literacy are the earliest stages of acquisition. One of the useful ideas emerging from the European Science Foundation study is from Klein and Perdue (1992, 1997), who observed a BASIC VARIETY with six characteristics commonly observed in learners' oral production, regardless of the L1 or the L2 involved.

(i) VO word order;
(ii) no movement (same word order);
(iii) no inflectional morphology or other grammatical morphemes;
(iv) optional DETERMINERS;
(v) lack of SUBORDINATION and lack of overt COMPLEMENTIZERS such as 'that'.

Schwartz (1997), however, argued that the Basic Variety ignores early L1-based word order differences: At the start of acquisition, regardless of the L2, in declarative clauses, the Punjabi and Turkish speakers used their L1-based OV order, and the Arabic and Italian speakers used their L1-based VO order. Researchers now generally agree, regardless of whether they think general cognitive or linguistic mechanisms/UG are involved, that adult L2 learners start acquisition with their basic L1 word order. If we disregard the pronominal subject, since beginners (both L1 children and L2 learners) do not always produce them, we can consider the following four scenarios:

(i) Both the L1 and L2 are VO: Spanish → English = no VP (verb phrase) word order change.

(ii) Both L1 and L2 are OV: Turkish → Farsi = no VP word order change.
(iii) The L1 is VO and the L2 OV: Arabic → Turkish = VP word order change.
(iv) The L1 is OV and the L2 VO: Farsi → Spanish = change needed in word order.

Vainikka and Young-Scholten (2005) argue that the six Basic Variety characteristics should be reconceptualized as two stages. A third stage could also be added, prompted by Myles' (2004) findings from her study of young adolescents in the United Kingdom learning French as a foreign language, which reflects what many researchers and teachers have long observed: There is an initial stage in which L2 learners produce verbless utterances, much like L1 children's early multi-word utterances.

Stage 1: No verbs.

Stage 2: The earliest Basic Variety data with L1 word order (VO or OV).

Stage 3: Slightly later Basic Variety data, where learners use L2 word order.

We now turn to further elaboration of how learners acquire morphosyntax and to another approach to stages, ORGANIC GRAMMAR (Vainikka & Young-Scholten, 1994, 1996, 2011). The idea emerged from Clahsen's (1991) idea that L1 children learning German incrementally build up linguistic competence guided by UG. The analysis involved oral production data from guest workers, from the ZISA study (L1 Italian, Portuguese and Spanish), from von Stutterheim (1984, 1987; L1 Turkish) and from Clahsen's LEXLERN study, along with longitudinal data from exchange students in Germany without prior knowledge of German who were exposed to their L2 naturalistically (Vainikka & Young-Scholten, 2011). These data combined led to the UG-driven stages of acquisition shown in Table 5.5. Each stage is represented by a **SYNTACTIC PROJECTION**.

Table 5.5 Organic Grammar stages for L2 German

Stage	Word order	Verb types	Agreement/ tense	Pronominal subjects	Syntax
VP	L1 order, then L2 order	Thematic (main) verbs	None	Absent	No verb raising, subordinate clauses or complex questions
TP	Head-initial, then head-final	Modals and auxiliaries emerge	Tense Emerging	Emerging	Verb raising emerging; absence of subordinate clauses and complex questions
AgrP	Head initial; then head final	Modals and auxiliaries acquired	Subject-verb agreement Acquired	Acquired	Verb raising acquired Subordinate clauses and complex questions emerging
CP	Head-initial	Modals and auxiliaries acquired	Acquired	Acquired	Subordinate clauses and complex questions acquired

VP = verb phrase, the lexical projection that forms the base of verbal morphosyntax
The rest of these are functional projections, involving functional morphemes. The columns in the table describe what is relevant for this projection.
TP = tense phrase
AgrP = agreement phrase
CP = complementizer phrase for subordinate clauses and complex questions

Table 5.6 L2 English (Vainikka *et al.*, 2017)

Stage	Word order	Verb types	Agreement/tense	Pronouns	Syntax
VP	L1 order, then L2 order	Thematic (main) verbs	None	Subject, object pronouns absent	None
NegP	Resembles the L1 apart from complex syntax	Thematic verbs; copula 'is'	None	Pronoun forms begin to emerge	Negation; single clauses; formulaic or intonation-based questions
TP	Resembles the L2 apart from complex syntax	Thematic verbs, modals; copula forms beyond 'is'	No agreement; some tense, some aspect, but not productive	More pronoun forms, but they can still be missing	Conjoined clauses; formulaic wh-Qs; yes/no Qs without inversion
AgrP	Resembles the L2 apart from complex syntax	Thematic verbs, modals, copula forms beyond 'is'; auxiliaries in all forms and tenses	Productive tense, aspect; some agreement, especially forms of 'be'	Pronouns obligatory, 'there' and existential 'it'	Simple subordination; wh-Qs but all Qs may lack inversion
CP	Always resembles the L2	Complex tense, aspect forms; range of thematic verb, modal, auxiliary forms	Forms usually correct, apart from newly attempted ones	Use of 'there' and 'it' beyond stock phrases	Complex subordination; all Qs with inversion

Under Organic Grammar, once learners produce utterances with verbs, their syntax is still simple and involves no functional morphology for verbs. In **GENERATIVE LINGUISTICS**, syntax has long been represented hierarchically as trees, and in linguistic terms, this simple syntax is a verb phrase (= VP) or a 'minimal tree', representing the trunk of the tree. A CP (= complementizer phrase), the syntax involved in questions and subordination, is the upper branches of the tree. As with some approaches described above and further below, OG involves stages that combine both functional morphology and syntax/word order.

Table 5.6 shows the Organic Grammar stages based on the cross-sectional study of English, whose morphosyntax differs from German in several ways. For example, in German, there is extensive subject-verb agreement, **VERB RAISING**, and head-final word order in the verb phrase (VP). Studies of L2 English include Young-Scholten and Ijuin (2006), based on guided written production from L2 English in the United States from a range of L1 backgrounds and a study of Arabic-, Somali- and Urdu-speaking migrants (literate as well as not literate) learning English (Vainikka *et al.*, 2017). NegP stands for negation phrase.

5.5 What are Independent of Stages of Development?

We now return to what Hawkins concludes is independent of these stages, the learner's L1, their age, the learner's educational background and type of exposure. The latter two are most relevant to adult migrants with little or no education or literacy.

5.5.1 Influence of the L1 and of age

An early observation by Zobl (1980) is that the learner's L1 can lead to a learner stalling at a stage of development in the L2 if it is similar to a construction in their L1 morphosyntax. For example, in Spanish, the way that sentences are negated resembles how researchers have found that learners negate sentences in L2 English, regardless of their L1. Like L1 learners of English, L2 learners omit the subject pronoun, and they produce the negator 'no' before the rest of the clause as in 'No have money', which is exactly the same in Spanish, except the verb is inflected for first person singular: *No tengo dinero*. Zobl observed that Spanish learners of English remained at this developmental stage longer than speakers of languages whose own negation patterns do not mimic this interlanguage stage.

Advances since the 1980s in formal linguistics have resulted in a much more sophisticated understanding of functional morphology and of syntax in a wide range of spoken and signed languages far beyond English and the European languages upon which early generative linguistics was based. In a highly influential hypothesis, FULL TRANSFER/FULL ACCESS, which revives the contrastive analysis ideas from the 1950s, adds Universal Grammar and also draws on developments in linguistic theory, Schwartz and Sprouse (1996) express the idea that the learner's L1 shapes acquisition of the L2 from the start and throughout. L1 influence/transfer (Full Transfer) is one component of the learner's mental INITIAL STATE upon starting to acquire an L2. The other component, Full Access, refers to the continued operation of UG, which enables the learner, regardless of the age at which they begin their acquisition of a new language, to go beyond full transfer.

The languages of the world vary in which grammatical functions they mark, and researchers have re-considered the difficulties that learners have when the learner's L1 differs from their L2 and when their exposure to the L2 is in adulthood. Some ask whether it is possible for an adult learner to acquire a FUNCTIONAL CATEGORY in the L2 that is absent in their L1 (Hawkins & Chan, 1997; Hawkins & Liszka, 2003). For example, articles and tense exist in many European languages, but not in Mandarin. Hawkins' and colleagues' FAILED FUNCTIONAL FEATURES HYPOTHESIS predicts that it will be impossible for an adult learner to acquire in the L2 features which are not in their L1. Research in this vein has not yielded definite answers, and two reasons for this may be that functional categories such as articles and tense are taught, and the majority of participants in studies carried out so far have experienced their initial exposure before puberty in the classroom.

5.5.2 Educational background

What role does educational background play in L2 acquisition? This can be considered more narrowly: what role does literacy play in the acquisition of morphosyntax? There are two different positions, one associated with the generative view and the other with a general cognition view under which noticing and interaction drive acquisition.

While literacy (and education) certainly expands certain aspects of language in its use (genre, register, variety, discourse), in increase in vocabulary and application of pragmatics (Olson, 2002) as well as in metalinguistic knowledge and skills (Gombert, 1992), it is less clear how it might affect the acquisition of language. After all, children are still not literate by the time they have completed their acquisition of the fundamentals of language around age four.

Non-literate adults seem to resemble young children in their use of only semantic strategies to process oral language rather than the semantic and phonological processing literates use (Kurvers, 2007, 2015; Kurvers *et al.*, 2010). In their study of low- and moderate-literate Somali L2 English learners in their uptake of the researcher's recasts of their erroneous utterances, Tarone and Bigelow (2005) concluded that literacy affects how one processes and takes in input during the acquisition of morphosyntax. This was based on the low literates' significantly worse recall of recasts and the significantly more changes that made in their attempts to correct their utterances, using more **BARE VERBS** and fewer dependent clauses than those with higher literacy.

In another study, of this time native-speaking non-literates vs. literates, Mishra *et al.* (2012) tracked the eye movements of very low-literate and high-literate Hindi – speaking Dalit adults in Uttar Pradesh, India, who heard and saw visual displays depicting sentence content. The eye movements of the low-literates showed that they were significantly slower than the high-literates at using syntactic cues from the sentences they heard to anticipate what came next in a given sentence. Mishra *et al.* conclude that this difference may simply be one of speed of processing.

For the teacher or tutor of migrant adults with little or no education or literacy, what these researchers conclude comes as no surprise. Even so, one must be careful not to draw premature conclusions about the source of slower progress. It's important to consider the myriad external factors that could also influence learners' progress from the social and political conditions surrounding their emigration and immigration to the lower amount of input they receive with fewer opportunities to interact with native L2 speakers due to weak L2 literacy along with less access to written text for the same reason. This may explain the very low levels (OG Stage 1) Young-Scholten and Strom (2006) found for the non-literates in their native language and with very weak L2 literacy in their study of 17 Somali and Vietnamese migrant adults with no and some native language literacy.

More recent research has examined whether patterns of development, in fact stages themselves, might be influenced by literacy. Two studies are relevant here. The first is a study by Julien *et al.* (2016) who tested a claim from previous research that those who are non-literate use **DUMMY AUXILIARIES** in during their acquisition of Dutch (Haberzettl, 2003; Huebner *et al.*, 1992; Jordens & Dimroth, 2006; Schimke, 2013 also consider these auxiliaries in languages other than Dutch). The researchers looked at oral production and also comprehension data from 40 Arabic-, Berber- and Turkish-speaking adults who either had no education or L1 literacy or up to secondary education in their L1. Their claim was not supported; rather, it turned out that their misuse and OVERGENERALIZATION of certain morphemes reflected their stage of development. They used these dummies to mark subject-verb agreement and to mark tense before they took the next step of attaching the correct Dutch suffixes to main verbs.

The second is a study of the acquisition of L2 English by 16 Arabic- Dari-, Pashto- and Urdu-speaking adults with no and low levels of L1 literacy (Vainikka *et al.*, 2017). Like Julien *et al.*'s L2 Dutch learners, their oral production contained overgeneralizations only at a certain point in their acquisition, in this case in the negated utterances that were part of one set of pictures they had to describe. Moreover, not only did they overgeneralize single morphemes, but they used words from different word classes, e.g. 'the' rather than a verbal morpheme such as 'is', and they used multi-word chunks such as 'in the' in the same way. Learners were recruited from a teaching program and frequency of exposure in the classroom may have prompted this. Interestingly, the chunks learners employed invariably involved functional morphemes rather than content words such as 'table' or 'pencil. Their acquisition is supported by internal linguistic mechanisms that enable them to subconsciously distinguish functional from content elements in the input and recruit only the FUNCTIONAL ELEMENTS as they grapple with acquiring functional projections in their English.

5.5.3 Type of exposure

Two questions were posed at the start of this chapter: Why don't learners always learn what teachers teach? How do learners acquire what hasn't been taught? The discussion above describes the line of generative-linguistics-based research on L2 morphosyntax that probes how learners go beyond the linguistic input they receive to create their own interlanguage systems. It is worth keeping in mind here that views in the wider field of SLA are divided; generative second language acquisitionists take the position that mental mechanisms are purely linguistic and operate entirely subconsciously while others hold the view that the mental mechanisms involved are of a general, cognitive nature and operate consciously. This implicates instruction.

What takes place during instruction often requires conscious analysis of language and the effortful learning and application of rules. This leads us back to the first question: Why don't learners always learn what teachers teach? This is addressed from two different perspectives: the memorization of multi-word expressions and application of learned rules both of which feature less or more prominently in the classroom, varying with the learner's age and their amount of formal education.

5.5.3.1 Multi-word expressions

Multi-word expressions are conventional expressions that are memorized in the same way that single words are. Much like a dictionary, a speaker's mental lexicon contains entries for single words, but it also contains entries of two or more words.

When we speak a language we know well, we rely on such expressions, and we recruit them as rapidly as single words from our mental lexicons. These expressions are also referred to as FORMULAIC SPEECH, FORMULAIC LANGUAGE, FORMULAIC SEQUENCES or HOLISTIC CHUNKS. These expressions include idioms such as 'kick the bucket', clichés such as 'the good old times', compounds such as 'motorway roundabout', collocations such as 'keep a secret', social expressions such as 'nice to meet you' and other fixed expressions such as 'I don't understand'. (See Wray, 2002 for further elaboration; and discussion in Chapter 4.)

Foreign language phrase books for tourists present lists of expressions that are useful in the various situations one might encounter. If one is actually going to use these expressions successfully, this requires considerable practice and a superior memory (especially for pronunciation) to produce them under communicative pressure and be understood. Fortunately for the tourist, there are now digital devices that act as interpreters. Then there is the danger that if the message the learner produces has been understood, the interlocutor's response will not be understood at all. Importantly, although expressions which end up in one's mental lexicon ought to be learned in the same way as individual words, there is evidence that they are more difficult (see, e.g. Martinez & Murphy, 2011, on younger migrants' problems with short multi-word expressions).

Expressions that learners memorize lend themselves to creative use. For example, Clark (1974) observed that when her three-year-old son started to say 'wait for it to cool' during mealtimes, he then later applied the 'wait for it' with other verbs as in 'wait for it to dry'. But there is the likelihood that such expressions will be overused, in contexts in which they are not correct. An example in L2 acquisition comes from the young boy, Homer, studied by Wagner-Gough (1978) who used these in his communication in his primary school classroom. For example, he used 'is it' to form questions such as 'Is it bicycle is Judy?' and used 'where's' to produce declaratives like 'Where's Mark is school' (=Mark is at school). Vainikka *et al.* (2017) found that migrant adults, some of whom were not literate in their native languages, deployed multi-word expressions similarly to Homer. Others have found similar patterns, including overgeneralization of certain morphemes in adult migrants' acquisition of other languages, for example, Dutch and German (Julien *et al.*, 2016; Haberzettl, 2003; van de Craats & van Hout, 2010).

In foreign language teaching, memorization of expressions can be traced in part to the dialogue memorization and to the pattern drills that were part of the AUDIO LINGUAL METHOD created in the United States in the 1940s (e.g. Fries, 1945). A pattern drill involves taking one of the patterns from a memorized dialogue and changing one component of the pattern, for example, changing a declarative: 'My name is Mary' to a question: 'What is your name?'

The usage-based view mentioned above in this chapter assumes that language is made up of such expressions, and in the process of amassing them, the learner becomes aware of the components of these expressions, extracts patterns, and then applies the patterns for creative use of the language. Addressing how this might work in relation to memorized expressions in L2 acquisition, Myles (2004; see also Myles *et al.*, 1999) proposes that the learner decomposes these expressions them over time, in much the same way as Clark (1974) found that her son did. Bardovi-Harlig and Stringer (2017) examined the case for decomposition as a driver of L2 acquisition and found little evidence to support Myles' proposal. They report on a study whose results indicated that the learner's route of acquisition is not affected by the expressions they had memorized. They first collected a corpus of such expressions used in the U.S. community in which the learners they were going to study lived. Then they created test scenarios in which these expressions were expected to be used, and they made sure that the native speakers they also recruited chose the answers they expected. Two-hundred and seventy-one English learners from various L1 backgrounds at four levels in a seven-level instructional program produced a conversation simulation and tried to imitate multi-word expressions. Results showed that they knew when to use which expressions, and they knew the essential words in these expressions but that they only mastered common but complex multi-word expressions until they reached higher levels of proficiency. Bardovi-Harlig and Stringer's conclusion was that the learners' morphosyntactic development had to catch up with the morphosyntax in these multi-word expressions before they could produce them automatically. Multi-word expressions were not acting as a catalyst for their acquisition of morphosyntax, but it was the other way around.

5.5.3.2 Instruction in rules

A long tradition exists of investigating whether L2 learners learn what they are taught. There is even a journal, *Instructed Second Language Acquisition,* which focuses entirely on classroom learning. Accompanying discussion about instruction is a decades-long debate about the distinction between what is unconsciously acquired vs. consciously learned, resulting in implicit knowledge and EXPLICIT KNOWLEDGE, or ACQUISITION VS LEARNING (Krashen, 1982, 1985; see also Felix, 1985). Rastelli (2018: 115) notes that the issue of explicit vs implicit teaching is 'among the most quoted and debated in the SLA literature'. In its strong form, implicit teaching is for the learner both unconscious and incidental. That is, the learner's attention is not directed to internalizing a certain aspect of language and, in fact, attention is focused on communication. Importantly, in his work on NEUROBIOLOGICAL REPRESENTATION OF LANGUAGE, Rastelli urges researchers to welcome on board more collaborators and includes teachers in his list. Those who work with migrant adults with little or no education and literacy would clearly be welcome.

The debate revolves around three issues: whether an acquisition-learning distinction exists; if so, how we can distinguish between these knowledge types; and if we can, whether this distinction is useful. Paradis (2009) recruits a range of evidence, including neurobiological evidence, to conclude that there is a distinction, allowing us to focus here on the second and third issues. This also raises an issue presented earlier in this chapter: the relationship between simplicity of a phenomenon and ease of learning or acquiring it. (See Spada & Tomita's, 2010, meta-analysis of a number of studies on the effectiveness of instruction which indicated no significant relationship between the simplicity of a phenomenon and effectiveness of teaching it.)

Slabakova *et al.* (2017) provide an example of the importance of understanding the relationship between what is assumed to be simple and ease of acquisition. All languages have pronouns, and the L2 learner can straightforwardly transfer knowledge of the concept of pronouns from their L1. However, lower proficiency learners may have difficulties with the meaning of these pronouns, including during listening to the L2, and may mis-assign meaning. Slabakova *et al.*'s focus was on **FULL** and **REDUCED OBJECT PRONOUNS** (e.g. 'him' vs. 'm' as in 'I saw him' vs. 'I saw'm' in English). We might assume that it is easier for learners to acquire what is pronounced clearly, what is perceptually salient, along the lines of the study referred to above by Goldschneider and de Keyser (2001). This means that 'him' should be acquired earlier than 'm'. However, in their study, the reverse turned out to be true. The reduced forms were acquired earlier. These results are compelling when reflecting on the language used with learners.

Whong and Gil (2018) also looked at a phenomenon assumed to be fairly simple to teach: the **QUANTIFIER** 'any' in English. They reviewed 26 popular English textbooks in worldwide use and found that the books only gave these rules: 'Any' is used in questions: 'Do you want any cake?' and in negative responses: 'No, I don't want any'. However, there were common, additional uses which no textbook included:

Conditional: If anyone comes, please shout. If you see any bears, call for help.

After before or without: Go before anyone sees you. I'd starve without any meat.

After a negative main clause: I'm sorry I said anything about your driving test.

Referring to free choice: Anyone can learn to bake a cake. Choose any cake that you like.

Whong and Gil recruited 97 Arabic-speaking adult learners of English, categorized them into three proficiency levels and asked them to judge sentences with grammatical and ungrammatical uses of 'any'. To see what they had learned from their textbooks and from their teachers, the researchers interviewed the learners to find out what they recalled about 'any'. Results showed that learners were best at judging grammatical and ungrammatical uses of 'any' based on what they had been taught, confirming that they were only aware of the simple rules which they had been taught and not of the additional four uses enumerated above. Learners also showed evidence of incorrect overgeneralization of these taught rules, even in cases where the interviews showed that the learners were not consciously aware of the rules. That is, the explicit teaching resulted in subconscious application. Most interestingly, the advanced groups were able to correctly judge the grammaticality of what they had not been taught; that is, they had also acquired some of the additional characteristics of 'any', not from the explicit instruction in the classroom or their text book, but from additional input they received.

Adopting the acquisition-learning distinction is Rothman (2007, 2009) in his COMPETING SYSTEMS HYPOTHESIS, whereby UG drives acquisition but there is interaction with other cognitive subsystems, with general cognitive mechanisms for learning an L2. Formal linguists' ongoing work on explaining native speakers' mental systems reinforces the idea that languages are highly complex, and Rothman points out that rules taught to learners regularly fail to reflect the complexity of language phenomena being taught. This underscores the usefulness for teachers and tutors to familiarize themselves with what linguists understand to inform their practice.

In his study of L2 Spanish, Rothman compared the use of ASPECT by native Spanish speakers with two groups of highly advanced English-speaking adults learning Spanish. Of the L2 group, 20 were instructed learners and 11 were naturalistic, uninstructed learners who had lived in a Spanish-speaking country for at least seven years. Learners were tested with examples of aspect in a multiple-choice story task and in a fill-in-the-blank task whose examples were drawn from how aspect is taught. The native speakers chose forms and filled in the blanks as expected, validating the test. With respect to the L2 Spanish learners, those with naturalistic exposure and those who were instructed did equally well. That is, the uninstructed learners were able to subconsciously acquire what the instructed learners were taught. However, the results showed differences between the instructed and uninstructed groups. On the one hand, the uninstructed learners were slightly better on the multiple-choice story task; on the other hand, the instructed learners applied the rules they had been taught and demonstrated the oversimplification of the Spanish aspect system that had been presented during instruction.

The preceding sections have addressed what we know about how L2 adults – including migrants with little or no education and literacy – acquire L2 morphosyntax. We now turn to the final topic in this chapter, how best to show outsiders what learners have attained.

5.6 Measuring Learner Attainment

How do we measure what learners have learned – be it morphosyntax, syntax, vocabulary or reading – in a valid and reliable way? Testing and assessment bring together in a very compelling way the ideas discussed above. We start by defining essential terms.

In the analysis of any set of data, RELIABILITY refers to consistency, to whether and how the data that were collected (in this case a test or assessment tool) measure a certain set of skills or knowledge in the same way every time it is used. VALIDITY refers to whether a test or assessment tool measures what it claims to measure. Three main factors can undermine validity: 'failing to measure adequately what ought to be measured, measuring something that should not be measured, and using a test in [the wrong or a different] manner than it was designed to be used' (Koretz, 2008: 220).

The constructs of reliability and validity are relevant in the critical examination of how we measure the skills and knowledge of migrant adults with limited education and limited or no literacy, because they have no or limited previous experience with the sort of testing and assessment that is typically used in the countries to which they immigrate.

On the one hand, 'testing' usually refers to the so-called high stakes exams used to measure the test-taker's knowledge and skills at a certain point in time. Examples range from institutional placement and end-of-year tests to STANDARDIZED, NORM-REFERENCED, DISCRETE-ITEM TESTS, such as the US-based Test of English as a Foreign Language (TOEFL), the UK-based International English Language Testing System (IELTS) and Cambridge tests of English as a second language. These are norm referenced, in that the tests have determined the validity and reliability of measuring a certain set of knowledge of skills for a given group of learners. On the other hand, 'assessment' usually refers to a continuous process of documenting the knowledge and skills as demonstrated in written or spoken samples that the learner produces.

Our example of testing and assessment of morphosyntax comes from a US community college system in the early 2000s. The student body was 58% permanent residents; 18% student visa holders; 15% naturalized citizens; 8% visitor/non-immigrant visa holders; and 2% refugees. The English as a second language program included students from a range of academic and language learning backgrounds, (1) who had completed secondary school in their native country, (2) who had completed secondary school after moving to the United States and (3) whose secondary school education was not completed, due to circumstances resulting from emigration. Admission to the college system required non-native English speakers to provide results from the Scholastic Aptitude Test (SAT) or the TOEFL. For college applicants who scored below a certain level on the verbal part of the SAT, an in-house reading and writing placement test was required. If the applicant was required to take English as a second language classes, progression from level to level was then a program-internal assessment of a written sample and a reading test.

In the United Kingdom, the practice of standardized, multi-level testing of adults – including non-native English speakers – who do not attend universities is widespread. Yet adult migrants without native language literacy or education have largely been ignored. Thus, while there are standardized tests for levels slightly above A1 of the Common European Framework of Reference referred to at the start of this chapter, there are no tests that measure the knowledge and skills of those below this level.

Consider the following categories of beginning learners:

(1) Well educated, highly literate learners with a background in a language that uses the Roman alphabet.
(2) Well educated, highly literate learners with a background in a language that uses a script other than the Roman alphabet.

(3) Learners who have had little or no schooling and no background in any other language (Burt *et al.*, 2008).

Although the first two groups are beginners, they have literacy skills to draw on. The third group not only have no or limited literacy skills in their native language, they might be grappling with the notion that 'print carries meaning' (DfES, 2001: 70). However, learners in many countries are tested against the same standards. Predictably, learners in the first two groups do well on tests and raise the average score for all three groups. However, those with limited native language and second language literacy skills in the third group struggle to pass tests.

There are also factors relating to context and to the test taker that have an impact on performance. This relates to the process of test development, which 'should begin ... by clearly defining the test-taking population in terms of the three sets of characteristics (physical, psychological and experiential) ... include[ing] the likely cognitive processing required for the successful completion of the test' (O'Sullivan, 2011: 263). One option for working with migrant adults is to rely on assessment in the form of a learner portfolio (see Stockmann, 2006).

Other options are based on the studies of adult migrants acquiring morphosyntax, which resulted in the stages shown above. Based on his early and later work, Pienemann (1998, 2001) developed a tool called RAPID PROFILING, which involves collecting oral questions produced by learners and whose use requires training in working with the oral samples of spontaneous speech required for this assessment. Along similar lines, Young-Scholten and Ijuin (2006) have applied the stages of Organic Grammar and have studied its reliability and validity. Looking at the written and oral production of several levels of learners in the US English community college program mentioned above, they used the stage descriptors of Organic Grammar to place learners at stages and then mapped these stages onto program levels. All learners in the study had been accurately placed except – crucially – learners who had been misplaced at too high a level and were struggling and in danger of being excluded from the program altogether.

If we just test and assess oral or written production, might we fail to capture the learner's complete linguistic competence? We know from considerable research on children acquiring their first language and from research on second language acquisition that comprehension precedes production. Babies produce their first identifiable single words between 10 and 12 months, but they comprehend words several months earlier. We also have plenty of evidence for adults that in L2 acquisition, comprehension precedes production. One line of research involves FIRST EXPOSURE STUDIES, which show how adults are similar to children in their ability to pick things up from what we call the speech stream. This indicates that in a second language, our listening can be considerably better than our production. Consider the CEF A1 listening descriptor: 'I can recognize familiar words and very basic phrases concerning myself, my family, and immediate concrete surroundings when people speak slowly and clearly'. Do tests that migrant adults are expected to take measure comprehension in a reliable and valid manner?

5.7 Conclusion

This chapter reviews the history and the state-of-the-art research on the acquisition of morphosyntax by adult second language learners. This includes discussion of the role of the learner's memorization of multiword expressions, the role of explicit teaching of morphosyntactic forms and rules and testing and assessment of the learning of morphosyntactic features. We hope that this chapter has stimulated new thinking about the considerable potential of adult learners with limited education and LITERACY LEARNERS, offered sufficient implications for working with these learners and provided tools to understanding current research.

6 Bilingualism and Multilingualism

Belma Haznedar

6.1 Introduction

Adults learning the language of their new country, who have limited education and literacy in their native/home language, often speak more than one language upon arrival and they often speak them well. Their children may also speak multiple languages to varying degrees of proficiency. Understanding the nature of the bilingualism (or multilingualism) of these learners from various perspectives gives teachers and tutors new insights into what migrant adults, as well as the younger members of their speech community, bring to the task of learning their new language.

There is an increasing focus among those who work with migrant adults on enabling them to deal effectively with their children's schooling. Indeed, many migrant adults are parents and if they are not parents, if the community is tightly knit, they will be aware of parents' concerns about the younger members of the community growing up with linguistic competence in at least two languages: the home language(s) and the new language that the older members of the community are now learning, the so-called majority language. Adults will not lose their home language(s) in the process of acquiring their new language. But children are vulnerable, and they may well grow up without the ability to speak or even comprehend the language(s) of the older members of their own family and community. Discussion of the difficult and often controversial issues that surround this situation is often neglected. Teachers and tutors can contribute to a more informed and positive way of handling issues which can negatively affect children's well-being and, in turn, the family and the community.

This chapter presents what is currently known, and important for teachers and tutors to know, about bilingualism and its benefits and challenges to individuals and to those around them. The second section of the chapter defines bilingualism and examines issues of linguistic diversity and CODE SWITCHING which apply to both younger and older individuals. The third section focuses on young children's bilingualism, starting with the distinction between SIMULTANEOUS BILINGUALISM and SUCCESSIVE BILINGUALISM, then moving to cognitive and neurological aspects of bilingualism, and to how researchers tackle the difficulty of distinguishing between TYPICAL and ATYPICAL development when the child is bilingual. The fourth and final section focuses on biliteracy and the place and value of heritage languages, migrants' home languages, in school and the community.

6.2 What is Bilingualism?

In this chapter, the term 'bilingual' is used to refer to the knowledge of two or more languages, to both individuals and groups, and to older and younger members of a community of learners. Bilingualism (and multilingualism) is a widespread phenomenon. A glance at the 7000 languages spoken in over 200 countries demonstrates how common it is (Bhatia & Ritchie, 2013; Eberhard *et al.*, 2019; Wei, 2007). Almost half of the population around the world speaks more than one language, and use of two languages in the same society is widespread in many African, Asian and European countries (Grosjean, 2008).

The broadest definition of a bilingual is someone who uses more than one language every day. In this chapter, unless the distinction is important, we use the word 'bilingual' to refer to those who know two or more languages. Figure 6.1 presents terms currently used to refer to different types and aspects of bilingualism. These definitions refer to how well and to what extent someone speaks the two or more languages that are spoken in their linguistic community (Edwards, 2013; Grosjean, 2008).

In this volume we adopt the widespread practice of calling adult learners 'second language learners' rather than 'late bilinguals' to make a distinction with those who have acquired more than one language since early childhood. 'Second' refers to an additional language, not literally the second language. The term 'heritage language' is relevant for the families and communities of migrant adults. While some researchers emphasize a 'particular family connection' with a language (e.g. Fishman, 2001), others define heritage learners as 'those who have been

Simultaneous bilinguals	Individuals who are exposed to two languages from infancy and, therefore, have spoken them since they began speaking (De Houwer, 1990)
Successive/sequential bilinguals	Individuals whose exposure to another language begins after the first language has been acquired; at the age of three to five years, before schooling starts (Haznedar, 2013; Unsworth, 2013)
Receptive bilinguals	Individuals who can understand the second language but have limited proficiency in using it (Wei, 2007)
Productive bilinguals	Individuals who can use/express themselves in both languages (Wei, 2007)
Additive bilingualism	Situations where both languages are used and supported in speakers' home, community and school settings (Wei, 2007)
Subtractive bilingualism	Situations where the mother tongue is lost at the expense of the acquisition of the majority language (Wei, 2007)
Family bilingualism/heritage language use	Situations where children and adults in migrant or non-migrant families speak the language of the family's home/first country (Valdés, 2000, Rothman, 2009)
Balanced bilingualism	The individual has similar levels of proficiency in both languages (Wei, 2007)

Figure 6.1 Types of bilinguals and bilingual situations

raised with a strong cultural connection to a particular language through family interaction' (e.g. Van Deusen-Scholl, 2003: 222) and others, with the ability to speak the language at some level (Valdés, 2001). The literature also presents a distinction between heritage and ANCESTRAL LANGUAGE, the latter referring to a language that was learned by the older generation, e.g. grandparents, as a mother tongue but is either only partially transmitted to new generations or is no longer used in the community, where a different language is spoken. The notion of ancestral language is usually used in the context of ethnicity, identity, or language loss (e.g. Imbens-Bailey, 1996).

6.3 Linguistic Diversity, Language Change and Code Switching

Wherever there is contact among languages, there will be bilingualism. However, its extent in some of today's urban areas in the world seems to be unprecedented. Political changes in the world influence the concept of nationhood, changing the linguistic situation in many societies. In Europe, for instance, there is a rise of European identity rather than national identities. With the EU's 55 officially recognized indigenous minority groups, recent years have seen the rise of English due to its lingua franca status, which adds to the complexity of the nation's linguistic situation. Linguists refer to the coexistence of multiple languages in the same place as SUPER-DIVERSITY (Blommaert, 2013; Vertovec, 2007).

A widespread phenomenon among bilinguals in such linguistically diverse settings is code switching. Code switching refers to the simultaneous use of two languages during interaction, and there is historical evidence of its contribution to language change. For example, modern English reflects the French of the Normans after they settled in Britain in the 12th century (Kibbee, 1991), and written records reveal this phenomenon; for example, in a letter written to King Henry IV at the start of the 15th century, the writer switched constantly between French and English (Crystal, 1997).

For some researchers, code switching refers to the incompetent use of a language by those with a poor command of one of the languages. However, it has now been established that speakers' use of two (or more) languages in the same conversation demonstrates linguistic creativity and versatility rather than lack of competence (Poplack, 1980; Zentella, 1999). It is also observed that the most common form of mixing involves inserting a word from one language while speaking in the other language. This is shown in the following Turkish-English example:

midterm*'ün* *tarihini değiştirebilir miyiz?*

midterm-of date change-could ques we

'Can we change the date of the midterm?'

The speaker uses the English word 'midterm' with a Turkish suffix. Such single-word switches with use of the morphology of that language are pervasive among those who regularly use the same languages. Why does the speaker in the above example use the word 'midterm' here? Turkish is her DOMINANT LANGUAGE, so this is not because she does not know the word in Turkish. Her use of 'midterm' could be due to communicative expectations, the nature of the context, or the identity of the interlocutors in the conversation.

When monolinguals use language to mark certain functions, they have dialects and registers at their disposal, but bilinguals have separate languages. Hence, the range of functions of code switching expands. The speaker can code switch to mark ethnic or linguistic identity, social role or social status. She or he can use it to establish interpersonal intimacy or distance (Myers-Scotton, 1993). An example comes from Chui *et al.* (2014), who studied immigrants in Hong Kong. The researchers found that code switching operated like social glue, where the code switching of the newly arrived revealed their motivation to fit in, while that of the longer-term residents demonstrated their identity.

Code switching can sometimes occur due to limited exposure to the languages involved, and learners of different ages during the lower stages of acquisition may be able to retrieve a word in one language but not in the other (see discussion in Chapter 4). Early research viewed bilingual children's code switching as a sign of both lack of linguistic competence and confusion (Volterra & Taeschner, 1978). Researchers have now overturned this view, but it persists in the general public and can lead to parents' concern that their children are unable to separate their languages and contribute to the decision to raise children monolingually in the majority language.

Studies showing young children's ability to separate languages includes Genesee *et al.*'s (1995) study of 2½ year-old English-French bilinguals, who were able to identify the different languages that the mother and the father spoke. The researchers examined the children's behavior in three different contexts to see which language they used – (i) with the mother alone, (ii) with the father alone, (iii) with both parents present – and found that they used more French with the French-speaking parent and more English with the English-speaking parent. However, although this study and other such studies show that bilingual children separate and appropriately use their languages at a young age, their languages interact with each other. Taking a closer look at bilingual development reveals where this occurs and where it does not.

As already noted, the controversial issues discussed above and in the rest of this chapter which surround the younger members of the family are relevant to the older members' support of their education in aiming to raise teachers' and tutors' awareness of the challenges that confront the adult migrants with whom they work. This becomes an unavoidable concern when schooling in the majority language begins and the status of the home language(s) is demoted. When teachers and tutors understand these issues, value the home language for both adults' and children's learning and language development, they can better support adult learners in making what are difficult decisions for the education of the younger members of their family and community.

6.4 Bilingual Children

We begin this section by considering monolingual children's language acquisition as a basis for comparison when there is exposure to more than one language. Linguists consider the acquisition of a first language in childhood to be an outstanding feat (Hoff & Shatz, 2007; Sebastian-Galles, 2010). Even before they start school, children have acquired a highly complex system that allows them to understand and produce an infinite number of utterances in the language. Despite differences in the environment in which they grow up, their social class, and the language input they receive, children end up with similar core linguistic competence in their language (e.g. Chomsky, 1965; Pinker, 1994). After only several years of exposure to a given language, children know how to form sentences, questions and other complex syntax at an age when their other cognitive, motor, perceptual and social skills remain immature.

Researchers have spent a good amount of time trying to find out what babies know at birth, including when they are exposed to more than one language. While still in the womb, outside sounds can be heard from 23 weeks onwards. This accounts for why, at birth, newborns can already distinguish and show preference for their mother's voice over others' voices (DeCasper & Fifer, 1980; Gervain & Mehler, 2010; Mehler *et al.*, 1988; Peña *et al.*, 2003). The fetus and neonates pick up on PROSODY and detect that sounds are grouped to create a rhythm and a tune in the language they listen to. However, they cannot yet identify the individual sounds of this language, since these are muffled in the womb. Two months after birth, babies start distinguishing utterances in their language from utterances in an unfamiliar language. This indicates that they are starting to form a mental representation of the phonology of their language (Mehler *et al.*, 1988). Babies thus have the tools to process more than one language at a time and to keep the languages separate (Paradis & Genesee, 1996).

Acquiring a language means coming to know its sound system (phonology), its words (vocabulary) and word formation system (morphology), and its grammar (syntax), and how to use the language in communication. The challenge might seem to be double for babies growing up in a bilingual context, and migrant parents might opt to focus on the majority language and minimize the home language. Research now tells us that children are easily able to deal with more than one language.

Humans acquire additional languages across the lifespan, whether the language is spoken or signed, and the brain imposes no limitations on how many languages can be learned. Figure 6.1, above, includes children who learn two languages simultaneously from infancy (simultaneous bilingualism) and individuals (children and adults) who learn a second language after the first language has been firmly established (successive or SEQUENTIAL BILINGUALISM; see, e.g. De Houwer, 1990; Haznedar, 2013; Unsworth, 2013). Bilingualism is actually a continuum, and more than one pattern of acquisition and use can apply (Valdés, 2001).

Early research asked whether bilingual children separate their two languages into two systems, and proponents of a UNITARY LANGUAGE SYSTEMS HYPOTHESIS held that at the early stages of acquisition, children did not differentiate languages (Volterra & Taeschner, 1978). Considerable research since the 1970s questions the Unitary Language Systems Hypothesis and, as mentioned previously, we now know that newborns can distinguish their mother's voice from others' voices on the basis of prosody. Within the first several months of life they have the ability to notice rhythmically distinct languages, such as English and Japanese, and discriminate between them on the basis of their rhythm. This does not necessarily mean that bilinguals and monolinguals are equivalent in their language discrimination capacities in differentiating closely related languages such as Catalan and Spanish (Bosch & Sebastian-Galles, 1997, 2001). In the study conducted by Bosch and Sebastian-Galles (1997), which tested Spanish and Catalan bilingual and monolingual babies, it was found that having two rhythmically similar languages did not hinder the development of babies' discrimination skills. However, the results were not conclusive enough to argue for greater discrimination skills in bilinguals than in monolingual 4- or 5-month-old babies.

Clearly, children in bilingual contexts may be exposed to two (or more) languages from different people and in different contexts (Grosjean, 2004) and experience less exposure to these languages than a monolingual baby, but they are able to deal efficiently with this situation. If parents share a language, it will usually be the one that is most often spoken around the child. One of the parents will then use the additional language when alone with the child. This imbalance of amount of input does not hamper babies' ability to distinguish languages. It is useful for the teacher or tutor to know that this might slightly – but not seriously – delay bilinguals' perception and discrimination of the sounds in the two languages (Bosch & Sebastián-Gallés, 2003; Polka *et al.*, 2007).

Rejection of the Unitary Language Systems Hypothesis suggests that simultaneous bilinguals are two monolinguals with one brain. There are some patterns of language development that are different from those of monolinguals. For example, monolingual and bilingual children produce their first words around the age of one, and their rate of word learning is similar (Nicoladis, 2001; Patterson & Pearson, 2004; Pearson *et al.*, 1997; Pearson *et al.*, 1993). There is evidence of a (again not serious) delay of several months for bilinguals, vocabulary size in one or both languages may be smaller than that of age-matched monolinguals, and they might know some words in only one of the two languages. If we consider that unlike learning of language systems (as in phonology, morphology and syntax), vocabulary items must be learned individually. The bilingual child indeed has a double learning task (two or more words are needed for every object or idea) and a more complicated learning situation (exposure to different people in different situations). We do not need to view this as a deficiency (Pearson *et al.*, 1997).

Studies of the acquisition of word order and INFLECTIONAL MORPHOLOGY (morphosyntax) in bilingual children present a different picture. These studies examine simultaneous bilingual children to see whether the path of development in each language is similar to the path of a monolingual child. There is a general consensus that bilingual children learn language-specific properties of each language early and that each path of development resembles that of monolingual children. Paradis and Genesee (1996) report that two-to-three-year-old children learning English and French followed the same path in each language as monolingual French- or English-learning children. The children usually showed the same rate of development as monolinguals, but their development was sometimes slower in the language in which they received less input (De Houwer, 2005). That said, research also shows that one language can affect the other for some aspects of syntax (Serrattice *et al.*, 2004). This CROSS-LINGUISTIC INFLUENCE has long been a widely addressed phenomenon. There can be cross-linguistic influence on the word order of the language being learned, which children otherwise pick up very early when the two languages differ. Döpke (2000) observed that two-year-old simultaneous bilingual German-English children produced object-verb sentences like monolingual German children, as in *Milch trinken* 'milk drink' ('I want some milk'), but unlike German monolinguals, they also produced a number of verb-object sentences, such as *Trinken Milch* in German, following the English word order, typically produced exclusively by monolingual English children.

Cross-linguistic influence also occurs for simultaneous bilinguals when the language is one such as English, which requires subject pronouns to be overt (pronounced), and a language such as Spanish and Turkish, which allows pronominal subjects to be dropped. In Paradis and Navarro's (2003) study of Spanish-English simultaneous bilinguals and in Haznedar's (2010) study of Turkish-English bilinguals, the children used more overt subjects in their Spanish and in their Turkish than monolingual children do in these languages. Children who are exposed to an additional language after they have acquired the core aspects of their first language (successive bilinguals) are older and therefore more cognitively, linguistically and physically advanced than simultaneous bilinguals. This means that their initial state of knowledge (Schwartz & Eubank, 1996) contains more cross-linguistic possibilities to subconsciously influence their acquisition of the additional language. In the past, the influence of the first language was believed to make a crucial difference between adult and child second language learners; it was thought that the influence of the first language impeded adults' but not children's mastery of a new language. A half century of research points to L1 influence on L2 learning for both adults and children and that the degree and type of influence are comparable. For example, in a study of a young successive bilingual, a four-year-old Turkish speaker learning English, Haznedar (1997) reported that during his first several months of exposure, the child adopted (subject)-object-verb Turkish word order in English and produced sentences such as 'Yes ball playing'.

Just like children learning two languages simultaneously, successive bilinguals take a while to master the morphosyntax and phonology of their new language, and initially they produce erroneous or non-target-like forms. It has long been known that in these two domains of language, errors are not random but rather highly systematic, demonstrating the learner's subconscious processing of the input as they creatively construct the mental system that we call language. Vocabulary learning is also a gradual process, which continues through primary school, secondary school and beyond (Kohnert, 2004). Research shows that both simultaneous and successive bilingual school children have smaller vocabularies (and successive bilinguals somewhat smaller than simultaneous bilinguals), weaker LEXICAL ACCESS and more limited vocabulary knowledge in their languages than monolinguals (Bialystok, 2007; Bialystok & Craik, 2010; Pelham & Abrams, 2014; Umbel *et al.*, 1992). Bialystok *et al.* (2010) found that monolingual English speakers aged three to ten scored better in *receptive vocabulary* measures when compared to bilinguals despite the bilingual children being deemed to be fluent in English, the language tested. Similarly, Michael and Gollan (2005) found that when bilinguals were tested in their dominant language, they were slower than monolinguals and made more errors in tasks involving picture naming and verbal fluency. Gollan and Acenas (2004) found that in comparison to their monolingual peers, bilinguals experienced more tip-of-the tongue phenomena, temporary inaccessibility of a word the child tries to retrieve. Given that a bilingual child may not be exposed to the same extent to both languages (even the dominant language) as a monolingual child, it is not surprising that s/he may manifest lexical access difficulties, especially in terms of the extra PROCESSING TIME needed to retrieve a word from the language a speaker is using at a given time. These findings should not be interpreted as disadvantages, but rather as the outcome of the bilingual's more complex mental organization. This and other challenges should not deter parents and others in the community from supporting children in developing two rather than one language. In fact, knowing more than one language seems to confer cognitive advantages.

6.5 Cognitive Aspects of Bilingualism

In the earliest years of research, a common misconception was that bilingualism was related to low IQ, learning problems and overall language delay. When the studies that gave rise to these misconceptions were critically examined, their rigor was questioned. For example, researchers did not match bilingual and monolingual children for age, social class, language proficiency or language exposure (Bialystok, 2015; Nanez, 2010). Peal and Lambert's (1962) seminal study marked the departure from a bilingualism-as-deficit approach toward an emphasis on its cognitive advantages (Bialystok, 2007; Cook, 1997).

One advantage is claimed to be better performance by bilinguals on tasks that involve the EXECUTIVE FUNCTIONING (EF) SYSTEM. The EF system is an umbrella term used to refer to the management of everyday cognitive processes such as memory, task flexibility, reasoning, problem solving, and planning (Miyake & Friedman, 2012). Researchers argue that the joint activation and constant use of two languages strengthen the processes of verbal and nonverbal executive control (Bialystok *et al.*, 2009). One early model held that bilinguals, whose management of competing systems trains their EF skills, perform better than monolinguals when an activity requires that they suppress information which is irrelevant in that context and direct their attention to a target stimulus (Bialystok, 2015; Green, 1998).

Researchers continue to explore what underlies the bilingual advantage observed. Costa and Sebastian-Galles (2014), for example, argue that high levels of Executive Functioning do not necessarily result from the deactivation of the language not being used during production, because bilinguals' cognitive superiority is observed in bilinguals who are as young as seven months and not yet producing language. Similarly, Kovacs (2015) reports that bilingual infants show specific adaptations to their environment that can be attributed to processing mixed language input rather than producing language. Bilinguals' environmental adaptations include greater attention to novel languages, to co-occurring patterns in unfamiliar speech and dealing with rapid changes in input in two languages. More support for the involvement of an inhibition mechanism in language production and processing comes from Britio and Barr (2012), who found that 18-month-old bilinguals were better at memory generalizations (using novel toys to imitate the same actions demonstrated by an experimenter), when compared to age-matched monolinguals, well before they started producing full language.

Early research on children's metalinguistic development also shows that bilinguals outperform their monolingual peers in tasks that involve conflicting information. In a number of studies, researchers noted that while monolingual and bilingual children between five and nine years old performed equally well in detecting ungrammaticality in sentences such as 'Apples growed on trees', bilinguals were more successful than monolinguals in dealing with semantically implausible sentences, such as 'Apples grow on noses' (Bialystok, 1986, 1988; Cromdal, 1999). The bilingual children disregarded semantic anomalies and focused on whether the target sentences were grammatical, whereas monolingual children were distracted by semantic anomalies and performed poorly. Bilinguals' performance reflects an enhanced awareness of language, which confers an advantage not only with respect to linguistic processing but also for the cognitive ability required to handle conflicting information (Bialystok, 2015).

The cognitive advantages of bilingualism go further. In a meta-analysis of the cognitive correlates of bilingualism by Adesope *et al.* (2010), data from 63 studies of 6022 participants showed that bilingualism is positively associated with a number of cognitive benefits, including higher performance in control of attention and metalinguistic awareness, working memory, abstract/symbolic reasoning and in creative thinking and problem solving. In addition, as a result of adjustment to different languages used in multiple contexts with various interlocutors, bilingual children have been reported to perform better in theory of mind tests, which measure understanding of others' feelings and opinions (Goetz, 2003; Kovacs, 2009).

Are benefits of bilingualism found only for those with high proficiency in each language? The answer to this question is not necessarily. One study of young school-aged children learning Hebrew and another study of children learning French, with varying levels of proficiency in these languages, showed that the bilingual executive control advantage was not connected to children's proficiency but to their length of exposure to the additional language (Bialystok & Barac, 2012).

The bilingual advantage in executive control seems also to be independent of socio-economic status, as explored in a study comparing working-class and middle-class monolingual and bilingual children at the same school. The bilinguals showed superiority in executive control tasks regardless of their socioeconomic background (Calvo & Bialystok, 2014). Bilinguals' executive control advantage is also found in adulthood where, with various forms of dementia, including Alzheimer's, symptoms after onset can be delayed for four to five years, based on a comparison of hospital records of monolinguals and bilinguals (Gollan *et al.*, 2011).

6.6 The Neurological Basis of Language

To provide a full picture of what is known about bilingualism, we now turn to the neurological properties of bilingual brains. This discussion also sheds light on the neurological correlates of the cerebral trauma and dementia that are not uncommon among older individuals (including migrant adults), which can selectively affect certain language domains. This section addresses the following questions: (i) Where is language represented in the brain? (ii) Which parts of the brain are responsible for various language tasks?

The brain amounts to only 2% of an adult's weight, yet it is highly complex. It contains roughly 86 billion neurons along with glial cells and blood vessels, which are organized into three main parts: (i) the cerebrum/cerebral cortex (19% of the neurons); (ii) the cerebellum (80% of the neurons); and (iii) the brain stem (1% of the neurons) (Azevedo *et al.*, 2009). The cerebrum is the largest part of the brain and is divided into right and left hemispheres, which communicate with each other via a longitudinal fissure and a bundle of fibers called the corpus callosum. Each cerebral hemisphere has frontal, temporal, occipital and parietal lobes.

At the end of the 19th century, two doctors working separately, Broca and Wernicke, discovered major language areas in the left hemisphere, which were then named after them. They connected symptoms of aphasia – language loss due to a trauma such as a stroke – to sites in the patient's brain, post-mortem. Individuals with Broca's aphasia cannot speak fluently or grammatically but can generally comprehend speech. Those with Wernicke's aphasia can speak fluently and grammatically, but their speech is nonsensical, and they cannot comprehend speech (Stowe *et al.*, 2005). Advanced technology has now revealed considerably more about the brain and language through use of techniques such as functional Magnetic Resonance Imaging (fMRI). When an area in the brain is activated by an individual's response to a language task and more oxygen is required, blood flow, as shown in fMRI, reveals where in the brain the oxygen is used (Scott & Wise, 2003). Some studies of bilinguals' cerebral blood flow show that they use the same brain areas for identical tasks for both languages tested (e.g. picture naming, verbal fluency), regardless of the differences in these languages in phonology, syntax, and the writing system. Other studies show that proficiency in and amount of exposure to the two languages influences the results. For example, when bilinguals produce sentences or words in their lower-proficiency language, there is greater activation in the prefrontal cortex, indicating more working memory involvement; the brain is working harder. However, this effect is moderated by longer exposure to the language, regardless of the speaker's proficiency. In some domains of language, such as syntax, studies show that the age at which the individual was first exposed to the language matters; the syntactic processing of those who begin acquiring the second language as adults differs from those who begin as children (Wartenburger *et al.*, 2003).

6.7 Distinguishing Typical and Atypical Bilingual Development

Some children display SPECIFIC LANGUAGE IMPAIRMENT or cognitive difficulties that are developmental in nature, not the result of injury but due to congenital impairment. Researchers around the world have been working on figuring out how we know when a bilingual child's development is typical and when it is atypical. Family members can easily confuse atypical and typical development in bilingual children, and well-informed teachers and tutors can offer support.

Atypical development affects members of our entire species, regardless of language, culture, education or socioeconomic status. Some problems persist and affect adults, including migrant adults. There is, however, very little research on this group of adults (see, e.g. Schwarz, 2009). Research indicates that 8% of boys and 6% of girls develop language atypically (Tomblin *et al.*, 1997), and clinical linguists have now identified atypical patterns of language development in a range of languages and have confirmed that while comprehension of language can be affected, it is more common for speech production to be impaired in some way (Conti-Ramsden & Hesketh, 2003). Some signs of atypical development are when compared to children of the same age, the child produces first words considerably later, has less intelligible speech, and has a smaller vocabulary. These problems exist alongside normal non-verbal IQ and otherwise normal cognitive and socio-emotional development. A smaller vocabulary of bilingual children has been mentioned above, and it is easy to see how this could prompt worries that the child is not developing typically. A specific type of atypical development known as language impairment (SLI) involves problems with morphosyntax, particularly production of functional morphology, discussed in Chapter 5 (see also Leonard, 1998). Because languages vary in the grammatical functions that words, prefixes, and suffixes mark, children's problems vary across languages (Abdalla & Crago, 2008; Leonard, 2000; Paradis & Crago, 2001). Because of its seriousness, SLI has received more attention by researchers.

By the age of five, children developing proficiency in English will typically have acquired the functional elements that mark tense and aspect, as in 'they are watching', where 'are' marks present tense and '–ing' marks progressive aspect. One sign of specific language impairment is the child's unstable and variable use of functional suffixes such as '-ing' and the auxiliary verb forms 'is' and 'are' (Rice & Wexler, 1996). Children learning Spanish show difficulties relevant to that language, such as correct use of articles to mark gender and number, as in *el libro* vs. *los libros* 'the book(s)s' and *la palabra* vs. *las palabras* 'the word(s)' (Restrepo & Guitiérrez-Clellen, 2004). German children have problems with the variable word order connected to subject-verb agreement on FINITE vs. no agreement on NON-FINITE VERBS, as in *Du trinkst den Wein* 'You drink the wine' vs. *Du sollst keinen Wein trinken* 'You shouldn't drink wine'. The SLI child might produce *Du sollen* or *du trinken*, both non-finite forms (Clahsen *et al.*, 1997). Turkish morphologically marks COUNTER-FACTUALS in a complex manner, and atypically developing children demonstrate difficulties not only in producing these but also in comprehending them (e.g. *(O) çok çalışmış olsaydı, görev ona verilmiş olurdu* 'If she had worked harder, she would have been given the position') (Yarbay-Duman *et al.*, 2015).

Accurate diagnosis of atypical development has considerable bearing not only on children's well-being and subsequent educational success, but also on family members' and school teachers' support of children growing up bilingually. On the one hand, it is a gross disservice to all parties concerned if a diagnosis of atypical development is incorrect due to the child's bilingualism. If the diagnosis is correct, the treatment need not involve focusing on monolingualism in the majority language; we have seen above that bilingualism affords advantages, and there is little evidence that these advantages are unavailable to atypically developing children. On the other hand, if the child's bilingual development masks atypical development, the child might fail to get timely treatment to master the linguistic competence necessary to underpin literacy (Rescorla, 2005). If family members and school teachers suspect that a bilingual child is atypical, they should take into account the typical characteristics of bilingual development discussed in the previous sections. These include code-switching patterns, cross-linguistic influence, the dominance of one language when the child is receiving different amounts of exposure to two languages and a relatively smaller vocabulary (Paradis *et al.*, 2011).

The body of work on atypical bilingual language development has been growing, but information is only slowly trickling down to guide families and school teachers in making informed, collaborative decisions in responding to problems. In a recent project conducted with monolingual and bilingual populations across Europe, researchers profiled BILINGUAL-SPECIFIC LANGUAGE IMPAIRMENT (BI-SLI) by establishing a network to identify cognitive and linguistic abilities of these bilingual children: http://www.bi-sli.org. This work has begun to dispel the now discredited view discussed above that bilingualism is too great a cognitive and linguistic burden on children and should be avoided. Evidence does not support the fear that bilingual children experience more delays, disorders, or impairments than their age-matched monolingual peers (Paradis *et al.*, 2011). Moreover, research on atypically developing bilingual children indicates that their development in each language is similar to atypically developing monolingual children. That is, their bilingualism does not exacerbate their atypical development (Paradis *et al.*, 2011). The unequivocal take-away message for family members and teachers is that children's bilingual development can and should be supported.

6.8 Bilingualism in Education

We now broaden our scope to consider bilingualism in education and address the ongoing issue of how those who work with migrant adults can support them in their interaction with their children's teachers. We first consider the literacy development of bilingual children and then look at the ways that migrant adults' home languages might be supported in school or after school in the community.

6.8.1 Biliteracy of children

If an individual is literate in two languages, bi-literate, they have 'literate competencies in two languages, to whatever degree, developed either simultaneously or successively' (Dworin, 2003: 171). Family members, educators and policy makers have long been concerned about whether bilingual children should learn to read and write only in the majority language of the country in which they are living, first learn to read in their home language, or learn to read in two languages simultaneously (Bialystok *et al.*, 2005). The first situation applies to most migrant children, while the second applies most often to children in families of higher socioeconomic status. When a child develops literacy in two languages, either simultaneously or successively, the same questions are asked as those asked concerning the acquisition of two languages. Do the writing systems of the languages involved influence each other? If so, how? Is this influence detrimental, beneficial, or neither? Does this depend on the characteristics of the two writing systems? In this section we provide answers through a review of six studies, whose results are often surprising.

The first study looked at the biliteracy development of bilingual Korean-English children. We are familiar with English as one of the most opaque spelling systems, using the Roman alphabet (see Chapter 3). The Korean writing system is also alphabetic in that it represents vowels and consonants, but unlike the linearly written Roman alphabet, letters in Korean (Hangul) are grouped in a syllable block, with six possible patterns to form the syllable block. Wang *et al.* (2006) tested the listening, word decoding and spelling processing of 45 bilingual children who were concurrently learning to read and write in both languages when they were six and again when they were seven. Results showed that phonological skills in Korean and English were strongly correlated, and Korean phonological skills explained a unique amount of variance in English pseudo-word reading beyond the children's English phonological and spelling skills. There was spelling skills transfer between the two language systems, but this cross-language transfer between a Roman alphabetic script and a non-Roman alphabetic script turned out to confer an advantage in their reading in each language.

In another study involving different writing systems, English (Roman alphabet); Hebrew (consonant alphabet with vowel diacritics, i.e. an abugida; see Chapter 3); and Cantonese (characters), Bialystok *et al.* (2005) collected data from three groups of six-year-olds: 29 Cantonese-English biliterate bilinguals, 30 Hebrew-English biliterate bilinguals and 33 Spanish-English biliterate bilinguals. The Hebrew-English children were attending a DUAL-LANGUAGE IMMERSION SCHOOL and received daily PHONICS instruction in both languages. The Cantonese-English children were learning to read in English and also had two hours of Chinese instruction every week. The Spanish-English bilinguals were learning to read in English and had weekly after-school Spanish classes. Toward the end of their first semester in school, all of the children were tested in English and the other language on working memory, receptive vocabulary, phoneme segmentation and word decoding. The results for word decoding showed a weak correlation between the two languages for the Cantonese-English bilinguals, a medium correlation for the Hebrew-English group and a high correlation for the Spanish-English group despite spending much less time on literacy than the Hebrew group and having a lower socioeconomic status. The conclusion is that simultaneous biliteracy is most achievable when the two languages share an alphabetic system.

Wang *et al.* (2005) also wondered whether cross-writing system transfer exists when the two languages do not share writing systems. They studied 46 English-Chinese bilingual/biliterate seven- and eight-year olds to look for cross-writing system influence on reading. The children were tested on their processing of spoken and written language for each language. Results revealed that the children's skills in noticing and manipulating rhymes in words correlated significantly in both languages and that their Chinese character reading correlated with word decoding in English. In another study of one five-year child, Buckwalter and Lo (2002) found that in Chinese and English, the child understood the morpho-syllabic features of Chinese and how characters differ from English letters and cannot be decoded through phonics. That is, the child was not confused by the two systems and kept them separate, as simultaneous bilinguals do with the spoken language.

Just as with successive bilingualism, where the child acquires an additional language after acquisition of the first language, there are countless examples of younger and older children who can read and write in their home/native language and then develop literacy in the additional language they are learning. Simply knowing how to read – regardless of the writing system – is helpful when developing literacy in another language (e.g. Cummins, 1979; Upton & Lee-Thompson, 2001). This means that when reading in a second language, readers might resort to what they know about their first language. However, with a focus on linguistic, cognitive, educational, and sociocultural factors, Grabe (2009) emphasizes the differences between L1 and L2 reading processes. While it is important to understand the role that L1 literacy skills play in L2 reading (Hudson, 2007), Grabe (2009) argues against the view that literacy skills in the L1 automatically transfer to reading in the L2. Among many issues, he stresses the magnitude of the task that the L2 reader has to deal with, in terms of the development of orthographic and morphosyntactic knowledge of the new language as well the lexical system, all of which require much effort before automatic use. (See Chapter 3 for more discussion of this complexity.)

From an educational perspective, research in bilingual education programs has shown that a key factor in enabling bilinguals to succeed in developing literacy in a second language is to maintain literacy in the mother tongue in a supportive sociocultural environment (Carder, 2013). Collier and Thomas (2007), for example, argue that in terms of long-term gains, it is important for bilinguals to maintain their home language while they improve their second language at an academic level during their school life. Bilinguals who are not yet fully biliterate transfer the reading skills that they have to support development of literacy skills in their additional language (Koda & Zehler, 2008; Leikin *et al.*, 2010). As with simultaneous biliterates, this transfer is most straightforward when both languages use the same writing system; e.g. the Roman alphabet (Durgunoğlu & Öney, 1999; Reyes, 2006). But as we have seen above, this transfer also occurs when they do not.

Leikin *et al.* (2010) compared Russian-Hebrew bilingual six-year olds learning to read and write in Hebrew in Israel. The Russian alphabet is transparent and represents both consonants and vowels, but Hebrew represents consonants and only long vowels, using diacritics for short vowels. The researchers assessed the early literacy acquisition of 39 Russian-Hebrew bilinguals who had received a year of weekly reading instruction in Russian and were then learning to read in Hebrew, 41 bilinguals learning to read in Hebrew with no Russian literacy and 41 monolinguals learning to read in Hebrew. At the start of schooling in Hebrew at six years old and then at the end of that school year, the children were tested on listening processing, awareness of phonemes, and word decoding in both languages. Results showed that the Russian-Hebrew biliterate children significantly outperformed the monoliterate bilinguals as well as monolinguals. The researchers concluded that children's knowledge of the highly regular Russian orthography conferred an advantage in their Hebrew reading. Like other studies, these results were not affected by children's non-verbal IQ or socioeconomic status.

On similar grounds, Hussein (2014) examined the reverse effect of cross-linguistic influence in biliteracy development. The aim was to explore the impact of opaque orthographies such as English over transparent ones. Based on data from 45 Arabic-English nine-year-old bilinguals, Hussein examined the effects of English literacy on Arabic literacy. The participants were tested on oral reading and spelling accuracy. The results showed that in comparison to 38 monolingual, mono-literate Arabic-speaking children, the biliterate bilinguals were significantly better not only in English but also in Arabic, the language in which they were receiving less literacy instruction.

It is important to note that while these studies involve children, they are indicative of the transfer effects that occur with migrant adults with little or no formal schooling: Those with a little literacy in their home or any other language have an advantage in tackling literacy in a new language.

6.8.2 Bilingual education in schools

Across generations, a shift is commonly observed, where first-generation speakers of a language that is not the majority language of the country are monolingual in their home language and starting to acquire the language of the country where they have resettled. The second generation is bilingual but may not be biliterate. The third generation is monolingual in the majority language. By the fourth and later generations, the home language is no longer used within the family (e.g. Fishman, 1991; Montrul, 2010; Portes & Hao, 1998; Portes & Schauffler, 1994). If there is no continued migration of speakers of the language into the community, that community becomes monolingual. 'Heritage language speaker' (see the start of this chapter) is a relatively recent term, used to refer not only to first-generation migrants but also to second and later generations who are exposed to the heritage language but may or may not speak it. The term was first introduced in Canada in the 1970s (Cummins, 2005) and started to receive attention in the United States in the 1990s (see, for example, Peyton *et al.*, 2001). Heritage language speakers can be bilinguals exposed to a language that is ethnolinguistically different from the majority language spoken by the majority of the population in that society (Montrul, 2010). Children around the world acquire their heritage language to varying degrees by listening to their parents, aunts and uncles, grandparents, and new immigrants in the community. In those cases, heritage language speakers do not have access to public or private education in their heritage language, and it is likely to be their weaker language. As a result, while they might have a good oral command of the language, their literacy skills in the language show variability, often far from being native speaker like.

There are controversies surrounding patterns of heritage language acquisition, the resolution of which bear on children's typical vs. atypical development. If teachers and tutors are informed, they can better anticipate the needs of migrant adults as parents. When comparing bilinguals' weaker language to the language of age-matched monolinguals, researchers find that second-generation children differ from their parents in the level to which they acquire the language. They acquire fewer registers, have smaller vocabularies, show less variety in their grammar and sometimes do not even acquire the more complex aspects of the language (Polinsky, 2007, 2008, 2011). Polinsky (2007) reports, for example, that for the six case markers in Russian (nominative, accusative, dative, instrumental, oblique and genitive), heritage language speakers tend to use only nominative and accusative. Polinsky (2008) shows that low-proficiency heritage language speakers make many errors with masculine, feminine and neuter gender marking in Russian, using only feminine and masculine. Montrul *et al.* (2008) report similar gender-marking problems in Spanish, which distinguishes masculine and feminine gender on articles preceding nouns, where heritage language speakers may use masculine articles for feminine nouns. However, Rothman *et al.* (2016) note that this may be due not only to input quantity (often limited to interactions with parents and extended family members) but also to input quality. For second- and third-generation migrants, the language variety to which they are exposed in the community may not be the *variety* that their parents or grandparents speak.

In addition to problems with NOMINAL MORPHOSYNTAX discussed above, heritage language speakers who have grown up hearing the language only from members of their family and the immediate community but not during their schooling experience difficulties with VERBAL MORPHOSYNTAX, in particular with subject-verb agreement and tense marking. These are the same vulnerable aspects of language with which children diagnosed as atypically developing struggle, and this is why it is very useful for teachers and tutors of migrant adults with children to know about bilingual language development in an immigrant situation. While the acquisition of verb tense has been reported to be non-problematic for heritage language speakers of Spanish and Russian, PERFECTIVE and IMPERFECTIVE forms in these languages pose challenges for them (Montrul, 2002; Polinsky, 2007; Silva-Corvalán, 1994). On similar grounds, based on data from heritage Brazilian Portuguese speakers, Rothman (2007) highlights the imperfect mastery of the heritage language and reports that the learners do not develop target knowledge of inflected INFINITIVES in Brazilian Portuguese. It should be noted, however, that in their recent work, Rothman *et al.* (2016) argue that the inconsistent nature of heritage speakers' knowledge of their heritage language(s) is not surprising due to some factors such as: (i) type of exposure; (ii) the way they use the heritage language; (iii) literacy skills they have in the heritage language; and (iv) the status of the heritage language in the community (Rothman *et al.*, 2016: 19). What they emphasize here is that despite the challenges that heritage language speakers face, it would be wrong to claim that their knowledge is completely different from that of monolinguals.

Further, above it is noted that by the third and fourth immigrant generations, the heritage language is often no longer spoken. With integration into the wider society, immigrants lose their home language(s). But with effort, a community's bilingualism (or multilingualism) can be maintained. One way to do this is through education in the home languages, where the language(s) is used and literacy in the language(s) is taught in school (Cummins, 2000). A range of challenging social, psychological, economic, administrative and instructional conditions apply to bilingual education (García, 2009: 137–157), and it is useful for teachers and tutors of migrant adults to be aware of the practicalities and realities of supporting migrants' home language(s).

These factors are:

- SITUATIONAL FACTORS refer to students' social and linguistic backgrounds, population diversity, language policies of the country, the role of the languages in school, the status of the languages in the society and the costs of providing bilingual education.
- OPERATIONAL FACTORS focus on curriculum and subjects taught in school; materials available and used in the language; students' initial literacy; languages used in assessments; and involvement of teachers, parents and community members.
- OUTCOME FACTORS are concerned with expectations regarding ultimate proficiency in the language, subject matter mastery and sociocultural maturity.

Goals for bilingual education range from students reaching equal proficiency in both languages to full proficiency in only the majority language, and these goals map on to several educational models (Baker & Wright, 2017). Under a dual-language immersion model, the goal is to reach balanced bilingualism and biliteracy. Such programs may start in either early or late primary school, and children may develop biliteracy either simultaneously or sequentially. Strict language compartmentalization by subject and equal numbers of students from each language are important for the success of this type of bilingual education.

Majority language or TRANSITIONAL BILINGUAL EDUCATION aims to support children in the heritage language until they gain sufficient majority language proficiency to cope with learning only in that language (Baker & Wright, 2017). This model is also found in non-migrant contexts (e.g. in sub-Saharan Africa, where after three or four years of instruction in their home language in primary school, children transition to learning in the national language, such as Amharic in Ethiopia, English in Nigeria or French in the Congo) (Obondo, 1997). There are criticisms of such practices in that they deprive the world of the talents of bilinguals in a range of languages and have a negative effect on the heritage communities, ultimately contributing to the extinction of languages (García, 2009). Educators and researchers now advocate that the heritage language be continued in school as long as possible (e.g. Simpson, 2015).

Research on children developing and maintaining their home language also addresses the issue of whether language teaching methodologies used with purely second language learners can be used with those with a heritage language background. Despite concerns noted by some researchers (e.g. Rothman *et al.*, 2016; Valdés *et al.*, 2006), Montrul (2010) notes that classroom second language acquisition research has a lot to offer to young heritage language users. A primary question concerns how and in what ways heritage language users respond to classroom instruction, which is usually explicit. As noted by Montrul (2010), heritage language users typically have high levels of communicative skills in their home language but still need to develop literacy skills to improve their grammatical and vocabulary knowledge and to be proficient with more formal and academic uses of the language. Moreover, while mainstream classrooms usually assume a homogeneous group of learners, heritage language users, in either migrant or non-migrant settings, are diverse linguistically and culturally (Baker & Wright, 2017). To this end, heritage language users will benefit more if they have access to a bicultural or multicultural curriculum, with multiple perspectives presented and opportunities to construct their own knowledge collaboratively with other students and in activities that are appropriate to their levels of grammatical and cultural knowledge (Cummins, 2000).

6.8.3 Bilingual education at the community level

In addition to these efforts and pedagogical concerns in schools, there has been a growing movement in recent years for heritage language maintenance and development, when individuals might have little oral proficiency in the language and little or no literacy. This movement is facilitated by what has been discussed above in terms of the growing understanding of the advantages of bilingualism and the dispelling of older myths regarding dangers associated with bilingualism. The aim of such steps has been to foster a sense of identity and to build linguistic and cultural strength and social cohesion and to promote multi-directional integration, not simply with the majority language. There is a range of unresolved and complex issues related to language policy and support for these languages in classroom settings (see discussions in Kagan *et al.*, 2017; Peyton *et al.*, 2001; Seals & Peyton, 2017; Wiley *et al.*, 2014).

Teaching of migrant as well as indigenous and other minority languages has not always been deemed culturally enriching; rather it has been actively discouraged in some contexts. As noted by Baker and Wright (2017), if a language is banned in school, this rapidly leads to its decline. For Fishman (2004: 417), who has long argued for the maintenance and development of heritage languages, 'it is just as scandalous and injurious to waste "native" language resources as it is to waste air, water, mineral, animal, and various non-linguistic human sources'.

Parents do not always rely on the school to make sure that their children acquire their heritage language. There are many examples worldwide of community-based programs, with classes offered after school, during the weekend, and/or during the summer. This requires involvement of the heritage language community, and new initiatives continue to be introduced around the world, some of which involve the migrant adults who are the focus of this volume. In her PhD dissertation, Aberdeen (2016) notes that unlike educated, literate and middle-class parents, migrant parents with little or no formal schooling are grappling with their own education and their survival. In addition, unlike non-migrant middle class adults, (i) many cannot travel to the home country; (ii) they may not have established a language community where they now live; (iii) their home language may have few if any books and other materials in the language; and (iv) they do not have the funds, the ability to raise funds or the time to do so for their children's extra-school heritage language support. Work on heritage language learning focuses on the link between what we know about successful additional language learning. As has been pointed out by Aberdeen in Canada (International & Heritage Languages Association, http://www.ihla.ca) and the US Coalition of Community-Based Heritage Language Schools (http://heritagelanguageschools.org/coalition/mission), to promote heritage language programs, the following issues need to be addressed: (i) space for classes; (ii) transportation for students; (iii) curriculum and instruction; (iv) teacher recruitment, quality and retention; and (v) health and safety. Given the complex nature of bilingual children whose home language is not the majority language of the country and who undergo a shift in language preference to the dominant language at school (Montrul, 2008), efforts to support the heritage language need to go beyond simply supporting its use. A programme should address social, affective, and educational issues and include, if necessary, the writing of textbooks and preparation of courses and programs specifically designed for heritage language speakers (Bayram *et al.*, 2017). Haznedar *et al.* (2018) discuss a new initiative, a heritage language hub to bring together online resources and to inform and provide reading resources for those who work with adult migrants with little or no formal schooling. The authors highlight the need for effective instruction and identification of materials in the heritage languages of migrants. On the assumption that heritage speaker linguistic competence differs from that of monolingual speakers of the same language in terms of lexicon, morphosyntax and phonology (Montrul, 2010), recent studies of heritage language learners endorse the increasingly widely held view that they differ from second and foreign language learners, which means that their instructional needs differ (cf. Rothman *et al.*, 2016). Instruction and creation of teaching materials, assessment tools and placement procedures for a typical heritage language classroom should reflect diversity, as each learner may have a different heritage language profile in terms of their level of oral language and literacy in the language.

6.9 Conclusion

This chapter aims to inform those who teach or tutor migrant adults about one of the most important aspects of the lives of the younger members of these migrants' community, as well as their own lives, their bilingual development. It describes bilingualism and development of bilingual proficiency in early childhood and issues that arise in relation to bilingualism across the lifespan through the themes of language contact, language differentiation in simultaneous and successive bilinguals and language maintenance in heritage language speakers. Special attention is given to cognitive and neurological aspects of bilingualism. Based on bilingual cognitive science research, we have specifically emphasized the bilingual advantage not only during childhood but also over the lifespan, in particular with respect to executive functions and cognitive reserves. This means that making constant use of two or more languages leads to increased abilities to engage in high-level cognitive functions such as decision making, suppressing irrelevant information, and attentional control. We have also noted that observed differences between monolinguals and bilinguals should not be taken as evidence of deficiency on the part of the latter group, precisely because they have access to two or more language systems, in different domains of life, with different people, and in different contexts.

The discussion has extended to maintenance and further development of the language and literacy of heritage language speakers who are migrant adults as well as their younger family members. If social, political, and educational contexts are unfavourable to these heritage language speakers, a shift to the majority language might lead to weakness in their home language in the next generation. A new initiative, led by this chapter's author and the editors of this volume, is underway to support those who work with migrant adults with little or no formal schooling in the maintenance and development of their heritage language.

7 Teaching and Tutoring Adult Learners with Limited Education and Literacy

Nancy Faux and Susan Watson

7.1 Introduction

In keeping with teachers' and tutors' interests and the professional development needs described in the introduction to this book, this chapter focuses on the skills for teaching and tutoring second language reading and writing to migrant adults with limited education and literacy and the attitudes necessary for working effectively with this learner population. We provide information so that teachers and tutors will be able to help learners develop literacy practices and be engaged in the communities in which they are living. The chapter starts with reference to the theory and research covered in the previous chapters and is then devoted to ideas for practice.

The chapter begins with an overview of the meaning and components of literacy and then discusses the following six topics:

(1) What it means to be a literacy learner.
(2) Preparing to teach an adult literacy class.
(3) Developing print awareness.
(4) Phonological awareness and sound-symbol correspondence.
(5) Instructional practices for MULTILEVEL CLASSES.
(6) Assessments.

7.2 Conceptualizing Literacy

Literacy is broadly understood to be reading and writing skills and what it means to use these skills in one's daily life. (See Chapter 3 for further discussion of literacy and society.) Discussions of what it means to be literate extend beyond a focus on basic skills and practices. For example, Brian Street and Shirley Brice Heath focus on the SOCIOCULTURAL ASPECTS OF LITERACY. According to Street (1984), literacy is a culturally and socially embedded practice that is infused with beliefs and ways of knowing within a particular context, rather than a set of isolated, transferable skills. In Heath's (1983) ethnographic work in rural American communities in North Carolina, literacy engagement begins with a text. Heath finds that people in different communities engage with texts in many different ways, that go beyond what is narrowly defined in formal, school settings as 'reading'.

The sociocultural perspective includes the notion of *multiliteracies* (Barton & Hamilton, 1998), the many ways that people practice literacy in their everyday lives outside of formal school settings. This includes reading recipes, newspapers, signs and online media; helping children with homework; and reading for self-improvement. Janks (2010), drawing on the work of Freire (1970/1993), argues that texts position readers and writers in specific ways and reflect the writers' and readers' contexts and perspectives. Gee (2015: 9) argues that texts contain the 'social and political ideas of those groups with the most power'. Therefore, it is important for teachers and tutors to consider the messages that materials used in instruction might convey and how they position literacy learners in the communities in which they are now living and learning.

Literacy, and what it might mean to be literate (or illiterate), is studied by scholars from a broad range of perspectives. In-depth discussion of these perspectives is beyond the scope of this chapter, but we acknowledge that becoming literate in a second or additional language (L2) is a complex process for adults with limited education and literacy, especially those who come from an oral tradition. Watson (2010), drawing on the work of Goody (1968, 1977) and others, suggests that literacy 'brings about major changes in the ways that people think about themselves and the world, because literacy fundamentally alters the structure of intellectual processes and cultural relations' (Goody, 1977: 34). Huettig (2015) contends that literacy skills can influence cognitive processes, which range from making predictions about the meanings of a text to the amount of attention that an individual is able to give to a text, for what period of time (ATTENTION SPAN). Bassetti (2009) writes that seeing a language in its written form during oral language learning acts as an additional form of language input, which can facilitate learning. We can see that literacy and becoming literate is more than learning to read and write. It is a different way of engaging with the world and thinking about language.

With ideas about literacy in society and in the mind described in Chapters 2 and 3, this chapter focuses on teaching L2 reading and writing skills and the attitudes necessary for working with literacy learners who are learning to read and write for the first time in a second language. By maintaining a focus on instruction, the chapter provides teachers and tutors with specific instructional practices for working with literacy learners in different instructional contexts.

7.3 Five Topics to Consider When Working With This Learner Population

7.3.1 What it means to be a literacy learner

Adults who have limited or no reading and writing skills in their home or any other language and who are developing literacy skills for the first time in the majority language of the country in which they are living are referred to by various terms.

Bigelow and Vinogradov (2011) use a term also used for children, emergent reader. In North America, the term *SLIFE*, or STUDENTS WITH LIMITED OR INTERRUPTED FORMAL EDUCATION, is often used (DeCapua & Marshall, 2013). In this chapter, we use emergent reader, adult learner and literacy learner interchangeably to acknowledge the agency and circumstances of adult learners. We recognize that learners may speak several languages but not read or write in any of them, and that some may speak a language that does not have a written form. Indeed, adult learners are a heterogeneous group.

Understanding that literacy learners may have difficulty with or little knowledge of reading and writing skills can help practitioners develop a deeper understanding of the challenges that these learners face when learning to read and write for the first time in a second language, as described in Chapters 2 and 3. We begin this chapter by stressing that that illiteracy is not a 'permanent condition or characteristic' (Bigelow & Vinogradov, 2011: 120), and educators need to be aware of assumptions they may hold about emergent readers. Unlike children or literate adults learning to read in a new language, these learners face the double challenge of learning oral forms of the L2 while simultaneously learning to read and write in that language (Koda, 2005; Vinogradov, 2008; Young-Scholten & Strom, 2006). Tarone *et al.* (2009) note that children acquiring L1 literacy have four or more years to develop oral skills before beginning to read and write. Additionally, adult learners are beyond the age of compulsory and cost-free schooling, they often work and have families and they have far less time to devote to schooling. This puts them in a very different position from their younger counterparts who are required to attend school and have few, if any, work and family commitments.

Adkins *et al.* (1999) observe that teachers and tutors are often involved in helping migrant adults cope with challenges of everyday life in the destination country, in which the simplest literacy tasks can pose barriers to communication. Misunderstandings that can arise from these tasks can result in refugees and immigrants believing that their identity is threatened (Ullman, 1997). In fact, these adults bring a great deal of commitment, knowledge and skills to the learning endeavor. In *Bringing Literacy to Life,* Wrigley and Guth (1992) describe the wealth of experience, life knowledge and strengths that they possess. In their new country, they may have secured jobs, enrolled their children in local school systems and accessed social services. Likewise, Vinogradov and Bigelow (2010) emphasize that these adult migrants, like all adults, develop social networks and are adept at problem solving in daily life. In the face of considerable educational challenges, their sense of humor, commitment and openness to learning create the sort of positive atmosphere in which learning flourishes. However, the loss of support systems, such as family, friends and community, can compound their challenges. According to Adkins *et al.* (1999), the pressure to integrate is an additional stressor that makes it difficult for adults to be fully engaged in their learning and may result in a lack of attention or sleepiness. If they are refugees or asylum seekers, they may have experienced trauma and they may not yet have legal status to remain in the country. Pynoos *et al.* (1993) discuss how the experience of trauma brings about psychological, social and physical changes that affect the speed and facility with which the L2 is learned. Observable behaviors include absences, withdrawal from participation and changes in progress.

Another important area of understanding for working with adult learners is their literacy background. Burt *et al.* (2008) offer the following six categories of literacy that range from:

(1) Pre-literate, because the L1 has no written form or is in the process of developing a written form.
(2) Nonliterate, having had no access to literacy instruction due to war, famine, economic issues and so forth.
(3) Semiliterate, having limited access to literacy instruction, such as a few years of formal schooling.
(4) Non-alphabet literate, being literate in a language written in a non-alphabetic script but not in an alphabetic script.
(5) Non-Roman alphabet literate, being literate in a language written in a non-Roman alphabet.
(6) Roman alphabet literate, being literate in a language written in a Roman alphabet script.

Additionally, there are adults who learn literacy through religion. Doing research in Iran, Street (1984) found that by attending *maktabs*, or Islamic religious schools, Farsi-speaking students learned to recite passages of the Koran, a book written in Arabic, a language they did not speak. Students could open the Koran to the correct page and follow along with their fingers as they listened to or recited the passage. They developed literacy with the Koran not by 'cracking the phonemic code' but through a habitual, cultural practice (Street, 1984: 133).

It is important to think about the different literacy backgrounds and practices that learners bring to the classroom in order to build an understanding of who they are, why they have limited reading and writing skills and why they may require more time to learn than their more literate classmates.

Limited literacy can hold adults back from engaging in the economic life of the new community. Any kind of writing – applying for jobs, filling out forms, writing notes to children's teachers – presents barriers to communication for those who do not read or write. Apter *et al.* (2008) note that adults may not admit to a lack of literacy skills or may be embarrassed to seek help. There may be cultural and religious differences that result in reluctance by learners to interact in certain ways with the teacher, tutor or classmates. Teachers and tutors who are sensitive to these feelings, barriers and challenges can provide encouragement and support to help emergent readers be successful. One way to accomplish this is to incorporate activities into instruction that are relevant to learners' needs and daily lives and to recognize the knowledge and strengths that they bring to the endeavor.

7.3.2 Preparing to teach an adult literacy class

7.3.2.1 Understanding learners and gathering materials

One way to prepare is to consider learners' needs, strengths and challenges, with the goal first of understanding who they are, what they need to learn, what countries they have come from, what languages they speak and at what levels. The previous five chapters will be helpful for this preparation. They also provide some ideas for instruction, but this chapter aims to provide many more options, particularly for the teacher or tutor new to working with this learner population. Preparation also involves gathering materials and designing instruction that will put learners at ease, build on their language proficiency in their home language, draw out their strengths and provide appropriate challenges, with guidance on how to address them. Instructional materials, particularly reading texts for adult emergent readers, can be difficult to locate. Appropriate texts are those that provide contextual clues, such as pictures, and use simple language. Wrigley (1993: 1) suggests 'starting with the images, concepts, words and expressions that are familiar to the learners, rather than with the alphabet [because] innovative programs provide opportunities for MEANING MAKING from the first day of literacy education'. As Vinogradov (2008) notes, making meaning from a visual text is the broader aim of reading, and engaging with pictures is an act of literacy. However, Strube *et al.* (2009) caution that pictures can be culturally biased and result in misunderstandings. Pictures, like other texts, represent the ideology of a culture. Photographs can be easier to decipher than illustrations. Therefore, careful selection of appropriate texts, including the images, is crucial to literacy instruction.

7.3.2.2 Connecting instruction to learners' lives

Another way to put learners at ease and draw on their strengths is to use authentic texts, or those that connect instruction with learners' lives outside of the classroom (see Auerbach, 1992; Purcell-Gates *et al.*, 2002). These might include texts in their home languages, when these are available. Fish *et al.* (2007: 2) remind us that adult learners 'are beginning readers, but they are not beginning problem solvers; therefore, it's important to utilize materials and methods that can connect to students' immediate needs'.

One way to connect instruction to learners' lives is the language experience approach (LEA), described also in Chapter 3. LEA engages learners in writing about an authentic experience or activity with the teacher's or tutor's help. The LEA-generated stories can then be used for reading lessons. An experience or activity for generating an LEA text might be a museum visit. Museums are suitable for literacy learners, because they often use sensory input, such as touching and hearing, to make sense of new information. The teacher or tutor prepares learners for the visit with instruction that explains the content to be viewed. He or she then accompanies the learners on the museum visit and helps them make sense of what is being seen and heard. Amoruso (2016) uses drama as a way for learners to act out their ideas and experiences. Young-Scholten and Limon (2015) advocate building a habit of reading for pleasure. These materials can be made available in class or the program premises, at learners' different reading levels.

7.3.2.3 Determining materials that are level appropriate

Wrigley and Guth (1992) recommend using a checklist or rubric to evaluate level-appropriate materials used for features such as authenticity, predictability, visual clues and relevance to learners' needs. Other factors to consider in selecting level-appropriate texts include appropriateness of pictures, photographs and art. Additionally, the teacher or tutor should think about clear labels, diagrams, graphs, maps, or other visuals in texts. Grabe (2009) recommends that teachers align use of reading texts with learners' oral language skills and continue to build those oral skills as reading and writing develop. At the same time, however, literacy learners' oral language skills are usually more advanced than their reading skills. Farrelly (2013) adds that teachers and tutors know their learners best and can use this knowledge to put learners at ease and draw on their strengths.

7.3.2.4 Using a variety of instructional materials

In addition to written texts, instructional materials such as lined paper and writing instruments, scissors, tape and sentence strips (large strips of heavy paper) are important for literacy instruction. Sentence strips give emergent writers a guide with lines and borders on which to practice forming letters and words. Wrigley and Guth (1992) suggest varying the materials and approaches to allow learners to experience learning and reading in diverse ways. For example, magnetic letters or Legos can be used for a TACTILE LEARNING experience. Common objects from everyday life, realia, can help learners make connections with text. Pictures and photographs are useful when trying to explain and understand different ideas and vocabulary. The teacher or tutor can ask learners to bring in objects and pictures of their own and incorporate them into instruction.

7.3.2.5 Creating a safe, engaging space for learning

Gathering texts and materials is one part of preparing to work with literacy learners, whether in a classroom or a one-on-one tutoring setting. Other considerations include creating a safe, comfortable space for learning (Santos & Shandor, 2012) and, if in a class, building a sense of community. Although learners are adults who bring many different and valuable life experiences to the classroom, if they have no formal schooling, they will lack the experience of a structured learning environment. They may not have school skills or know what to expect when learning to read and write. Wrigley (2009) refers to these skills as COGNITIVE ACADEMIC SKILLS, or skills necessary for success in school. If learners feel nervous about their ability to use these skills, this could raise their stress level, or affect. Krashen's (1982) AFFECTIVE FILTER HYPOTHESIS suggests that motivation, self-confidence, self-esteem and anxiety play a role in second language acquisition. MacIntyre and Gardner (1991) describe one of these emotions as language anxiety, or the inability to adequately express thoughts and ideas because of fear of negative social evaluation and the need to impress others. Rubin and Thompson (1994) add that language learning requires taking risks and a high self-esteem, which can contribute to learners' willingness to engage and has been positively correlated with success in language learning (Brodkey & Shore, 1976; Gardner & Lambert, 1972; Heyde, 1979; Watkins *et al.*, 1991).

The role of emotions in second language learning is complex. Teachers and tutors can address learners' comfort and safety, and promote engagement, by creating a supportive learning environment. One idea for creating a learning environment in the classroom is use of interactive activities that help learners get acquainted with each other. The teacher can do an **ICE-BREAKER**, or introductory activity, to promote learner interaction. For example, learners might walk around the room and talk with five other learners, and each one says to the other their name and the country they are from. In a later icebreaker, they might share one thing interesting about their country. The complexity of the sharing can increase over time. Tutors working with learners one-on-one can modify these activities and interact directly with the learner.

Keeping learners engaged can be another challenge. A **LEARNER-CENTERED APPROACH**, which emphasizes learner agency, includes conducting a needs assessment and involving learners in the choice of instructional topics. These strategies are in keeping with principles of adult learning theory (Merriam *et al.*, 2007). A needs assessment can be used to better determine learners' goals and desires for learning. For example, pictures provide an easy, visual way to gather information about learners' needs. The teacher or tutor can use pictures from magazines or drawings that represent common curriculum themes such as community, housing or transportation. Classroom teachers can post the pictures around the room, and learners can vote for the topics of their choosing by placing a checkmark beside the picture(s) that best represent what they want to learn. They can also vote with their feet, or stand beside the picture of the subject area they want to study most. Picture dictionaries also allow learners to communicate their choices of what they want to study in class. The whole class can identify the themes that are selected most often to determine a content focus for class. Since interests and needs might change over time, these activities might be done several times during a semester or year.

One example of a learner-centered approach is found in the Reflect ESOL program (http://www.reflect-action.org/reflectesol). Reflect ESOL is a **DIALOGIC APPROACH** in which the teacher steps back, and the learners not only determine the topic(s) for instruction but also express the concerns of the class as a community. The goal is to shift the power dynamic between teacher and student in favor of the student. Further examples of learner-centered approaches are seen in the work of Amoruso *et al.* (2016) and Di Benedetto *et al.* (2017). Both worked with unaccompanied, refugee-background minors who had crossed the Mediterranean Sea and arrived in Sicily. With support as needed, these youth wrote autobiographies describing their journeys, including maps that traced the routes they had taken to get there.

Teachers and tutors can plan how to meet learners' concerns and needs by doing a needs assessment activity. Different from a language assessment, which evaluates learners' skills, a needs assessment helps determine what language students want and need to learn. For example, students may be interested in language around the topic of health, communication with their children's schools, or how to use local transportation. Classes become more engaging for literacy learners when instruction focuses on topics they want and need to study.

7.3.2.6 Considering learning factors when planning instruction

Other considerations for planning instruction include program features, such as length of the teaching session, number of meetings per week, and total number of hours of instruction. For example, if a teaching session is 12 weeks, with classes meeting two nights a week for two hours, one or two instructional topics should be adequate. Theme-based teaching may be new to some teachers and tutors, but this approach contextualizes language learning and addresses the need for learner engagement. Planning a unit and lessons using a thematic approach, rather than focusing solely on grammar (form-focused instruction), is an effective strategy with learners who do not yet read and write. For example, the theme for a 12-week class might be health, with topics including reading prescriptions, describing illnesses to the doctor and accessing emergency care.

7.3.2.7 Considering approaches to teaching reading

Finally, the teacher or tutor can consider different approaches to teaching reading. In some countries, there is a debate about whether to begin with a top-down or with a bottom-up approach. A top-down, or whole language approach, begins with words and simple phrases, and instruction includes use of all language skills – speaking, listening, reading and writing – in all lessons. A bottom-up, linguistic or phonics approach begins with the alphabet, sounds and syllables, with a focus on learning those, often in isolation from meaning, and gradually building to working with longer texts. For learners of English, Vinogradov (2008) advocates the balanced approach, also known as a whole-part-whole approach (see also Hempenstall, 2005; Trupke-Bastidas, 2007). A whole-part-whole approach begins with oral discussion of specific topics related to the unit or semester theme and moves to reading and writing about those topics, using words, sentences, paragraphs and longer texts (top-down). At relevant times, the teacher provides specific instruction on phonemes (sounds) in words, phoneme-grapheme correspondence (the ways that sounds are represented in print), syllables of words and vocabulary that is important for working with the theme. (Phoneme-grapheme correspondence is explained in Section 7.3.4 below.)

Another consideration for a teaching approach is the writing and spelling system of the target language. It is important for teachers and tutors to understand how the orthographies (spelling systems) of languages using the Roman alphabet, such as Dutch, English, German, Finnish, Italian, Spanish or Turkish, present different degrees of regularity in the correspondence between oral language and written symbols. This is discussed in depth in Chapter 3. Written symbols, such as letters, are called graphemes. Individual sounds of oral language are called phonemes. The strength of the phoneme (sounds)-grapheme (letters) correspondence in a language is referred to as ORTHOGRAPHIC DEPTH. Orthographic depth is typically depicted using a continuum of shallow to deep or transparent to opaque. For example, English (depending on the dialect) has as many as 1120 letter combinations for (ways of writing) 40 phonemes (Hempenstall, 2005: 21). This relationship, 1120 to 40, is far from a one-to-one correspondence, making English a deep or opaque orthography (see Goswami & Bryant, 1992). On the other hand, Italian has 33 graphemes to its 25 phonemes (Paulesu *et al.*, 2001), making it a shallow, more transparent orthography. The strength of the grapheme-phoneme correspondence is something to consider in developing an instructional approach. For languages with shallow orthographies, a bottom-up or phonics-based approach may be appropriate. For languages with deep orthographies, such as English or French, beginning with themes and words and sentences used to develop those themes, a top-down approach may be more appropriate.

7.3.2.8 Considering learning that takes place outside the classroom

Finally, it is important to remember that language learning takes place both inside and outside of the classroom. Learners are immersed to varying degrees in the L2-speaking environment; they are parents, workers and citizens in the community. At the same time, these factors may limit their access to the L2, if the language of the home and the immediate community is not the L2. An important goal of adult education is to create independent learners who can employ learning strategies wherever opportunities present themselves (Merriam *et al.*, 2007). Developing independence with L2 learning begins during instruction. However, Dalderop *et al.* (2008) theorize that adult literacy learners may be more teacher dependent than their more literate peers. They are often learning how to learn and may rely on the teacher as a learning strategy.

7.3.2.9 Adjusting the teacher's or tutor's attitudes and beliefs

Teachers' and tutors' beliefs about what learners can do affects instruction, making it important to be self-aware and develop a reflective practice. Vinogradov (2008) provides a helpful way for teachers and tutors to raise their awareness of learners' potential, using the following six principles for working with these learners:

(1) Keep teaching in context by building on what learners already know and can do.
(2) Take a balanced approach between whole language and phonics (particularly for English) and use objects that represent words and ideas that are familiar to learners.
(3) Break down the sound-symbol correspondence for words that learners struggle with.

(4) Provide instruction that appeals to different learning styles, preferences, current strengths, such as including tactile learning.
(5) Build on learners' strengths, especially L2 oral skills, to connect oral and written language.
(6) Nurture learner confidence.

In summary, preparing to work with adult L2 learners with limited education and literacy will likely involve extra planning time and effort to gather instructional materials. As literacy learners, they may not have attended school and may have limited experience with academic environments. One way to prepare is to build on their strengths by carefully selecting instructional materials that are relevant and authentic to their needs. A needs assessment can also serve to foster communication and support the creation of a comfortable environment where language learning can take place. This is not a quick process, and teachers can expect learning to proceed slowly, with frequent repetition. Adult emergent readers, like their younger counterparts, are learning how to learn and are developing academic skills for the first time. Unlike children, though, they are accomplishing these difficult tasks in a new language.

7.3.3 Developing print awareness

Print awareness includes being able to recognize the functions and uses of print, being comfortable with using a writing instrument, being able to recognize letters of the alphabet and being able to recognize high-frequency words (see discussion in Chapter 3). Print awareness skills and oral language skills are connected. Therefore, in this section, we focus on activities that will build print awareness, using both oral and literate skills.

The goal of print awareness instruction is for learners to recognize the functions and uses of text on labels, schedules and forms. Learners need to understand that print can be found in many places other than books (e.g. warnings, descriptions, signs, newspapers, magazines, the internet). Wrigley and Guth (1992) suggest using real-world objects, or realia, as part of print-awareness instruction. Realia can be food packages, signs, a tube of toothpaste, money and other commercial items with print on them. For an activity, learners can predict the meaning and function of the text on these objects, using contextual clues. After the learners spend time thinking and talking about this, the teacher or tutor can reveal what the text says. Print awareness activities can be used with thematic instruction focused on family, work, school, health, transportation, the community and so forth. Wrigley and Guth (1992) suggest helping learners to develop a sense of what print looks like, such as how it is different from a picture or the wallpaper, which merely exists as decoration. Students who are not familiar with the Roman alphabet may also need to develop a global sense of the shape and look of English writing (and Roman alphabet writing in other languages) before focusing on individual words and letters.

Additionally, learners may need help understanding that written texts have a beginning, middle and end; or that text is read from left to right and from the top of a page down; and that written words can represent a story or a message (August & Shanahan, 2006). Spending instructional time teaching the structure of texts is also important.

Another aspect of print awareness is comfort with writing instruments. According to Schwarz (2008), literacy learners may need practice with copying words, writing on lines or in boxes and understanding that some letters need capitalization and that there are spaces between words. In teaching how to write letters of the alphabet, Burt *et al.* (2008) recommend first helping students practice with writing in a specific direction and with shapes and sizes; then practicing letters, consonants, vowels and – particularly for deep orthographies – sight words, and eventually longer utterances, such as sentences. Schwarz (2008) adds that learning to write requires fine motor skills that these learners may not have developed. Kinesthetic activities, such as following dots to complete a picture, tracing letters and numbers and coloring pictures to help distinguish figures and background, can help strengthen learners' fine motor skills as they learn to write. Adult literacy learners may experience cognitive overload, because they are tackling many new ideas at one time: school skills, oral language and literacy skills. They may tire easily and require breaks. Their eyes may be unaccustomed to the focused work that reading and writing require, making it important to vary the activities, with short periods of focused reading and writing that can be repeated and times to talk with each other about what they are doing or about other topics. Some suggested activities include:

- Coloring in adult coloring books.
- Drawing a red line down the left margin of a paper and across a paper from left to right, to help focus on directionality when writing.
- Taking occasional breaks from reading and writing to prevent eyestrain and use oral language in interactions or in specific exercises.
- Getting up out of their seats to write or draw on the blackboard or a poster.
- Cutting out photos from magazines.
- Organizing photos into an album.
- Playing games such as BINGO and using flashcards for practice.
- Making a picture dictionary.
- Singing or chanting the alphabet.

Teachers and tutors might:

- Cover up additional text (for example, text attached to the board in a classroom from another teacher who uses the room) with large poster board paper, to avoid extra visual distraction when students read from the board.
- Design documents so they are easy to read, with a larger font, double spacing and lots of white space.

In summary, print awareness addresses the functions and uses of print, being comfortable with using a writing instrument and being able to automatically recognize letters of the alphabet and high-frequency words and process written text. Using realia and activities that involve movement (kinesthetic activities) such as coloring, copying and drawing are some ways to help learners develop these skills. Dance and drama are also effective ways to develop not only oral language skills but also print awareness (Pecoraro, 2017).

7.3.4 Grapheme-phoneme correspondence

Grapheme-phoneme correspondence is the connection between written symbols and sounds. An example of a grapheme, or written symbol, is the letter <m> in the Roman alphabet. An example of a phoneme is /m/, or the sound that this letter represents in a word like *mother* or *may*. Awareness of abstract units of sound, known as phonological awareness, develops in part before children start school and expands as they begin learning to read and write. Adult literacy learners who have not had the opportunity to attend school, or who come from an oral tradition, will not have the same phonological awareness as their educated L2 counterparts and will need time to develop this as part of literacy instruction. (See Chapter 2, Reading, for discussion of phonological awareness and phonemic awareness.)

Adults with limited literacy skills in any language may not be able to distinguish phonemes – individual sounds in words and the concepts of beginning, middle and end sounds – and understand that changing a single sound changes the meaning of a word. For pre- and non-literate adult learners, language is likely to be perceived as a string of continuous sounds.

For learners without formal schooling and for those whose home language does not have a written form, Schwarz (2008) notes that they have no words for discussing language, such as *syllable, sentence, grammar* or *tense*. These are concepts that evolve with knowledge of written language. Learners whose first language has a written form can learn the words in their language to start to understand the concepts in the second language.

Like teaching reading overall, instruction for building grapheme-phoneme correspondence can take either a balanced, bottom-up (grapheme-phoneme), or top-down (whole word) approach. For example, teachers and tutors can use pictures, photos and posters representing different sounds that help learners build awareness of these in the L2 through the repetition of seeing the grapheme-phoneme connections. With learners with some literacy, a CLOZE ACTIVITY can be used, where learners insert a missing letter, in word-initial or word-final position, for example, into a written word. For example, a learner could insert an <m> into the word <_other>. The activity can be supported by pictures or realia. The teacher or tutor can also dictate the word, and the learner(s) write in the missing letter. This can be repeated with any number of familiar words and letters. Another activity requires learners to fill in a missing word from a dictated sentence. For example, the teacher or tutor dictates the sentence 'The cat sleeps' but omits a word on the worksheet; e.g. 'The cat ______' or 'The _____ sleeps', using words that the learners know and are learning to spell. Other ways to practice grapheme-phoneme correspondence is minimal pairs, an activity in which learners are prompted to choose the right answer from one of two options. For example, learners can be prompted to indicate which sound they hear by choosing from one of two sounds (e.g. /b/ or /v/). When prompted, they indicate the correct answer in a number of ways, such as holding up letters or words written on different pieces of paper. Learners can also indicate the answer by raising or not raising their hand.

Introducing rhyming words builds phonemic awareness by helping learners distinguish one sound in a word. For an activity, the teacher or tutor provides many examples of rhyming and non-rhyming words. It is best to focus on short, high-frequency words, such as 'cat', 'bat', 'fat', 'car'. When learners seem to grasp the concept that something is different about the sound in one of the words, the teacher or tutor checks for comprehension by asking learners to indicate which word is different, or does not RHYME. For example, the teacher or tutor slowly reads the list of words and learners raise their hands when they hear the word that does not rhyme (e.g. car). For a variation, ask learners to indicate precisely where words differ when they do not rhyme, such as beginning, middle or end sounds, to develop phonemic awareness. Using a simple set of rhymes, such as 'cat', 'bat', 'fat', teachers and tutors can show how changing the initial sound changes the meaning of a word. For this activity, Vinogradov (2008) suggests using manipulatives, things the learner can handle such as Scrabble-type letter tiles or letters used for children's early literacy, to change the beginning sound so that learners experience tacitly what they are doing. These activities can help build phonological awareness in the L2 and, in particular, the phonemic awareness that underpins alphabetic reading. Puco (2007) finds that the use of tactile objects such as those described here makes learning more enjoyable for learners, which promotes engagement.

Once learners have a bank of words and are moving beyond single word decoding to higher-level comprehension, sentence strips can help them create their own sentences without the added challenge of writing. Individual words are cut out from a sentence written on a strip of paper, mixed up in a different order, and then learners reassemble the sentence by placing the words in the right order. This activity can be done in small groups, pairs, or individually. Sentence strip activities give learners hands-on practice with word order and when read aloud, practice with pronunciation. They also help learners become aware of individual word boundaries. Additionally, use of sentence strips is helpful for learners who prefer kinesthetic activities. Sentence strip words can also be used to create simple cloze activities in which learners add the missing word, or a word is written with a missing letter that is filled in (We went to the ____. We saw a lot of _ood.). These activities help to build confidence by putting into writing the useful social phrases from learners' oral language discussed in Chapter 5.

7.3.5 Text comprehension

As discussed above, a language experience approach (LEA) activity can also help build awareness of the relationship of words and text to print and can contribute to development of reading comprehension. One LEA activity involves learners relating something from their lives to another person, who writes down what was said. (Care is taken to ensure that learners are not put in a situation where they are talking about traumatic aspects of their past or events that they prefer not to talk about; see Santos & Shandor, 2012, on safe spaces in the classroom.) The text can then be used for reading, vocabulary development, pronunciation and building morphosyntactic competence. LEA texts are sometimes used with one common theme, with each learner sharing information related to the theme. For example, learners describe their families or other aspects of their current lives. In one-on-one tutoring sessions, LEA provides rich instructional material with maximal student interest due to its immediate relevance to their lives.

Another LEA option is an activity such as a field trip, and, with the teacher's or tutor's facilitation, writing an account of the activity after it is completed. Field trips can be a visit to the local library or government office, a museum, a shopping center, a park, among other locations. Pictures can be taken while on the field trip and then used to create a journalistic-type story about the experience. Individually, in pairs, or in groups, learners generate sentences to describe the pictures, which are then used for practice activities, such as reading, cloze activities, grammar activities, phonics-related activities, SEQUENCING ACTIVITIES and dialogue practice.

LEA writing can be used at all language proficiency levels, and this is a great way to spark learners' motivation and create lessons that match their abilities and draw on their experiences. LEA texts may be created based solely on visuals; for example, a learner writes about a picture or a short series of pictures. Wrigley and Guth (1992) describe a variation on the traditional LEA approach in which learners put together something cohesive solely using photographs and no text. For example, an urban literacy class takes a trip on the city's bus and metro system, and learners take photographs of the ticket machines, purchasing instructions and the bus and metro maps. When they return to the classroom, they study their photographs, discuss strategies they used to get their tickets and find their way around the city and then organize the photographs logically. In this way, picture-based accounts of activities from daily life build vocabulary and sequencing skills. Learners can also use the Internet to find photographs about a common theme. One example from the United States is *Picture Stories for Adult ESL Health Literacy* (Singleton, n.d.) with pictures that show examples of activities in daily life, and learners add comments based on their own experiences. Many activities can be developed that use the words and phrases produced by the learners. Likewise, pictures and photographs can help to relate needed information as well as provide crucial survival information. In Australia, Williams and Chapman (2007) used staged photographs to convey safety in the home where dangerous situations could develop. These photographs became part of the readers for the learners along with other materials, including picture cards and word flash cards.

7.3.6 Instructional practices for multilevel classes

Adult literacy classes are usually multilevel along one or more dimensions of learning, because adult learners' literacy, linguistic and education backgrounds, experiences, skills and even views of themselves as learners vary (see DeCapua & Marshall, 2015). Some learners may have stronger L2 oral skills, some may have L1 literacy but weak L2 oral skills, while others need to build basic oral L2 skills and have no L1 literacy skills. Addressing the learning needs of a multilevel class presents challenges for the teacher and a need for careful planning. While this section focuses on instruction in the multilevel classroom, the suggestions are also relevant for work with learners in smaller, homogenous groups or in one-on-one scenarios.

7.3.6.1 Separating learners into different groups

For classroom teachers, Schwarz (2005, 2008) advocates separating learners with little or no literacy into different classes from more literate peers in order to address their print awareness and grapheme-phoneme correspondence needs. Unfortunately, many adult education programs do not have the resources to offer separate classes for these learners and instead offer multilevel classes, which include learners from varied education and literacy backgrounds. Then the teacher will need to create groups within a given class.

7.3.6.2 Providing one-on-one tutoring

One way to address multilevel needs in a class is to pull out literacy learners for one-to-one tutoring, for example, on skills related to literacy components (sounds, letters, syllables, basic words). A tutor or teaching assistant can serve well in this model. The classroom teacher identifies which learners need tutoring support and what skills the tutoring will focus on. A typical PULL-OUT MODEL for phonics instruction in English-speaking countries might use a basal reader such as the US series, *Sam and Pat* (Hartel *et al.*, 2006). Assistants are given a lesson plan, so they know what to cover in any given session, and they keep the classroom teacher advised on the learner's progress. Teachers and assistants should be careful not to make the pull-out tutoring seem punitive. To reduce this perception, feedback should be provided to learners at every session, so they can see how the tutoring is helping them progress.

7.3.6.3 Time management and differentiated instruction

Another method for organizing multilevel classes is through time management and DIFFERENTIATED INSTRUCTION. Time management includes scheduling activities where all of the learners focus on a particular need or skill, which differs by group. For example, if class time is devoted to writing, some groups might copy letters or write their names while other groups write paragraphs. Differentiated instruction involves activities that have simpler and more complex versions to meet the needs of learners at different proficiency levels.

Organizing learners in groups within the classroom has the added social benefit of fostering cooperation and building community, as discussed above. Moreover, groups can be formed with like-ability or mixed-ability learners. Wrigley and Guth (1992) suggest mixing up existing groups from time to time, so that less proficient learners do not feel stigmatized as the slow learners. With like-ability groups, or groups composed of learners with approximately the same proficiency level, instructional materials can be tailored to meet the specific needs of the group. In mixed-ability groups, or groups in which the learners are of various proficiency levels, more knowledgeable peers can support the learning of lower-level learners. Learning between different-level individuals can take place in the Zone of Proximal Development, or ZPD (Vygotsky, 1978), discussed in Chapter 2. These are activities that learners can do with help, when they are not yet able to do them without help. As Chapter 2 discusses, learning occurs when a more knowledgeable other (teacher, classmates, friends and so forth) acts as a scaffold/help/support to help the less knowledgeable learner reach a higher level of understanding and skill. While learners work together, the teacher can circulate among the groups to ensure that they are on track, more knowledgeable learners are providing support, and less knowledgeable learners are progressing.

7.3.6.4 Classroom centers and learning stations

Another means of differentiating instruction advocated by Schwarz (2008) and Wrigley and Guth (1992) is classroom centers, or LEARNING STATIONS, where learners can choose what they want to do and work toward mastery of specific skills. Based on Montessori (1964) principles, classroom centers provide learners the opportunity to develop at their own pace (Lillard, 2011). Centers can be designed around any language or literacy skill and include different proficiency-level tasks that learners complete and then self-assess. This way, learners manage their own progress and move to the next proficiency level only after they have mastered the task at the current level. Reading centers might include some of the authentic texts that students encounter in daily life, including magazines, newspapers, coupons, posters, pictures and notes from their children's school. However, reading authentic text can be challenging for literacy learners, because it often contains difficult vocabulary, slang, idioms, or humor. The font may be very small or decorative, making it more difficult for learners to decode. Teachers can mitigate some of these challenges by breaking texts into small chunks and providing scaffolds such as pictures, graphic organizers, realia, strategies, and making the print larger. Centers can also include digital tools that help students negotiate meaning from texts, such as talking dictionaries, translators, or screen readers. Whatever the design and content of a reading center, students can work at their own pace. With centers, teachers are free to monitor the larger class and better track everyone's progress.

7.3.6.5 Project-based learning

Use of PROJECT-BASED LEARNING is another strategy that is effective in a multilevel classroom. Learners work in small groups or pairs, with each person assigned a specific role and task to complete which fits their interests (Peterson & Nassaji, 2016). This can incorporate the ZPD mentioned above. Strube (2007) observes that peer-to-peer work on projects is one of many scaffolding strategies used by teachers to support learners who would not be able to complete these on their own. Working in groups with more proficient peers allows learners to find other ways to excel, such as with oral storytelling, taking photographs or drawing. Some drawbacks to differentiated instruction and grouping are the time and effort needed for planning and convincing learners of the benefits of group work with those from other language backgrounds and cultures and at different proficiency levels. However, once the groups are operating independently, the teacher has the opportunity to continually observe their progress and provide feedback.

One example of a classroom project is a class newsletter in which learners report on a topic, such as what they did over the weekend, what they studied in class, activities that they enjoy with their family or current events. For weaker learners, use of pictures will reduce literacy demands. A newsletter project provides learners at all proficiency levels with doable tasks such as finding pictures, writing, editing, managing resources and organizing texts and pictures. It automatically scaffolds learning through the shared goal of creating a newsletter, and it raises learners' awareness of an important written genre. The newsletter becomes a text that can be shared with outsiders as well as used for further reading practice. Those working in one-on-one tutoring contexts can consider collaborating with other tutors to involve learners in contributing to community newsletters.

Similarly, students can create picture books about classmates and teachers, families and friends, revolving around their interests. Like newsletters, these books generate relevant vocabulary and provide real documents in an additional genre where learners can share what's important to them. A book project works well in a multilevel class, because it allows each author the opportunity to work independently at their level. For learners with greater literacy challenges, a technique borrowed from LEA (the learner dictates what they want to share to another person, who writes it) enables learners to express themselves without having to worry about their insufficient writing skills. Learners might then copy what is written. As with newsletters, these are ideal for sharing with outsiders.

7.3.6.6 Engaging in dramatic productions

Drama is a less used but highly engaging means of promoting collaboration and exploring a range of issues, while also expanding oral proficiency and literacy skills. At the Italian Language School for Foreigners at the University of Palermo (Amoruso, 2016), a group of learners with very low literacy met for twelve Saturdays to organize a theatrical production reflecting their shared experiences with and feelings about leaving their homes (Pecoraro, 2017). Teachers in Finland have been working with these learners on a documentary project known as *Toinen koti,* Other Home, which involves refugee musicians, actors, singers, poets and rap artists (see Pöyhönen & Simpson, 2017). In such projects, there are multiple opportunities for scaffolding. The teacher can support learners in the development of these projects by breaking the project down into smaller sequential tasks, by assigning specific tasks to learners with special skills, by providing multiple examples or templates to be filled in by learners and by working with the learners to correct language inaccuracies.

7.3.6.7 Engaging with the community and people outside the class

Other projects suggested by Wrigley and Guth (1992) include: (1) a field trip planned by learners to a place in addition to those listed above, which they would not normally have the chance to see; (2) inviting a guest speaker of the learners' choosing to come to class to discuss a specific community issue; or (3) writing a letter to a famous person or someone involved with local government or in the community. Although multilevel instruction requires careful planning and classroom management to address adult learners' diverse backgrounds and experiences, the teacher (or tutor) can make use of learners' strengths in creative and rewarding ways.

7.3.7 Assessment of learners

The use of commercially developed, standardized tests for formally assessing learners' language skills for both class placement and documenting progress is required by most publicly funded adult education programs. (See also Chapter 5.) The challenges of using standardized testing with language learners are well documented in the literature. Notably, these tests may not capture fine-grained linguistic changes, such as those seen in pragmatics or oral fluency (Pettitt & Tarone, 2015; Strube, 2014). Test scoring does not accommodate the many ways that students might interpret the language and instead, requires one right answer. Simpson (2006) adds that test administrators vary in their skills and expectations in putting test data into practice. Vermeersch *et al.* (2008) warn that formal assessments often position learners with static labels, such as *low-beginning learner* or *basic user*, in alignment with systems such as the Common European Framework of Reference (CEFR, Council of Europe, 2001), the National Reporting System in the United States (https://www.nrsweb.org) and the Canadian Language Benchmarks (Centre for Canadian Language Benchmarks, 2012). As discussed above, Bigelow and Vinogradov (2011) caution that labels are not a permanent characteristic of the learners, and we need to be ready to look beyond labels and recognize learners' full potential and their steps toward realizing it. Nevertheless, formal testing is a reality in adult education, and test data are typically used to both place students and mark learning progress.

For informal, or FORMATIVE ASSESSMENT, Croydon (2005) suggests creating an assessment grid to better inform instruction and track learner progress over the course of a teaching session. An example is shown in Figure 7.1. When using this grid, students 'read' the pictures and indicate whether they enjoy the particular food by writing either a check mark or an 'x'. Teachers and tutors can adapt grids to accommodate learners' interests, needs and skill levels by using different pictures or

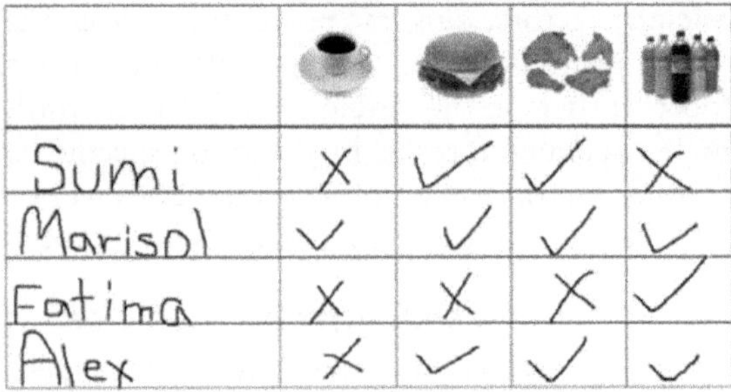

Figure 7.1 Formative assessment grid (adapted from Croydon, 2005)

words. Learners might use words, such as 'yes' or 'no' instead of checks or 'x's' to indicate their answers.

Spiegel and Sunderland (2006) promote the use of a reading progress checklist to informally document fine-grained skills such as reading with a left-to-right orientation, word and number discrimination, upper- and lower-case letter discrimination and knowledge of specific grapheme-phoneme correspondences. For writing, teachers and tutors use the checklist to indicate whether learners can copy text, such as a sentence written on the board; compose a short text, such as writing the date; and write personal words, such as name and address. Examples would be adjusted according to the focus of the class and levels of the learners in the class. As informal assessments, the reading and writing checklists can be used as a basis for designing level-appropriate instruction as well as a means for tracking learner progress over time. The checklists could also serve a means for providing feedback to learners on their progress. The reading and writing checklists are shown in Table 7.1.

Table 7.1 Reading and writing progress checklist

Reading The learner is able to ...
Read from left to right
Read numbers as different from words
Recognize upper case and lower-case versions of letters
Recognize a sound (phoneme) and its associated letters(s) (graphemes, for the following letters: -- -- -- --

Writing The learner is able to ...
Write his/her name
Write his/her address
Copy a text
Compose a short text

Dalderop *et al.* (2008) and Stockmann (2006) advocate use of portfolios assessment to document learners' work. Portfolios are dossiers of a learner's work, including authentic documents such as postcards and notes to teachers. As a form of assessment, portfolios reflect and encourage learner autonomy and responsibility. Stockmann (2006) and Nuwenhoud (2015) show that portfolios serve multiple functions, including a space to keep learner's work, the opportunity to use their work as reference materials during examinations and providing evidence for reporting and accountability purposes. When the portfolio is aligned with a checklist of skills and abilities, it can provide a broader and more detailed picture of the learner's progress.

Dalderop *et al.* (2008) propose creating the portfolio with the learner so that the process itself contributes to learning and goal setting. Both Stockmann (2006) and Nuwenhoud (2015) note that using a literacy portfolio alongside a literacy framework, such as the one shown in Table 7.2, has proven to be very successful for both assessing learners' progress and allowing learners to set up and track their own development on life- and work-based tasks. Feldmeier (2015) observes that learners, even at the lowest literacy levels, use supports to create their own portfolios and make learning contracts to assess their progress.

The use of standardized tests as an accountability measure in adult education is a reality for publicly funded programs, which are often required to use specific assessments and report results regularly in order to receive funding. As noted above,

Table 7.2 Global characterization of the three literacy levels: Literacy framework (Stockmann, 2006)

	Alfa A	**Alfa B**	**Alfa C**
Autonomy	Can carry out reading and writing tasks with help and/or with the help of examples.	Can carry out known and trained tasks without any help.	Can carry out new tasks without help, is able to transfer things learnt in another context.
Fluency	Can read and write character by character.	Can spell and write no longer character by character, but by (consonant) clusters.	Can analyze and synthesize in silence; only long, unknown words cause problems. Can recognize words as a unit and can write them as a unit.
Word complexity	Can read and write global words trained, CVC words, words in which two graphemes represent one phoneme.	Can read and write the global words trained, all short words, long words if known, all grapheme combinations; words may contain consonant clusters and morphemes.	Can read and write all words except for long and semantically unknown words.
Text properties	Texts are very short and concern familiar subjects. Texts have a clear typeface and line spacing. Capitals and punctuation marks occur in the text but are not relevant for understanding.	Texts are selected with purpose, are short and concern familiar subjects. Texts contain concrete and well-known words. Typeface may vary. Characters written by hand are recognized.	Texts are short and simple and concern familiar subjects. Texts contain high-frequency words and short and simple sentences with visual support. Typeface is clear. Capitals and punctuation marks are used as a source of information.

test scores do not capture all that a learner has achieved. Teachers usually have some freedom to develop more appropriate and additional ways of assessing learning and helping learners make sense of their own progress, which might include exit cards (on which students write something they have learned that day and give it to the teacher before leaving class) and circulating while students are working in pairs or small groups to determine how they are doing and where they need help and specific instruction, as described above.

7.4 Conclusion

This chapter provides ideas for those who are just getting started in working with adult migrants with little or no formal schooling. The strategies and resources described provide guidance for teachers and tutors working with this learner population, who can adopt, adapt and build on them. Teachers and tutors know best the needs and interests of the learners in their classes and can start by considering the feasibility and the usefulness of the ideas presented here as they suit their contexts.

References

Abdalla, F. and Crago, M. (2008) Verb morphology deficits in Arabic-speaking children with specific language impairment. *Applied Psycholinguistics* 29 (2), 315–340.

Aberdeen, T. (2016) Understanding community heritage language schools in Alberta. Unpublished PhD thesis, University of Alberta.

Adesope, O.O., Lavin, T., Thompson, T. and Ungerleider, C. (2010) A systematic review and meta-analysis of the cognitive correlates of bilingualism. *Review of Educational Research* 80 (2), 207–245.

Adkins, M.A., Sample, B. and Birman, D. (1999) Mental health and the adult refugee: The role of the ESOL teacher. See http://www.cal.org/caela/esl_resources/digests/mental.html (assessed November 2019).

Aebersold, J.A. and Field, M.L. (2003) *From Reader to Reading.* New York, NY: Cambridge University Press.

Aitchison, J. (2012) *Words in the Mind: An Introduction to the Mental Lexicon.* Toronto: John Wiley and Sons.

Alderson, J.C. (2005) *Assessing Reading.* Cambridge: Cambridge University Press.

Alencar, A, Kondova, K. and Ribbens, W. (2018) The smartphone as a lifeline: An exploration of refugees' use of mobile communication technologies during their flight. *Media, Culture & Society* 41 (6), 1–17.

Allwright, R. (1984) Why don't learners learn what teachers teach? The interaction hypothesis. In D.M Singleton and D.G. Little (eds) *Language Learning in Formal and Informal Contexts* (pp. 3–18). Dublin: IRAAL.

Amoruso, M. (2016) Foreign unaccompanied minors – from Barges University. See http://minorinonaccompagnatialluniversita.wordpress.com/le-storie-in-valigia/ (assessed November 2019).

Amoruso, M., Cipolla, N., Piraneo, C. and Salvato, V. (2016) *Odisseo arriving alone. Un laboratorio, una mostra, un libro. Un percorso di inclusione lungo dieci anni.* Palermo: Palermo Academic Press.

Anderson, R.C. and Freebody, P. (1981) Vocabulary knowledge. In J.T. Guthrie (ed.) *Comprehension and Teaching: Research Reviews* (pp. 77–117). Newark, DE: International Reading Association.

Anthony, J. and Lonigan, C. (2004) The nature of phonological awareness: Converging evidence from four Studies of preschool and early grade school children. *Journal of Educational Psychology* 96 (1), 43–55.

Anthony, J.L., Lonigan, C.J., Burgess, S.R., Driscoll Bacon, K., Phillips, B.M. and Cantor, B.G. (2002) Structure of preschool phonological sensitivity: Overlapping sensitivity to rhyme, words, syllables, and phonemes. *Journal of Experimental Child Psychology* 82 (1), 65–92.

Apter, A., Paasche-Orlow, M., Remillard, J., Bennett, I., Ben-Joseph, E., Batista, R., Hyde, J. and Rudd, R. (2008) Numeracy and communication with patients: They are counting on us. *Journal of General Internal Medicine* 23 (12), 2117–2124.

Auerbach, E. (1992) *Making Meaning Making Change.* Washington, D.C.: Center for Applied Linguistics.

Auerbach, E. and Wallerstein, N. (2005) *Problem-Posing at Work: English for Action.* Edmonton: Grassroots Press.

August, D. and Shanahan, T. (eds) (2006) *Developing Literacy in Second-Language Learners: Report of the National Literacy Panel on Language-Minority Children and Youth.* Mahwah, NJ: Erlbaum.

Azevedo, F.A.C., Carvalho, L.R.B., Grinberg, L.T., Farfel, J.M., Ferretti, R.E.L., Leite, R.E.P., Filho, W.J., Lent, R. and Herculano-Houzel, S. (2009) Equal numbers of neuronal and nonneuronal cells make the human brain an isometrically scaled-up primate brain. *Journal of Comparative Neurology* 513 (5), 532–541.

Bailey, N., Madden, C. and Krashen, S. (1974) Is there a 'natural sequence' in adult second language learning? *Language Learning* 24 (2), 235–243.

Baker, C. and Wright, W.E. (2017) *Foundations of Bilingual Education and Bilingualism* (6th edn). Bristol: Multilingual Matters.

Bamford, J. and Day, R.R. (2004) *Extensive Reading Activities for Teaching Language.* Cambridge: Cambridge University Press.

Bardovi-Harlig, K. and Stringer, D. (2017) Unconventional expressions. Productive syntax in the L2 acquistion of formulaic language. *Second Language Research,* 33, 61–90.

Barton, D. and Hamilton, M. (1998) *Local Literacies Reading and Writing in One Community.* New York, NY: Routledge.

Bassetti, B. (2009) Orthographic input and second language phonology. In T. Piske and M. Young-Scholten (eds) *Input Matters in SLA* (pp. 191–206). Bristol: Multilingual Matters.

Bayram, F. Prada, J., Pascual y Cabo, D. and Rothman, J. (2017) Why should formal linguistic approaches to heritage language acquisition be linked to heritage language pedagogies? In P.P. Trifonas and T. Aravossitas (eds) *Handbook of Research and Practice in Heritage Language Education* (pp. 187–206). New York, NY: Springer International.

Becker, A., Dittmar, N., Gutmann, M., Klein, W., Rieck, B-0., Senft, G., Senft, I., Steckner, W. and Thielicke, E. (1977) *Heidelberger Forschungsprojekt 'Pidgin-Deutsch spanischer und italienischer Arbeiter in der Bundesrepublik': Die ungesteurerte Erlernung des Deutschen durch spanische und italienischer Arbeiter. Eine soziolinguistische Untersuchung.* [Heidelberg research project 'The pidgin German of Spanish and Italian workers in West Germany': The uninstructed acquisition of German by Spanish and Italian workers: A sociolinguistic study] Osnabrücker Beiträge zur Sprachtheorie (OBST). Beihefte 2: Osnabrück.

Ben-Dror, I., Bentin, S. and Frost, R. (1995) Semantic, phonologic and morphologic skills in reading-disabled and normal children: Evidence from perception and production of spoken Hebrew. *Reading Research Quarterly* 30 (4), 876–893.

Berker, E.A., Berker, A.H. and Smith, A. (1986) Translation of Broca's 1865 report: Localization of speech in the third left frontal convolution. *Archives of Neurology* 43 (10), 1065–1072.

Bernhardt, E. (2011) *Understanding Advanced Second Language Reading.* New York, NY: Routledge.

Bhatia, T.K. and Ritchie, W.C. (2013) *The Handbook of Bilingualism and Multilingualism.* Oxford: Wiley/ Blackwell.

Bialystok, E. (1986) Factors in the growth of linguistic awareness. *Child Development* 57 (2), 498–510.

Bialystok, E. (1988) Levels of bilingualism and levels of linguistic awareness. *Developmental Psychology* 24 (4), 560–567.

Bialystok, E. (2007) Cognitive effects of bilingualism: How linguistic experience leads to cognitive change. *International Journal of Bilingual Education and Bilingualism* 10 (3), 210–223.

Bialystok, E. (2015) Bilingualism and the development of executive functions: The role of attention. *Child Development Perspective* 9 (2), 117–121.

Bialystok, E. and Hakuta, K. (1999) Confounded age: linguistic and cognitive factors in age differences for second language acquisition. In D. Birdsong (ed.) *Second Language Acquisition and the Critical Period Hypothesis* (pp. 161–181). London: Lawrence Erlbaum.

Bialystok, E. and Craik, F.I.M. (2010) Cognitive and linguistic processing in the bilingual mind. *Current Directions in Psychological Science* 19 (1), 19–23.

Bialystok, E. and Barac, R. (2012) Emerging bilingualism: Dissociating advantages for metalinguistic awareness and executive control. *Cognition* 122 (1), 67–73.

Bialystok, E., Luk, G. and Kwan, E. (2005) Bilingualism, biliteracy and learning to read: Interactions among language and writing systems. *Scientific Studies of Reading* 9 (1), 17–42.

Bialystok, E., Craik, F.I.M., Green, D.W. and Gollan, T.H. (2009) Bilingual minds. *Psychological Science in the Public Interest* 10 (3), 89–129.

Bialystok, E., Luk, G., Peets, K.F. and Yang, S. (2010) Receptive vocabulary differences in monolingual and bilingual children. *Bilingualism: Language and Cognition* 13 (4), 525–531.

Bigelow, M. and Vinogradov, P. (2011) Teaching adult second language learners who are emergent readers. *Annual Review of Applied Linguistics* 31, 120–136.

Bigelow, M. and King, K. (2016) Peer interaction while learning to read in a new language: Pedagogical potential and research agenda. In S. Masatoshi and S. Ballinger (eds) *Peer Interaction and Second Language Learning* (pp. 349–375). Amsterdam: John Benjamins.

Bley-Vroman, R. (1989) The logical problem of language learning. *Linguistic Analysis* 20 (1), 3–49.

Bliss, H. (2006) L2 acquisition of inflectional morphology: Phonological and morphological transfer effects. In M. Grantham O'Brien, C. Shea and J. Archibald (eds) *Proceedings of the 8th Generative Approaches to Second Language Acquisition Conference (GASLA 2006)* (pp. 1–8). Somerville, MA: Cascadilla Proceedings Project.

Blommaert, J. (2013) Citizenship, language and superdiversity: Towards complexity. *Journal of Language, Identity and Education* 12 (3), 193–196.

Bloom, L. (2000) *Pushing the Limits on Theories of Word Learning*. Toronto: John Wiley and Sons.

Bosch, L. and Sebastián-Gallés, N. (1997) Native-language recognition abilities in 4-month-old infants from monolingual and bilingual environments. *Cognition* 65 (1), 33–69.

Bosch, L. and Sebastián-Gallés, N. (2001) Evidence of early language discrimination abilities in infants from bilingual environments. *Infancy* 2 (1), 29–49.

Bosch, L. and Sebastián-Gallés, N. (2003) Simultaneous bilingualism and the perception of a language specific vowel contrast in the first year of life. *Language and Speech* 46 (2–3), 217–243.

Botha, R. and Knight, C. (eds) (2009) *The Cradle of Language*. Oxford: Oxford University Press.

Brady, S. and Shankweiler, D. (1991) *Phonological Processes in Literacy*. Hillsdale NJ: Lawrence Erlbaum.

Brandt, D. (2009) Writing over reading: New directions in mass literacy. In M. Baynham and M. Prinsloo (eds) *The Future of Literacy Studies* (pp. 54–74). London: Palgrave MacMillan.

Britio, N. and Barr, R. (2012) Influence of bilingualism on memory generalization during infancy. *Developmental Science* 15 (6), 812–816.

Brodkey, D. and Shore, H. (1976) Student personality and success in an English language program. *Language Learning* 26 (1), 153–159.

Brown, R. (1973) *A First Language: The Early Stages*. Cambridge, MA: Harvard University Press.

Brown, R. and McNeill, D. (1966) The 'tip of the tongue' phenomenon. *Journal of Verbal Learning and Verbal Behavior* 5 (4), 325–337.

Buckwalter, J.K. and Gloria Lo, Y-H. (2002) Emergent biliteracy in Chinese and English. *Journal of Second Language Writing* 11 (4), 269–293.

Burt, M., Peyton, J.K. and Schaetzel, K. (2008) Working with adult English language learners with limited literacy: Research, practice, and professional development. See http://www.cal.org/caelanetwork/resources/limitedliteracy.html (accessed November 2019).

Burtoff, M. (1985) *Haitian Creole Literacy Evaluation Study. Final Report*. Washington D.C.: Center for Applied Linguistics.

Bynum, W.F. (2002) The childless father of eugenics. *Science* 296 (5567), 472.

Calderón, M.E. and Soto, I.M. (2017) *Academic Language Mastery: Vocabulary in Context*. Thousand Oaks, CA: Corwin Publishing.

Calderón, M.E. and Sinclair-Slakk, S. (2018) *Teaching Reading to English Learners, Grades 6–12: A Framework for Improving Achievement in the Content Areas* (2nd edn). Thousand Oaks, CA: Corwin.

Calderón, M.E. and Slakk, S. (2019) *Success with Multicultural Newcomers and English Learners: Proven Practices for School Leadership Teams*. Alexandria, VA: ASCD.

Calvo, A. and Bialystok, E. (2014) Independent effects of bilingualism and socioeconomic status on language ability and executive functioning. *Cognition* 130 (3), 278–288.

Cambridge Dictionary (2019) Reading. See https://dictionary.cambridge.org/dictionary/english/reading (accessed November 2019).

Carder, M. (2013) English language teaching in an international school: The change in students' language from 'English only' to 'linguistically diverse'. In R. Pearce (ed.) *International Education and School: Moving Beyond the First 40 Years*. London: Bloomsbury.

Carey, S. (1978) *The Child as a Word Learner.* Cambridge, MA: MIT Press.

Cassany, D., Sanz, G. and Luna Sanjuán, M. (1998) *Enseñar Lengua*. Barcelona: Graó.

Cazden, C., Cancino, H., Rosansky, E. and Schumann, J. (1975) *Second Language Acquisition Sequences in Children, Adolescents and Adults*. Cambridge, MA: Harvard University Graduate School of Education.

Centre for Canadian Language Benchmarks (2012) Canadian language benchmarks: English as a second language for adults. See http://www.cic.gc.ca/english/pdf/pub/language-benchmarks.pdf (accessed November 2019).

Chambers, F. (1997) What do we mean by fluency? *System* 25 (4), 535–544.

Chomsky, N. (1957) *Syntactic Structures*. The Hague: Mouton.

Chomsky, N. (1965) *Aspects of the Theory of Syntax*. Cambridge, MA: MIT Press.

Chomsky, N. (1981) Principles and parameters in syntactic theory. In N. Hornstein and D. Lightfoot (eds) *Explanation in Linguistics: The Logical Problem of Language Acquisition* (pp. 32–75). London: Longman.

Chui, H.L., Liu, Y. and Mak, B.C.N. (2014) Code-switching for newcomers and veterans: A mutually-constructed discourse strategy for workplace socialization and identification. *International Journal of Applied Linguistics* 26 (1), 25–51.

Clahsen, H. (1991) Constraints on parameter setting. A grammatical analysis of some acquisition stages in German child language. *Language Acquisition* 1 (4), 361–391.

Clahsen, H. and Muysken, P. (1986) The availability of Universal Grammar to adult and child learners – A study of the acquisition of German word order. *Second Language Research* 2 (2), 93–119.

Clahsen, H. and Muysken, P. (1989) The UG paradox in L2 acquisition. *Second Language Research* 5 (1), 1–29.

Clahsen, H., Meisel, J. and Pienemann, M. (1983) *Deutsch als Zweitsprache: Der Spracherwerb Ausländischer Arbeiter*. Tübingen: Gunter Narr.

Clahsen, H., Bartke, S. and Göllner, S. (1997) Formal features in impaired grammars: A comparison of English and German SLI children. *Journal of Neurolinguistics* 10 (2-3), 151–171.

Clark, E. (1974) Performing without competence. *Journal of Child Language* 1 (1), 1–10.

Clark, M.C. (1993) *Transformational Learning*. Toronto: Wiley Periodicals.

Collier, V.P. and Thomas, W.P. (2007) Predicting second language academic success in English using the prism model. In J. Cummins and C. Davison (eds) *International Handbook of English Language Teaching* (pp. 333–348). Boston, MA: Springer.

Coltheart, M. (1978) Lexical access in simple reading tasks. In G. Underwood (ed.) *Strategies of Information Processing* (pp. 151–216). London: Academic Press.

Condelli, L., Cronen, S., Bos, J., Tseng, F. and Altuna, J. (2010) *The Impact of a Reading Intervention for Low-Educated Adult ESL Learners*. Alexandria, VA: U.S. Department of Education, National Center for Education, Evaluation, and Regional Assistance. Institute of Education Sciences.

Condelli, L., Spruck Wrigley, H.K., Yoo, K., Sebring, M. and Cronen, S. (2003) *What Works for Adult ESL Literacy Students*. Volume II. Final Report. Washington, DC: American Institutes for Research and Aguirre International.

Conti-Ramsden, G. and Hesketh, A. (2003) Risk markers for SLI: A study of young language-learning children. *International Journal of Language and Communication Disorders* 38 (3), 251–263.

Cook, V. (1997) The consequences of bilingualism for cognitive processing. In A.M.B. de Groot and J.F. Kroll (eds) *Tutorials in Bilingualism: Psycholinguistic Perspectives* (pp. 279–299). Mahwah, NJ: Lawrence Erlbaum.

Cooke, M. and Simpson, J. (2008) *ESOL: A Critical Guide*. Oxford: Oxford University Press.

Cope, B. and Kalantzis, M. (2000) *Multiliteracies: Literacy Learning and the Design of Social Futures*. London: Routledge.

Corder, S.P. (1967) The significance of learner's errors. *International Review of Applied Linguistics* 5 (4), 161–170.

Costa, A. and Sebastian-Galles, N. (2014) How does the bilingual experience sculpt the brain? *Nature Reviews: Neuroscience* 15 (5), 336–345.

Council of Europe (2001) *Common European Framework of Reference for Languages: Learning Teaching Assessment (CEFR)*. Cambridge: Cambridge University Press.

Cox, M. (2005) L2 English morpheme acquisition order: The lack of consensus examined from a case study of four L1 Chinese Pre-School Boys. *Working Papers in Educational Linguistics* 20 (2), 59–78.

Craik, F.I.M. and Lockhard, R.S. (1972) Levels of processing: A framework for memory research. *Journal of Verbal Learning and Verbal Behaviour* 11 (6), 671–684.

Crain, S. (1993) Language acquisition in the absence of experience. In P. Bloom (ed.) *Language Acquisition: Core Readings* (pp. 364–409). London: Harvester Wheatsheaf.

Crandall, J.A. and Peyton, J.K. (1993) *Approaches to Adult ESL Literacy Instruction*. McHenry, IL and Washington, DC: Delta Systems and Center for Applied Linguistics.

Creese, M. (2016) On the assessment of English and math skills levels of prisoners in England. *London Review of Education* 14 (3), 13–30.

Cromdal, J. (1999) Childhood bilingualism and metalinguistic skills: Analysis and control in young Swedish–English bilinguals. *Applied Psycholinguistics* 20 (1), 1–20.

Crossley, S.A., Allen, D. and McNamara, D.S. (2012) Text simplification and comprehensible input: A case for an intuitive approach. *Language Teaching Research* 16 (1), 89–108.

Croydon, A. (2005) *Making It Real: Teaching Pre-literate Adult Refugee Students*. Tacoma, WA: Department of Health and Social Services.

Crystal, D. (1987) *The Cambridge Encyclopedia of Language*. Cambridge: Cambridge University Press.

Crystal, D. (1997) *English as a Global Language*. Cambridge: Cambridge University Press.

Crystal, D., Fletcher, P. and Garman, M. (1976) *The Grammatical Analysis of Language Disability: A Procedure for Assessment and Remediation*. London: Edward Arnold.

Cucchiarini, C., Dawidowicz, M., Filimban, E., Tammelin-Laine, T., van de Craats, I. and Stik, H. (2015a) The Digital Literacy Instructor: Developing automatic speech recognition and selecting learning materials for opaque and transparent orthographies. In I. van de Craats, J. Kurvers and R. van Hout (eds) *Adult Literacy, Second Language and Cognition* (pp. 251–278). Nijmegen: Center for Language Studies.

Cucchiarini, C., Ganzeboom, M., Doremalen, J. and Strik, H. (2015b) Becoming literate while learning a second language – practicing reading aloud. In S. Steidl, A. Batliner and O. Jokisch (eds) *SLaTE-2015 Workshop on Speech and Language Technology in Education Proceedings* (pp. 77–82). Leipzig: International Speech Communication Association.

Cummins, J. (1979) Linguistic interdependence and the educational development of bilingual children. *Review of Educational Research* 49 (2), 222–251.

Cummins, J. (2000) *Language, Power and Pedagogy: Bilingual Children in the Crossfire*. Clevedon: Multilingual Matters.

Cummins, J. (2005) A proposal for action: Strategies for recognizing language competence as a learning resource within the mainstream classroom. *Modern Language Journal* 89 (4), 585–591.

Curtiss, S. (1977) *The Case of Genie, A Modern Day 'Wild Child'*. New York, NY: Academic Press.

Dalderop, K., Janssen-van Dieten, A-M. and Stockmann, W. (2008) Literacy: Assessing progress. In I. van de Craats and J. Kurvers (eds) *Low-educated Adult Second Language and Literacy Acquisition: Symposium Proceedings* (pp. 85–96). Antwerp: Landelijki Onderzoekschool Taalwetenschap (LOT).

Davidson, D., Jergovic, D., Imami, Z. and Theodos, V. (1997) Monolingual and bilingual children's use of the mutual exclusivity constraint. *Child Language* 24 (1), 3–24.

DeCapua, A. and Marshall, H.W. (2013) *Breaking New Ground: Teaching Students with Limited or Interrupted Formal Education in U.S. Secondary Schools*. Ann Arbor, MI: University of Michigan Press.

DeCapua, A. and Marshall, H.W. (2015) Implementing a mutually adaptive learning paradigm in a community-based adult ESL literacy class. In M. Santos and A. Whiteside (eds) *Low Educated Second Language and Literacy Acquisition. Proceedings of the Ninth Symposium* (pp. 151–171). San Francisco, CA: City College of San Francisco.

DeCasper A.J. and Fifer, W.P. (1980) Of human bonding: Newborns prefer their mothers' voices. *Science* 208 (4448), 1174–1176.

DeFrancis, J. (1996) How efficient is the Chinese writing system? *Visible Language* 30 (1), 6–44.

De Houwer, A. (1990) *The Acquisition of Two Languages from Birth: A Case Study*. Cambridge: Cambridge University Press.

De Houwer, A. (2005) Early bilingual acquisition: Focus on morphosyntax and the Separate Development Hypothesis. In J. Kroll and A. de Groot (eds) *The Handbook of Bilingualism* (pp. 30–48). Oxford: Oxford University Press.

Del Percio, A. (2016) The governmentality of migration: Intercultural communication and the politics of (dis) placement. *Language and Communication* 51, 87–98.

Del Percio, A. (2017) Engineering commodifiable workers: Language, migration and the governmentality of the self. *Language Policy* 17 (2), 239–259.

De Villiers, J. and Roeper, T. (eds) 2011. *Handbook of Generative Approaches to Language Acquisition.* Berlin: Springer.

De Villiers, P. and de Villiers, J. (1973) A cross-sectional study of the acquisition of grammatical morphemes in child speech. *Journal of Psycholinguistic Research* 2 (3), 267–78.

DfES/Department for Education and Skills. (2001) United Kingdom.

Di Benedetto, L., Salvato, V., and Tiranno, C. (2017) The value of language in linguistic autobiography: Teaching experience with low educated unaccompanied multilingual minors. In M. Sosinski (ed.) *Alfabetización y aprendizaje de idiomas por adultos: Investigación, política educativa y práctica docente* (pp. 99–108). Granada: Universidad de Granada.

Djikic, M., Oatley, K., Zoeterman, S. and Peterson, J. B. (2009) On being moved by art: How reading fiction transforms the self. *Creativity Research Journal* 21 (1), 24–29.

Dolch, E.W. (1948) *Problems in Reading*. Champaign, IL: Garrard.

Döpke, S. (2000) Generation of and retraction from cross-linguistically motivated structures in bilingual first language acquisition. *Bilingualism: Language and Cognition* 3 (3), 209–226.

Doyé, P. (2004) Intercomprehension. Rezeptive Mehrsprachigkeit als Alternative. (2004). *Praxis Fremdsprachenunterricht* 1 (1), 4–7.

Dubin, F. and Olshtain, E. (1977) *Facilitating Language Learning: A Guidebook for the ESL/EFL Teacher.* New York, NY: McGraw Hill.

Dufva, H., Suni, M. Aro, M. and Salo, O-P. (2011) Languages as objects of learning: Language learning as a case of multilingualism. *Apples – Journal of Applied Language Studies* 5 (1), 109–124.

Dulay, H. and Burt, M. (1973) Should we teach children syntax? *Language Learning* 23 (2), 245–258.

Dulay, H. and Burt, M. (1974) Natural sequences in child second language acquisition. *Language Learning* 24, 37–53.

Duncan, S. (2014) *Reading for Pleasure and Reading Circles for Adult Emergent Readers.* Leicester: National Institute for Adult Continuing Education.

Durgunoğlu, A.Y. and Öney, B. (1999) A cross-linguistic comparison of phonological awareness and word recognition. *Reading and Writing* 11 (4), 281–299.

Du Plessis, J., Solin, D., Travis, L. and White, L. (1987) UG or not UG, that is the question: A reply to Clahsen and Muysken. *Second Language Research* 3 (1), 56–75.

Dworin, J. (2003) Insights into biliteracy development: Toward a bidirectional theory of a bilingual pedagogy. *Journal of Hispanic Higher Education* 2 (2), 171–186.

Eberhard, D.M., Simons, G.F. and Fenning, C.D. (eds) (2019) Ethnologue: Languages of the world. See https://www.ethnologue.com (accessed November 2019).

Ecalle, J., Magnan, A. and Biot-Chevrier, C. (2008) Alphabet knowledge and early literacy skills in French beginning readers. *European Journal of Developmental Psychology* 5 (3), 303–325.

Edwards, J. (2013) Bilingualism and multilingualism: Some central concepts. In T.K. Bhatia and W.C. Ritchie (eds) *The Handbook of Bilingualism and Multilingualism* (pp. 5–25). Oxford: Wiley/Blackwell.

Ehri, L.C. (1992) Reconceptualizing the development of sight word reading and its relationship to recoding. In P.B. Gough, L.C. Ehri and R. Treiman (eds) *Reading Acquisition* (pp. 107–143). Hillsdale, NJ: Lawrence Erlbaum.

Elley, W.B. and Mangubhai, F. (1983) The impact of reading on second language learning. *Reading Research Quarterly* 19 (1), 53–67.

Ellis, R. (1990) *Instructed Second Language Acquisition*. Oxford: Blackwell.

Ellis, R. (ed.) (2001) *Form-focused Instruction and Second Language Learning*. London: Lawrence Erlbaum.

Elmeroth, E. (2003) From refugee camp to solitary confinement: Illiterate adults learn Swedish as a second language. *Scandinavian Journal of Educational Research* 47 (4), 431–449.

Eskildsen, S.W. (2009) Constructing another language: Usage-based linguistics in second language acquisition. *Applied Linguistics* 30 (1), 335–357.

European Commission (2012) *Intercomprehension. Studies on translation and multilingualism*. Luxembourg: European Commission.

Faretta-Stutenberg, M. and Morgan-Short, K. (2018) The interplay of individual differences and context of learning in behavioural and neurocognitive second language development. *Second Language Research* 34 (1), 67–102.

Farrelly, R. (2013) Converging perspectives in the LESLLA context. In T. Tammelin-Laine, L. Nieminen and M. Martin (eds) *Low-educated Second Language and Literacy Acquisition: Proceedings of the 8th Symposium* (pp. 25–45). Jyväskylä: Jyväskylä University.

Feldmeier, A. (2015) Encouraging learner autonomy: Working with portfolios, learning agreements and individualized materials. In I. van de Craats and R. van Hout (eds) *Adult Literacy, Second Language, and Cognition: Proceedings of the 2014 LESLLA Symposium* (pp. 149–164). Nijmegen: Centre for Language Studies.

Felix, S. (1985) More evidence on competing cognitive systems. *Second Language Research* 1 (1), 47–72.

Filimban, E. (2019) The effectiveness of a computer software programme for developing phonemic awareness and decoding skills for low-literate adult learners of English. Unpublished PhD thesis, Newcastle University.

Finnish National Agency for Education (2019a) *Curriculum Guidelines for Literacy Training in Liberal Adult Education 2017. Regulations and Guidelines 2018:2c*. Finnish National Agency for Education: Helsinki.

Finnish National Agency for Education (2019b) *National Core Curriculum for Basic Education for Adults 2017. Literacy Training Phase and Introductory Phase. Regulations and Guidelines 2017:9c*. Finnish National Agency for Education: Helsinki.

Finnish National Board of Education (2012) *National Curriculum of Integration Training for Adult Immigrants*. Publications 2012: 6. Helsinki: Finnish National Board of Education.

Finnish National Board of Education (2014) *National Core Curriculum for Basic Education 2014*. Helsinki: Finnish National Board of Education.

Fish, B., Knell, E. and Buchanan, H. (2007) Teaching literacy to preliterate adults: The top and the bottom. *TESOL Adult Interest Section Electronic Newsletter* 5, 2.

Fishman, J.A. (1991) *Reversing Language Shift: Theoretical and Empirical Foundations of Assistance to Threatened Languages*. Clevedon: Multilingual Matters.

Fishman, J.A. (2001) 300-Plus Years of Heritage Language Education in the United States. In J.K. Peyton, D.A. Ranard and S. McGinnis. (eds) *Heritage Languages in America: Preserving a National Resource* (pp. 81–89). McHenry, IL: Delta Systems.

Fishman, J.A. (2004) Language maintenance, language shift, and reversing language shift. In T. Bhatia and W. Ritchie (eds) *The Handbook of Bilingualism* (pp. 406–436). Malden, MA: Blackwell Publishing.

Franker, Q. and Christensen, L. (2013) Description of teachers' competence in initial and functional literacy for adults with non-Nordic mother tongues. Alfarådet, The Nordic Adult Literacy Network. www.alfaradet.net.

Freire, P. (1970/1993) *Pedagogy of the Oppressed*. (Ramos, trans.) New York, NY: Continuum/Herder and Herder.

Freire, P. and Macedo, D. (1987) *Literacy: Reading the Word and the World*. London: Routledge.

Fries, C. (1945) *Teaching and Learning English as a Foreign Language*. Ann Arbor, MI: University of Michigan Press.

Frith, U. (1985) Beneath the surface of developmental dyslexia. In K. Patterson, J. Marshall and M. Coltheart (eds) *Surface Dyslexia: Neurological and Cognitive Studies of Phonological Reading* (pp. 301–330). Hillsdale, NJ: Lawrence Erlbaum.

Fromkin, V., Krashen, S., Curtiss, S., Rigler, D. and Rigler, M. (1974) The development of language in Genie: A case of language acquisition beyond the 'Critical Period'. *Brain and Language* 1 (1), 81–107.

Gairns, R. and Redman, S. (2004) *Working with Words. A Guide to Teaching and Learning Vocabulary*. Cambridge: Cambridge University Press.

Galloway, S. (2017) Flowers of argument and engagement? Reconsidering critical perspectives on adult education and literate practices. *International Journal of Lifelong Education* 36 (4), 458–470.

García, O. (2009) *Bilingual Education in the 21st Century: A Global Perspective*. Oxford: Blackwell Publishing.

Gardner, R. and Lambert, W. (1972) *Attitudes and Motivation in Second Language Learning*. Rowley, MA: Newbury House.

Gass, S. and Madden, C. (1985) *Input in Second Language Acquisition*. Rowley, MA: Newbury House.

Gass, S. and Varonis, E. (1994) Input, interaction, and second language acquisition. *Studies in Second Language Acquisition* 16 (3), 283–302.

Gathercole, S.E. and Baddeley, A.D. (1989) Evaluation of the role of phonological STM in the development of vocabulary in children: A longitudinal study. *Journal of Memory and Language* 28 (2), 200–213.

Gee, J.P. (1991) Socio-cultural approaches to literacy (literacies). *Annual Review of Applied Linguistics* 12 (1), 31–48.

Gee, J.P. (2000) Identity as an analytic lens for research in education. *Review of Research in Education* 25 (1), 99–125.

Gee, J.P. (2015) *Social Linguistics and Literacies: Ideology in Discourses*. New York, NY: Routledge.

Gelb, I. (1963) *A Study of Writing*. Chicago, IL: University of Chicago Press.

Genesee, F., Nicoladis, E. and Paradis, J. (1995) Language differentiation in early bilingual development. *Journal of Child Language* 22 (3), 611–632.

Gentner, D. and Boroditsky, L. (2001) Individuation, relativity and early word learning. In M. Bowerman and S.C. Levinson (eds) *Language Acquisition and Conceptual Development* (pp. 215–256). Cambridge: Cambridge University Press.

Gervain J. and Mehler J. (2010) Speech perception and language acquisition in the first year of life. *Annual Review of Psychology* 61 (1), 191–218.

Gillon, G.T. (2017) *Phonological Awareness: From Research to Practice*. London: Guilford Publications.

Giroux, H. (1993) Literacy and the politics of difference. In P.L. McLaren and C. Lankshear (eds) *Critical Literacy: Politics, Praxis, and the* Postmodern. Albany, NY: State University of New York Press.

Glück, C.W. (1999) Wortfindungsstörungen von Kindern in kognitionspsychologischer Perspektive. *Der Sprachheilpädagoge* 31 (1), 1–27.

Glück, C.W. (2003) Semantisch-lexikalische Störungen bei Kindern und Jugendlichen. In M. Grohnfeldt (ed.) *Lehrbuch der Sprachheilpädagogik und Logopädie. Beratung, Therapie und Rehabilitation* (pp. 178–184). Stuttgart: Kohlhammer.

Glück, C.W. (2007) *Wortschatz- und Wortfindungstest für 6- bis 10-Jährige (WWT 6-10)*. München: Elsevier.

Glushko, R.J. (1979) The organization and activation of orthographic knowledge in reading aloud. *Journal of Experimental Psychology: Human Perception and Performance* 5 (4), 674.

Goetz, J.P. (2003) The effects of bilingualism on theory of mind development. *Bilingualism: Language and Cognition* 6 (1), 1–15.

Goldberg, A.E. (1995) *Constructions: A Construction Grammar Approach to Argument Structure*. Chicago, IL: University of Chicago Press.

Goldberg, A.E. (2007) *Constructions at Work: The Nature of Generalizations in Language*. Oxford: Oxford University Press.

Golden, A. and Lanza, E. (2012) Narratives on literacies: Adult migrants' identity construction in interaction. In A. Pitkänen-Huhta and L. Holm (eds) *Literacy Practices in Transition: Perspectives from the Nordic Countries* (pp. 27–53). Bristol: Multilingual Matters.

Goldschneider, J. and de Keyser, R. (2001) Explaining the 'natural order of L2 morpheme acquisition' in English: A meta-analysis of multiple determinants. *Language Learning* 51 (1), 1–50.

Golinkoff, R.M. and Hirsh-Pasek, K. (2000) Word learning: Icon, index, or symbol? In R.M. Golinkoff and K. Hirsh-Pasek (eds) *Becoming a Word Learner. A Debate on Lexical Acquisition* (pp. 3–18). Oxford: Oxford University Press.

Gollan, T.H. and Acenas, L.A. (2004) What is a TOT? Cognate and translation effects on tip-of-the-tongue states in Spanish–English and Tagalog–English bilinguals. *Journal of Experimental Psychology: Learning, Memory, and Cognition* 30 (1), 246–269.

Gollan, T.H., Salmon, D.P., Montoya, R.I. and Galasko, D.R. (2011) Degree of bilingualism predicts age of diagnosis of Alzheimer's disease in low-education but not in highly educated Hispanics. *Neuropsychologia* 49 (14), 3826–3839.

Gombert, J.É. (1992) *Metalinguistic Development*. London: Harvester Wheatsheaf.

Goody, J. (ed.) (1968) *Literacy in Traditional Societies*. Cambridge: Cambridge University Press.

Goody, J. (1977) *The Domestication of the Savage Mind*. Cambridge: Cambridge University Press.

Goswami, U. and Bryant, P. (1990) *Phonological Skills and Learning to Read*. London: Lawrence Erlbaum.

Goswami, U. and Bryant, P. (1992) Rhyme, analogy and children's reading. In P. B. Gough, L.C. Ehri and R. Treiman (eds) *Reading Acquisition* (pp. 49–62). Hillsdale, NJ: Erlbaum.

Grabe, W. (2009) *Reading a Second Language: Moving from Theory to Practice*. Cambridge: Cambridge University Press.

Grabe, W. and Kaplan, R.B. (1996) *Theory and Practice of Writing: An Applied Linguistic Perspective*. New York, NY: Longman.

Grabe, W. and Stoller, F.L. (2002) *Teaching and Researching Reading*. London: Longman.

Grabe, W. and Stoller, F.L. (2011) *Teaching and Researching Reading* (2nd edn). Harlow: Pearson Education.

Graff, G. (1993) *Beyond the Culture Wars*. New York, NY: Norton.

Graham, W.G. (1987) *Beyond the Written Word. Oral aspects of Scripture in the History of Religion*. Cambridge: Cambridge University Press.

Graves, M.F., August, D. and Mancilla-Martinez, J. (2013) *Teaching Vocabulary to English Language Learners*. New York, NY: Teachers College Press.

Green, D.W. (1998) Mental control of the bilingual lexico-semantic system. *Bilingualism: Language and Cognition* 1 (2), 67–81.

Gregg, K. (1996) The logical and developmental problems of second language acquisition. In W.C. Ritchie and T.K. Bhatia (eds) *Handbook of Second Language Acquisition* (pp. 50–81). London: Academic Press.

Grosjean, F. (2004) Studying bilinguals: Methodological and conceptual issues. In T.K. Bhatia and W.C. Ritchie (eds) *The Handbook of Bilingualism* (pp. 32–63). Oxford: Blackwell.

Grosjean, F. (2008) *Studying Bilinguals*. Oxford: Oxford University Press.

Gullberg, M., Roberts, L., Dimroth, C. and Indefrey, P. (2010) Adult language learning after minimal exposure to an unknown natural language. *Language Learning* 60 (2), 5–24.

Gutek, G.L. (1995) *A History of the Western Educational Experience* (2nd edn). Long Grove, IL: Waveland Press.

Haberzettl, S. (2003) 'Tinkering' with chunks: Form-oriented strategies and idiosyncratic utterance patterns without functional implications in the IL of Turkish speaking children learning German. In C. Dimroth and M. Starren (eds) *Information Structure and the Dynamics of Language Acquisition* (pp. 45–64). Amsterdam: Benjamins.

Halliday, M.A.K. (1994) *Introduction to Functional Grammar* (2nd edn). London: Edward Arnold.

Hansen, M.B. and Markman, E.M. (2009) Children's use of mutual exclusivity to learn labels for parts of objects. *Developmental Psychology* 45 (2), 1651–1664.

Harju-Luukkainen, H., Nissinen, K., Sulkunen, S., Suni, M. and Vettenranta, J. (2014) *Avaimet osaamiseen ja tulevaisuuteen: Selvitys maahanmuuttajataustaisten nuorten osaamisesta ja siihen liittyvistä taustatekijöistä PISA 2012 – tutkimuksessa*. Jyväskylä: Finnish Institute for Educational Research.

Hartel, A., Lowry, B. and Hendon, W. (2006) *Sam and Pat 1: Beginning Reading and Writing*. Boston, MA: Thomson Heinle.

Haudeck, H. (2008) *Fremdsprachliche Wortschatzarbeit außerhalb des Klassenzimmers. Eine qualitative Studie zu Lernstrategien und Lerntechniken in den Klassenstufen 5 und 8*. Tübingen: Gunter Narr.

Hausmann, F.J. (1993) Was ist eigentlich Wortschatz? In W. Börner and K. Vogel (eds) *Wortschatz und Fremdsprachenerwerb* (pp. 2–21). Bochum: AKS-Verlag.

Hawkins, R. (2001) *Second Language Syntax. A Generative Introduction*. Malden, MA: Blackwell.

Hawkins, R. (2018) *How Languages are Learned. An Introduction*. Cambridge: Cambridge University Press.

Hawkins, R. and Chan, Y.-H.C. (1997) The partial availability of Universal Grammar in second language acquisition: The 'Failed Functional Features Hypothesis'. *Second Language Research* 13 (3), 187–226.

Hawkins, R. and Liszka, S. (2003) Locating the source of defective past tense marking in advanced L2 English speakers. In A. van Hout, A. Hulk, F. Kuiken and R. Towell (eds) *The Lexicon-Syntax Interface in Second Language Acquisition* (pp. 21–44). Amsterdam: John Benjamins.

Haznedar, B. (1997) L2 acquisition by a Turkish-speaking child: Evidence for L1 influence. In E. Hughes, M. Hughes and A. Greenhill (eds) *Proceedings of the 21st Annual Boston University Conference on Language Development 21* (pp. 245–256). Somerville, MA: Cascadilla Press.

Haznedar, B. (2010) Transfer at the syntax-pragmatics interface: Pronominal subjects in bilingual Turkish. *Second Language Research* 26, 355–378.

Haznedar, B. (2013) Child second language acquisition from a generative perspective. *Linguistic Approaches to Bilingualism* 3 (1), 26–47.

Haznedar, B., Peyton, J.K. and Young-Scholten, M. (2018) Teaching adult migrants: A focus on the language they speak. *Critical Multilingualism Studies: An Interdisciplinary Journal* 6 (1), 155–183.

Heath, S.B. (1983) *Ways with Words: Language, Life, and Work in Communities and Classrooms*. Cambridge: Cambridge University Press.

Hempenstall, K. (2005) The whole-language-phonics controversy: A historical perspective. *Australian Journal of Learning Disabilities* 10 (3 and 4), 19–33.

Herschensohn, J. (2007) *Language Development and Age*. Cambridge: Cambridge University Press.

Huebner, T., Carroll, M. and Perdue, C. (1992) The acquisition of English. In W. Klein and C. Perdue (eds) *Utterance Structure: Developing Grammars Again* (pp. 1–121). Amsterdam: Benjamins.

Heyde, A. (1979) The relationship between self-esteem and the oral production of a second language. *TESOL Quarterly* (13) 3, 429–429.

Hidalgo Navarro, A. and Quilis Merín, M. (2012) *La voz del lenguaje: fonética y fonología del español*. Valencia: Tirant humanidades.

Hill, D. (2008) Graded readers in English. *ELT Journal* 62 (2),184–204.

Hilles, S. (1986) Interlanguage and the pro-drop parameter. *Second Language Research* 2 (1), 33–52.

Hirsh-Pasek, K., Golinkoff, R.M. and Hollich, G. (2000) An emergentist coalition model for word learning: Mapping words to objects is a product of the interaction of multiple cues. In R.M. Golinkoff and K. Hirsh-Pasek (eds) *Becoming a Word Learner. A Debate on Lexical Acquisition* (pp. 136–164). Oxford: Oxford University Press

Hoff, E. and Shatz, M. (2007) (eds) *Blackwell Handbook of Language Development*. Oxford: Blackwell.

Honko, M. (2013) *Alakouluikäisten leksikaalinen tieto ja taito. Toisen sukupolven suomi ja S1-verrokit*. Tampere: University of Tampere.

Hudson, T. (2007) *Teaching Second Language Reading*. Oxford: Oxford University Press.

Hussien, A.M. (2014) The effect of learning English (L2) on learning of Arabic literacy (L1) in the primary school. *International Education Studies* 7 (3), 88–99.

Huettig, F. (2015) Literacy influences cognitive abilities far beyond the mastery of written language. In I. van de Craats, J. Kurvers and R. van Hout (eds) *Adult Literacy, Second Language and Cognition* (pp. 115–127). Nijmegen: Center for Language Studies.

Imbens-Bailey, A.L. (1996) Ancestral language acquisition: Implications for aspects of ethnic identity among Armenian American children and adolescents. *Journal of Language and Social Psychology* 15 (4), 422–443.

Ingram, D. (1989) *First Language Acquisition*. Cambridge: Cambridge University.

Intke-Hernandéz, M. (2015) Migrant stay-at-home mothers learning to eat and live the Finnish way. *Nordic Journal of Migration Research* 5 (2), 75–82.

Ionin, T., Ko, H. and Wexler, K. (2004) Article semantics in L2 acquisition: The role of specificity. *Language Acquisition* 12 (1), 3–69.

Janks, H. (2010) *Literacy and Power*. New York: Routledge.

Jordens, P. and Dimroth, C. (2006) Finiteness in children and adults learning Dutch. In N. Gagarina and I. Gülzow (eds) *The Acquisition of Verbs and their Grammar: The Effect of Particular Languages* (pp. 173–200). Dordrecht: Springer.

Juffs, A. and Rodríguez, G.A. (2008) Some notes on working memory in college-educated and low-educated learners of English as a second language in the United States. In M. Young-Scholten (ed.) *Low-educated*

Second Language and Literacy Acquisition. Research, Policy and Practice (pp. 33–48). Durham: Roundtuit.

Julien, M., van Hout, R. and van de Craats, I. (2016) Meaning and function of dummy auxiliaries in adult acquisition of Dutch as an additional language. *Second Language Research* 32 (1), 49–73.

Kagan, O., Carreira, M. and Chik, C. (2017) *The Routledge Handbook of Heritage Language Education: From Innovation to Program Building*. New York: Routledge.

Kahoul, W., Vainikka, A. and Young-Scholten, M. (2018) The mystery of the missing inflections. In C. Wright, T. Piske and M. Young-Scholten (eds) *Mind Matters in SLA*. Bristol: Multilingual Matters.

Kaminski, J., Call, J. and Fischer, J. (2004) Word learning in a domestic dog: Evidence for 'fast mapping'. *Science* 304 (5677), 1682–1683.

Karmiloff-Smith, A., Grant, J., Sims, K., Jones, M.C. and Cuckle, P. (1996) Rethinking metalinguistic awareness: Representing and accessing knowledge about what counts as a word. *Cognition* 58 (2), 197–219.

Katz, L. and Frost, R. (1992) The reading process is different for different orthographies: The orthographic depth hypothesis. *Advances in Psychology* 94 (1), 67–84.

Kibbee, D.A. (1991) *For to Speke Frenche Trewely: The French Language in England, 1000-1600: Its Status, Description and Instruction*. Amsterdam: Benjamins.

Kintsch, W. (1998) *Comprehension: A Framework for Cognition*. New York, NY: Cambridge University Press.

Klein, E.C., Stoyneshka, I., Adams, K., Pugach, Y., Solt, S. and Rose, T. (2004) Past tense affixation in L2 English. In A. Brugos, L. Micciulla and C.E. Smith (eds) *Proceedings Supplement of the 28th Boston University Conference on Language Development (BUCLD)* (pp. 553–564). Somerville, MA: Cascadilla Press.

Klein, R.G. (2000) Archeology and the evolution of human behavior. *Evolutionary Anthropology: Issues, News, and Reviews* 9 (1), 17–36.

Klein, W. and Perdue, C. (eds) (1992) *Utterance Structure: Developing Grammars Again*. Amsterdam: John Benjamins.

Klein, W. and Perdue, C. (1997) The Basic Variety (or: Couldn't natural languages be much simpler?) *Second Language Research* 13 (4), 301–347.

Knapp-Potthoff, A. (1997) Sprach(lern)bewusstheit im Kontext. In W. Edmondson and J. House (eds) *Themenschwerpunkt: Language Awareness* (pp. 9–23). Tübingen: Narr.

Koda, K. (2005) *Insights into Second Language Reading: A Cross-Linguistic Approach*. Cambridge: Cambridge University Press.

Koda, K. and Zehler, A.M. (2008) *Learning to Read Across Languages: Crosslinguistic Relationships in First and Second Language Literacy Development*. Mahwah, NJ: Routledge.

Kohnert, K. (2004) Processing skills in early sequential bilinguals. In B. Goldstein (ed.) *Bilingual Language Development and Disorders in Spanish–English Speakers* (pp. 53–76). Baltimore, MD: Brookes.

Koretz, D. (2008) *Measuring Up. What Educational Testing Really Tells Us*. Cambridge, MA: Harvard University Press.

Kovacs, A.M. (2009) Early bilingualism enhances mechanisms of false-belief reasoning. *Developmental Science* 12 (1), 48–54.

Kovacs, A.M. (2015) Cognitive adaptations induced by a multi-language input in early development. *Current Opinion in Neurobiology* 35 (1), 80–86.

Krashen, S. (1973) Lateralization, language learning and the Critical Period: Some new evidence. *Language Learning* 23 (1), 63–74.

Krashen, S. (1982) *Principles and Practice in Second Language Acquisition*. Oxford: Pergamon.

Krashen, S. (1985) *The Input Hypothesis*. London: Longman.

Krashen, S. (1989) We acquire vocabulary and spelling by reading: Additional evidence for the input hypothesis. *Modern Language Journal* 73 (4), 440–464.

Krashen, S. (1993) The case for free voluntary reading. *Canadian Modern Language Review* 50 (1), 72–82.

Krashen, S. (1998) Comprehensible output? *System* 26 (2), 175–182.

Krashen, S. (2004) *The Power of Reading*. Portsmouth, NH: Heinemann.

Kurhila, S. (2006) *Second Language Interaction*. Amsterdam: John Benjamins.

Kurvers, J. (2007) Development of word recognition skills of adult L2 beginning readers. In N. Faux (ed.) *Low Educated Second Language and Literacy Acquisition: Research, Policy and Practice* (pp. 23–44). Richmond, VA: The Literacy Institute at Virginia Commonwealth University.

Kurvers, J. (2015) Emerging literacy in adult second-language learners: A synthesis of research findings in the Netherlands. *Writing Systems Research* 7 (1), 58–78.

Kurvers, J., Stockmann, W. and van de Craats, I. (2010) Predictors of success in adult L2 literacy acquisition. In T. Wall and M. Leong (eds) *Low-Educated Second Language and Literacy Acquisition* (pp. 47–62). Calgary: Bow Valley College.

Kurvers, J., van de Craats, I. and Young-Scholten, M. (2006) Research on low-educated second language and literacy acquisition. In J. Kurvers, I. van de Craats and M. Young-Scholten (eds) Low-educated Adult Second Language and Literacy Acquisition (pp. 7–23). *Proceedings of the Inaugural LESLLA conference*. Utrecht: LOT.

Labov, W. and Waletzky, J. (1997) Narrative analysis: Oral versions of personal experience. *Journal of Narrative and Life History* 7 (1–4), 3–38.

Lado, R. (1957) *Linguistics Across Cultures. Applied Linguistics for Language Teachers*. Ann Arbor, MI: University of Michigan Press.

Lahikainen, A.R., Mälkiä, T. and Repo, K. (2017) Introduction: Media and family interaction. In A.R. Lahikainen, T. Mälkiä and K. Repo (eds) *Media, Family Interaction, and the Digitalization of Childhood* (pp. 1–30). Cheltenham: Edgar Elgar.

Lakoff, G. (1987) *Women, Fire, and Dangerous Things: What Categories Reveal about the Mind*. Chicago, IL: CSLI.

Lankshear, C. and Knobel, M. (2003) *New Literacies: Changing Knowledge and Classroom Learning*. Buckingham: Open University Press.

Länstyrelsen Östergötland (2016) *Kartläggning föredrarstöd – slutredovisning*. Linköping: Länstyrelsen Östergötland.

Lardiere, D. (2003) Second language knowledge of [+/-past] vs. [+/-finite]. In J. Liceras, H. Goodluck and H. Zobl (eds) *Proceedings of the 6th Generative Approaches to Second Language Acquisition Conference (GASLA 2002)* (pp. 176–189). Somerville, MA: Cascadilla Press.

Laymon, L. (2013) Extensive reading in low-level ESL: Can it be done? Unpublished manuscript, San Francisco State University.

Lee, J.F. (1997) Non-native reading research and theory. In K. Bardovi-Harlig and B. Hartford (eds) *Beyond Methods: Components of Second Language Teacher Education* (pp. 152–171). New York, NY: McGraw-Hill.

Lee, S-K. (2009) Topic congruence and topic of interest: How do they affect second language reading comprehension? *Reading in a Foreign Language* 21 (2), 159–178.

Leikin, M., Schwartz, M. and Share, D.L. (2010) General and specific benefits of bi-literate bilingualism: A Russian-Hebrew study of beginning literacy. *Reading and Writing* 23 (3), 269–292.

Lenneberg, E. (1967) *The Biological Foundations of Language*. New York, NY: Wiley.

Leonard, L.B. (1998) Language learnability and specific language impairment. *Applied Psycholinguistics* 10 (2), 179–202.

Leonard, L.B. (2000) Specific language impairment across languages. In D.V.M. Bishop and L.B. Leonard (eds) *Speech and Language Impairments in Children: Causes, Characteristics, Intervention and Outcome* (pp. 99–113). Hove: Psychology Press.

Levelt W.J. (1989) *Speaking: From Intention to Articulation*. Cambridge, MA: MIT Press.

Lewis, M. (1993) *The Lexical Approach: The State of ELT and the Way Forward*. Hove: Language Teaching Publications.

Liberman, I.Y., Shankweiler, D., Fischer, F.W. and Carter, B. (1974) Explicit syllable and phoneme segmentation in the young child. *Journal of Experimental Child Psychology* 18 (2), 201–212.

Lightbown, P.M. (1985) Great expectations: Second language acquisition research and classroom teaching. *Applied Linguistics* 6 (2), 173–189.

Lilja, N. (2010) *Ongelmista oppimiseen. Toisen aloittamat korjausjaksot kakkoskielisessä keskustelussa. Jyväskylä Studies in Humanities 309*. Jyväskylä: University of Jyväskylä.

Lilja, N. and Piirainen-Marsh, A. (2018) Connecting the language classroom and *the wild*. Re-enactments of language use experiences. *Applied Linguistics* 40 (4), 1–31.

Lillard, P.P. (2011) *Montessori Today: A Comprehensive Approach to Education from Birth to Adulthood*. New York, NY: Knopf Doubleday.

Linell, P. (2005) *The Written Language Bias in Linguistics: Its Nature, Origins and Transformations*. Abingdon: Routledge.

Long, M. (1985) Input and second language acquisition theory. In S. Gass and C. Madden (eds) *Input in Second Language Acquisition* (pp. 377–393). Rowley, MA: Newbury House.

Long, M. (1996) The role of the linguistic environment in second language acquisition. In W. Ritchie and T. Bhatia (eds) *Handbook of Second Language Acquisition* (pp. 413–468). San Diego, CA: Academic Press.

McCarter, S. and Jakes, P. (2009) *Uncovering EAP.* London: Macmillan Education.

Ma, Q. (2009) *Second Language Vocabulary Acquisition*. Berlin: Peter Lang.

Maag, L.K. (2007) *Measuring Morphological Awareness in Adult Readers: Implications for Vocabulary Development*. Gainesville, FL: University of Florida.

MacIntyre, P. and Gardner, R. (1991) Language anxiety: Its relationship to other anxieties and to processing in native and second languages. *Language Learning* 41 (4), 85–117.

MacWhinney, B. (ed.) (1999) *The Emergence of Language*. Mahwah, NJ: Lawrence Erlbaum.

MacWhinney, B. (2000) *The CHILDES Project: Tools for Analyzing Talk* (3rd edn). Mahwah, NJ: Lawrence Erlbaum.

MacWhinney, B. and Snow, C. (1985) The child language data exchange system. *Journal of Child Language* 12 (2), 271–295.

Malessa, E. and Filimban, E. (2017) Exploring what log files can reveal about LESLLA learners' behaviour in an online CALL environment. In M. Sosinski (ed.) *Alfabetización y aprendizaje de idiomas por adultos: investigación, política educative y práctica docente / Literacy Education and Second Language Learning by Adults: Research, Policy and Practice* (pp. 149–159). Granada: Universidad de Granada.

Malin, A., Sulkunen, S. and Laine, K. (2013) *PIAAC 2012: Kansainvälisen aikuistutkimuksen ensituloksia. Opetus- ja kulttuuriministeriön julkaisuja 2013: 19*. Helsinki: Ministry of Education and Culture.

Marcel, A.J. (1980) Conscious and preconscious recognition of polysemous words: Locating the selective effects of prior verbal context. In R.S. Nickerson (ed.) *Attention and Performance VIII* (pp. 436–457). Hillsdale, NJ: Erlbaum.

Mar, R.A. and Oatley, K. (2008) The function of fiction is the abstraction and simulation of social experience. *Perspectives on Psychological Science* 3 (3), 173–192.

Marinis, T. and Cunnings, I. (2018) Using psycholinguistic techniques in a second language teaching setting. In C. Wright, T. Piske and M. Young-Scholten (eds) *Mind Matters in SLA* (pp. 185–202). Bristol: Multilingual Matters.

Markman, E.M. (1989) *Categorization in Children: Problems of Induction*. Cambridge, MA: MIT Press.

Markman, E.M. and Hutchinson, J.E. (1984) Children's sensitivity to constraints on word meaning: Taxonomic vs thematic relations. *Cognitive Psychology* 16 (1), 1–27.

Marsh, G., Friedman, M., Desberg, P. and Saterdahl, K. (1981) Comparison of reading and spelling strategies in normal and reading disabled children. In M.P. Friedman, J.P. Das and N. O'Connor (eds) *Intelligence and Learning* (pp. 363–367). Boston, MA: Springer.

Martinez, R. and Murphy, V.A. (2011) Effect of frequency and idiomaticity on second language reading comprehension. *TESOL Quarterly* 45 (2), 267–290.

Masonheimer, P.E., Drum, P.A. and Ehri, L.C. (1984) Does environmental print identification lead children into word reading? *Journal of Reading Behavior* 16 (4), 257–271.

Mehler, J., Jusczyk, P.W. and Lambertz, G., Halsted, N., Bertoncini, J. and Amiel-Tison, C. (1988) A precursor of language acquisition in young infants. *Cognition* 29 (2), 143–178.

Mellars, P., Boyle, K., Bar-Yosef, O. and Stringer, C. (eds) (2007) *Rethinking the Human Evolution: New Behavioural and Biological Perspectives on the Origin and Dispersal of Modern Humans*. Cambridge: McDonald Institute Archaeological Publications.

Merriam, S., Caffarella, R. and Baumgartner, L. (2007) *Learning in Adulthood: A Comprehensive Guide*. San Francisco, CA: John Wiley and Sons.

Mervis, C.B. and Bertrand, J. (1994) Acquisition of the novel name - nameless category (N3C) principle. *Child Development* 65 (6), 1646–1662.

Minuz, F. and Borri, A. (2016) Literacy and language teaching: Tools, implementation and impact. *Italiano LinguaDue* 8 (2), 220–231.

Mißler, B. (1999) *Fremdsprachenlernerfahrungen und Lernstrategien. Eine empirische Untersuchung.* Tübingen: Stauffenburg Verlag.

Michael, E.B. and Gollan, T.H. (2005) Being and becoming bilingual: Individual differences and consequences for language production. In J.F. Kroll and A.M.B. de Groot (eds) *Handbook of Bilingualism: Psycholinguistic Approaches* (pp. 389–407). Oxford: Oxford University Press.

Miller, M. and King, K.P. (2009) Introduction. In M. Miller and K.P. King (eds) *Empowering Women through Literacy: Views from Experience* (pp. xi–xviii). Charlotte, NC: Information Age Publishing.

Mishra, R.K., Singh, N. Pandey, A. and Huettig. F. (2012) Spoken language-mediated anticipatory eye-movements are modulated by reading ability – Evidence from Indian low and high literates. *Journal of Eye Movement Research* 5 (1), 1–10.

Miyake, A. and Friedman, N.P. (2012) The nature and organization of individual differences in Executive Functions: Four general conclusions. *Current Directions in Psychological Science* 21 (1), 8–14.

Möller, R. (2014) Sieb Kognaten. In B. Hufeisen and N. Marx (eds) *EuroComGerm-Die sieben Siebe: Germanische Sprachen lesen lernen* (pp. 23–46). Aachen: Shaker.

Montessori, M. (1964) *The Montessori Method* (George, Trans.). Oxford: Bentley.

Montrul, S. (2002) Incomplete acquisition and attrition of Spanish tense/aspect distinctions in adult bilinguals. *Bilingualism: Language and Cognition* 5 (1), 39–68.

Montrul, S. (2008) *Incomplete Acquisition in Bilingualism. Re-examining the Age Factor*. Amsterdam: John Benjamins.

Montrul, S. (2010) Current issues in heritage language acquisition. *Annual Review of Applied Linguistics* 30 (1), 3–23.

Montrul, S., Foote, R. and Perpiñán, S. (2008) Gender agreement in adult second language learners and Spanish heritage speakers: The effects of age and context of acquisition. *Language Learning* 58 (3), 503–553.

Morais, J., Cary, L., Alegria, J. and Bertelson, P. (1979) Does awareness of speech as a sequence of phones arise spontaneously? *Cognition* 7 (4), 323–331.

Morais, J., Content, A., Bertelson, P., Cary, L. and Kolinsky, R. (1988) Is there a critical period for the acquisition of segmental analysis? *Cognitive Neuropsychology* 5 (3), 347–352.

Murphy, B.M. (1987) Bad books in easy English. *Modern English Teacher* 14 (3), 22–23.

Mussett, P. (2015) *Building Skills for All: A Review of Finland. Policy Insights on Literacy, Numeracy and Digital Skills from the Survey of Adult Skills. OECD Skills Studies*. Paris: OECD Publishing.

Myles, F. (2004) From data to theory: The over-representation of linguistic knowledge in SLA. *Transactions of the Philological Society* 102 (2), 139–168.

Myles, F., Hooper, J. and Mitchell, R. (1999) Interrogative chunks in French L2: A basis for creative construction? *Studies in Second Language Acquisition* 21 (1), 49–80.

Myers-Scotton, C. (1993) *Social Motivation for Code-switching: Evidence from Africa*. Oxford: Oxford University Press.

Nanez Sr., J.E. (2010) Bilingualism and cognitive processing in young children. In E.E. García and E.C. Frede (eds) *Young English Language Learners: Current Research and Emerging Directions for Practice and Policy* (pp. 80–99). New York: Teachers College Press.

Nassaji, H. (2002) Schema theory and knowledge-based processes in second language reading comprehension: A need for alternative perspectives. *Language Learning* 52 (2), 439–481.

Nation, I.S. (1990) *Teaching and Learning Vocabulary*. Boston, MA: Heinle and Heinle.

Nation, I.S. (2001) *Learning Vocabulary in Another Language*. Cambridge: Cambridge University Press.

Nessel, D. and Dixon, C. (2008) *Using the Language Experience Approach with English Language Learners: Strategies for Engaging Students and Developing Literacy*. Thousand Oaks, CA: Crowing Press.

Neuman, S.B. and Celano, D. (2001) Access to print in low income and middle income communities: An ecological study of four neighborhoods. *Reading Research Quarterly* 36 (1), 8–26.

Newport, E., Gleitman, L.R. and Gleitman, H. (1977) Mother, I'd rather do it myself: Some effects and non-effects of maternal speech style. In C. Snow and C.A. Ferguson (eds) *Talking to Children: Language Input and Acquisition* (pp. 109–149). Cambridge: Cambridge University Press.

Nicoladis, E. (2001) Finding first words in the input. In J. Cenoz and F. Genesee (eds) *Trends in Bilingual Acquisition* (pp. 131–147). Amsterdam: John Benjamins.

Nirenberg, S. and Raskin, V. (2004) *Ontological Semantics (Language, Speech, and Communication)*. Cambridge, MA: The MIT Press.

Norton Peirce, B. (1995) Social identity, investment, and language learning. *TESOL Quarterly* 29 (1), 9–31.

Nuwenhoud, A. (2015) The red book: A role-based portfolio for non-literate immigrant language learners. In I. van de Craats, J. Kurvers and R. van Hout (eds) *Adult Literacy, Second Language and Cognition* (pp. 217–223). Nijmegen: Center for Language Studies.

O'Grady, W. (2005) *Syntactic Carpentry: An Emergentist Approach to Syntax*. London: Erlbaum.

O'Grady, W. (2018) Syntax and acquisition: The emergentist story. In C. Wright, T. Piske and M. Young-Scholten (eds) *Mind Matters in SLA* (pp. 35–51). Bristol: Multilingual Matters.

O'Sullivan, B. (2011) Language testing. In J. Simpson (ed.) *The Routledge Handbook of Applied Linguistics* (pp. 259–273). Oxford: Routledge.

Obondo, A.M. (1997) Bilingual Education in Africa: An overview. In J. Cummins and D. Corson (eds) *Encyclopedia of Language and Education: Bilingual Education* (pp. 25–32). Dordrecht: Springer.

OECD (2000) *Literacy in the Information Age. Final Report of the International Adult Literacy Survey*. Paris: OECD Publication service.

OECD (2013) What do immigrant students tell us about the quality of education systems? *PISA in focus* 33. dx.doi.org/10.1787/22260919.

OECD (2019) Employment and unemployment rates by gender and place of birth. OECD International Migration Statistics (database). See https://www.oecd-ilibrary.org/social-issues-migration-health/data/oecd-international-migration-statistics/employment-and-unemployment-rates-by-gender-and-place-of-birth_data-00722-en (accessed November 2019).

Ohta, A.S. (2013) Sociocultural theory and the zone of proximal development. In J. Herschensohn and M. Young-Scholten (eds) *Cambridge Handbook of Second Language Acquisition* (pp. 648–669). Cambridge: Cambridge University Press.

Olson, D.R. (2002) There are x kinds of learners in a single class: Diversity without individual differences. In J.S. Gaffney and B.J. Askew (eds) *Stirring the Waters: The Influence of Marie Clay* (pp. 17–25). Portsmouth: Heinemann.

Oxford, R.L. (1990) *Language Learning Strategies: What Every Teacher Should Know*. New York, NY: Newbury House.

Paradis, M. (2009) *Declarative and Procedural Determinants of Second Languages*. Amsterdam: John Benjamins.

Paradis, J. and Genesee, F. (1996) Syntactic acquisition in bilingual children: Autonomous or interdependent? *Studies in Second Language Acquisition* 18 (1), 1–25.

Paradis, J. and Crago, M. (2001) The morphosyntax of specific language impairment in French: Evidence for an Extended Optional Default account. *Language Acquisition* 9 (4), 269–300.

Paradis, J. and Navarro, S. (2003) Subject realization and crosslinguistic interference in the bilingual acquisition of Spanish and English. *Journal of Child Language* 30 (2), 371–393.

Paradis, J., Genesee, F. and Crago, M. (2011) (eds) *Dual Language Development and Disorders: A Handbook on Bilingualism and Second Language Learning*. Baltimore, MD: Brookes Publishing Company.

Patterson, J.L. and Pearson, B.Z. (2004) Bilingual lexical development: Influences, contexts and processes. In B.A. Goldstein (ed.) *Bilingual Language Development and Disorders in Spanish-English Speakers* (pp. 77–104). Baltimore, MD: Paul H. Brookes.

Paulesu, E., Demonet, J-F., Fazio, F., McCrory, E., Chanoine, V., Brunswick, N., Cappa, S.F., Cossu, G., Habib, M., Firth, C.D. and Firth, U. (2001) Dyslexia: Cultural diversity and biological unity. *Science* 291 (5511), 2165–2167.

Peal, E. and Lambert, W.E. (1962) The relation of bilingualism to intelligence. *Psychological Monographs: General and Applied* 76 (27), 1–23.

Pearson, B.Z., Fernández, S.C. and Oller, D.K. (1993) Lexical development in bilingual infants and toddlers. *Language Learning* 43 (1), 93–120.

Pearson, B.Z., Fernández, S.C., Lewedeg, V. and Oller, D.K. (1997) The relation of input factors to lexical learning by bilingual infants. *Applied Psycholinguistics* 18 (1), 41–58.

Pecoraro, F. (2017) Teaching and learning L2 literacy using corporeal movement (dance). Workshop presented at the 13th Literacy Education and Second Language Learning for Adults (LESLLA) Symposium. (Portland, OR, 10–12 August).

Pelham, S.D. and Abrams, L. (2014) Cognitive advantages and disadvantages in early and late bilinguals. *Journal of Experimental Psychology: Learning, Memory, and Cognition* 40 (2), 313–325.

Peña, M., Maki, A., Kovacić, D., Dehaene-Lambertz, G., Koizumi, H., Bouquet, F. and Mehler, J. (2003) Sounds and silence: An optical topography study of language recognition at birth. *Proceedings of the National Academy of Sciences of the United States of America* 100 (20), 11702–11705.

Pennycook, A. and Otsuji, E. (2015) *Metrolingualism – Language in the City.* London: Routledge.

Peres Rodrigues, J.H. (1999) Para umha classificaçom e avaliaçom dos sistemas gráficos: os sistemas gráficos do galego-português e o do espanhol, *Agália* 57 (1), 103–129.

Peterson, C. and Nassaji, H. (2016) Project-based learning through the eyes of teachers and students in adult ESL classrooms. *The Canadian Modern Language Review* 72 (1), 13–39.

Pettitt, N. and Tarone, E. (2015) Following Roba: What happens when a low-educated multilingual adult learns to read. *Writing Systems Research* 7 (1), 20–38.

Peyton, J.K., Ranard, D.A. and McGinnis, S. (eds) (2001) *Heritage Languages in America: Preserving a National Resource.* McHenry, IL: Delta Systems.

Phillips, C. and Ehrenhofer, L. (2015) The role of language processing in language acquisition. *Linguistic Approaches to Bilingualism* 5 (4), 409–453.

Pinker, S. (1994) *The Language Instinct. How the Mind Creates Language.* London: William Morrow.

Pienemann, M. (1998) *Language Processing and Second Language Development. Processability Theory.* Amsterdam: John Benjamins.

Pienemann, M. (2001) Rapid profiling. Paper presented at the 9th EUROCALL Conference (Nijmegen, 29 August–1 September).

Pienemann, M. (2003) Language processing capacity. In C.J. Doughty and M.H. Long (eds) *The Handbook of Second Language Acquisition* (pp. 679–715). Oxford: Blackwell.

Pliatsikas, C., Johnstone, T. and Marinis, T. (2014) fMRI evidence for the involvement of the procedural memory system in morphological processing of a second language. *PLoS One* 9 (5), e97298.

Polinsky, M. (2007) Incomplete acquisition: American Russian. *Journal of Slavic Linguistics* 14 (2), 191–262.

Polinsky, M. (2008) Gender under incomplete acquisition: Heritage speakers' knowledge of noun categorization. *Heritage Language Journal* 6 (1), 40–71.

Polinsky, M. (2011) Reanalysis in adult heritage language. New evidence in support of attrition. *Studies in Second Language Acquisition* 33 (2), 305–328.

Polka, L., Rvachew, S. and Mattock, K. (2007) Experiential influences on speech perception and speech production in infancy. In E. Hoff and M. Shatz (eds) *Blackwell Handbook of Language Development* (pp. 153–172). Oxford: Blackwell Publishing.

Poplack, S. (1980) 'Sometimes I start a sentence in English y termino en espanõl': Toward a typology of code-switching. *Linguistics* 18 (7), 581–618.

Portes, A. and Hao, L. (1998) Bilingualism and language loss in the second generation. *Sociology of Education* 71 (4), 269–294.

Portes, A. and Schauffler, R. (1994) Language and the second generation: Bilingualism yesterday and today. *International Migration Review* 28 (4), 640–661.

Pöyhönen, S. and Simpson, J. (2017) The story of Tailor F: Seeking asylum in the Northern periphery. Paper presented at the 50th British Association for Applied Linguistics conference (Leeds, 31 August – 2 September).

Puco, N. (2007) Using manipulatives to improve decoding skills. Unpublished MA dissertation, Caldwell College.

Purcell-Gates, V., Degener, S., Jacobson, E. and Soler, M. (2002) Impact of authentic adult literacy instruction on adult literacy practices. *Reading Research Quarterly* 37 (1), 70–92.

Pynoos, R.S., Sorenson, S.B. and Steinberg, A.M. (1993) Interpersonal violence and traumatic stress reactions. In L. Goldberger and S. Bresnitz (eds) *Handbook of Stress: Theoretical and Clinical Aspects* (pp. 573–590). New York, NY: The Free Press.

Rastelli, S. (2018) Neurolinguistics and second language teaching: A view from the crossroads. *Second Language Research* 34 (1), 103–124.

Raude, E. and Winsnes, K. (2010) *Learning Basic Skills while Serving Time. Reading, Writing and Numeracy Training.* Oslo: Norwegian Agency for Lifelong Learning.

Read, C., Zhang, Y-F., Nie, H-Y. and Ding B-Q. (1986) The ability to manipulate speech sounds depends on knowing alphabetic writing. *Cognition* 24 (1–2), 31–44.

Reis, A. and Castro-Caldas, A. (1997) Illiteracy: A cause for biased cognitive development. *Journal of the International Neuropsychological Society* 3 (5), 444–450.

Rescorla, L. (2005) Age 13 language and reading outcomes in late-talking children. *Journal of Speech, Language and Hearing Research* 48 (2), 459–472.

Restrepo, M.A. and Guitiérrez-Clellen, V.F. (2004) Grammatical impairments in Spanish-English bilingual children. In B.A. Goldstein (ed.) *Bilingual Language Development and Disorders in Spanish-English Speakers* (pp. 213–234). Baltimore, MD: Brookes.

Reyes, I. (2006) Exploring connections between emergent biliteracy and bilingualism. *Journal of Early Childhood Literacy* 6 (3), 267–292.

Rice, R. and Wexler, K. (1996) Toward tense as a clinical marker of specific language impairment. *Journal of Speech, Language and Hearing Research* 39 (6), 1236–1257.

Roberge, P.T. (2011) Pidgins, creoles, and the creation of language. In M. Tallerman and K. Gibson (eds) *The Oxford Handbook of Language Evolution* (pp. 537–544). Oxford: Oxford University Press.

Robinson, P. and Ellis, N.C. (eds) (2008) *Handbook of Cognitive Linguistics and Second Language Acquisition*. London: Routledge.

Robson, B. (1982) Hmong literacy, formal education, and their effects on performance in an ESL class. In B. Downing and O. Douglas (eds) *The Hmong in the West* (pp. 201–225). Minneapolis, MN: Center for Urban and Regional Affairs.

Rodrigo, V., Greenberg, D., Burke, V., Hall, R., Berry, A., Brinck, T., Joseph, H. and Oby, M. (2007) Implementing an extensive reading program and library for adult literacy learners. *Reading in a Foreign Language* 19 (2), 106–119.

Rohde, A. (2005) *Lexikalische Prinzipien im Erst- und Zweitsprachenerwerb.* Trier: Wissenschaftlicher Verlag Trier.

Rohde, A. and Tiefenthal, C. (2002) On L2 lexical learning abilities. In P. Burmeister, T. Piske and A. Rohde (eds) *An Integrated View of Language Development: Papers in Honor of Henning Wode* (pp. 449–472). Trier: Wissenschaftlicher Verlag Trier.

Rothman, J. (2007) Heritage speaker competence differences, language change and input type: Inflected infinitives in heritage Brazilian Portuguese. *International Journal of Bilingualism* 11 (4), 359–389.

Rothman, J. (2008) Aspectual selection in adult L2 Spanish and the competing systems hypothesis: When pedagogical and linguistic rules conflict. *Languages in Contrast* 8 (1), 74–106.

Rothman, J. (2009) Understanding the nature and outcomes of early bilingualism: Romance languages as heritage languages. *International Journal of Bilingualism* 13 (2), 155–163.

Rothman, J., Tsimpli, I. and Pascual y Cabo, D. (2016) Formal linguistic approaches to heritage language acquisition: Bridges for pedagogically oriented research. In D. Pascual y Cabo (ed.) *Advances in Spanish as a Heritage Language* (pp. 13–26). Amsterdam: John Benjamins.

Rubin, J. and Thompson, I. (1994) *How to be a More Successful Language Learner* (2nd edn). Boston, MA: Heinele and Heinele.

Ruuska, K. (2016) Between ideologies and realities: Multilingual competence in a languagised world. *Applied Linguistics Review* 7 (3), 353–374.

Saeed, J.I. (2016) *Semantics.* Oxford: Wiley Blackwell.

Sampson, G. (1985) *Writing Systems. A Linguistic Introduction*. Stanford, CA: Stanford University.

Sandwall, K. (2013) *Att hantera praktiken. Om sfi-studerandes möjligheter till interaktion och lärande på praktikplatser. Göteborgstudier in nordisk språkvetenskap 20*. Gothenburg: University of Gothenburg.

Santos, M.G. and Shandor, A. (2012) The role of classroom talk in the creation of 'safe spaces' in adult ESL classrooms. In P. Vinogradov and M. Bigelow (eds) *Low Educated Second Language and Literacy Acquisition. Proceedings of the 7th Symposium* (pp. 110–134). Minneapolis, MN: University of Minnesota.

Saville-Troike, M. (1991) Teaching and testing for academic achievement: The role of language development. *NCBE FOCUS: Occasional Papers in Bilingual Education* 4 (1), 1–11.

Schellekens, P. (2007) *The Oxford ESOL Handbook*. Oxford: Oxford University Press.

Schellekens, P. (2011) *Teaching and Testing the Language Skills of First and Second Language Speakers*. Cambridge: Cambridge ESOL.

Schimke, S. (2013) Dummy verbs and the acquisition of verb raising in L2 German and French. In E. Blom, I. van de Craats and J. Verhagen (eds) *Dummy Auxiliaries in First and Second Language Acquisition* (pp. 307–338). Berlin: De Gruyter Mouton.

Schmidt, R.W. (1990) The role of consciousness in second language learning. *Applied Linguistics* 11 (2), 129–158.

Schwartz, B.D. (1993) On explicit and negative data effecting and affecting competence and linguistic behavior. *Studies in Second Language Acquisition* 15 (2), 147–163.

Schwartz, B.D. (1997) On the basis of the Basic Variety. *Second Language Research* 13 (4), 386–403.

Schwartz, B.D. and Eubank, L. (1996) Introduction: What is the 'L2 initial state'? *Second Language Research* 12 (1), 1–5.

Schwartz, B.D. and Sprouse, R.A. (1996) L2 cognitive states and the Full Transfer/Full Access model. *Second Language Research* 12 (1), 40–72.

Schwartz, B.D. and Sprouse, R. (2013) Generative approaches and the poverty of the stimulus. In J. Herschensohn and M. Young-Scholten (eds) *Cambridge Handbook of Second Language Acquisition*. Cambridge: Cambridge University Press.

Schwartz, B.D. and Tomaselli, A. (1990) Some implications from an analysis of German word order. In W. Abraham, W. Kosmeijer and E. Reuland (eds) *Issues in Germanic Syntax* (pp. 251–274). Berlin: Mouton de Gruyter.

Schwarz, R. (2005) Taking a closer look at struggling ESOL learners. *Focus on Basics Connecting Research and Practice* 8 (A), 29–33.

Schwarz, R. (2008) Assuring Success for Non/pre-literate ESOL Learners. See https://slideplayer.com/slide/6294261/ (accessed November 2019).

Schwarz, R. (2009) Issues in identifying learning disabilities for English language learners. In J. Taymans (ed.) *Learning to Achieve: A Review of the Research Literature on Serving Adults with Learning Disabilities* (pp. 73–117). Washington, DC: National Institute for Literacy.

Scott, S.K. and Wise, R.J. (2003) Functional imaging and language: A critical guide to methodology and analysis. *Speech Communication* 41 (1), 7–21.

Seals, C.A. and Peyton, J.K. (2017) Heritage language education: Valuing the languages, literacies, and cultural competencies of immigrant youth. *Current Issues in Language Planning* 18 (1), 87–101.

Sebastian-Galles, N. (2010) Bilingual language acquisition: Where does the difference lie? *Human Development* 53 (5), 245–255.

Seidenberg, M.S. and McClelland, J.L. (1989) A distributed, developmental model of word recognition and naming. *Psychological Review* 96 (4), 523–568.

Seliger, H.W. (1978) Implications of a multiple critical period hypothesis for second language learning. In W.C. Ritchie (ed.) *Second Language Research: Issues and Implications* (pp. 11–19). London: Academic Press.

Selinker, L. (1972) Interlanguage. *International Review of Applied Linguistics in Language Teaching* 10 (3), 209–231.

Senghas, A. and Coppola, M. (2001) Children creating language: How Nicaraguan Sign Language acquired a spatial grammar. *Psychological Science* 12 (4), 323–328.

Serratrice, L., Sorace, A. and Paoli, S. (2004) Crosslinguistic influence at the syntax–pragmatic interface: Subjects and objects in English–Italian bilingual and monolingual acquisition. *Bilingualism: Language and Cognition* 7 (3), 183–205.

Seymour, P.H., Aro, M. and Erskine, J.M. (2003) Foundation literacy acquisition in European orthographies. *British Journal of Psychology* 94 (2), 143–174.

Silva-Corvalán, C. (1994) *Language Contact and Change. Spanish in Los Angeles.* Oxford: Oxford University Press.

Simpson, J. (2006) Differing expectations in the assessment of the speaking skills of ESOL learners. *Linguistics and Education* 17 (1), 40–55.

Simpson, J. (2015) English language learning for adult migrants in superdiverse Britain. In J. Simpson and A. Whiteside (eds) *Adult Language Education and Migration: Challenging Agendas in Policy and Practice* (pp. 200–213). London: Routledge.

Singleton, K. (n.d.) Picture stories for adult ESL health literacy. See http://www.cal.org/caela/esl_resources/Health/healthindex.html (accessed November 2019).

Slabakova, R., White, L. and Brambatti Guzzo, N. (2017) Pronoun interpretation in the second language: Effects of computational complexity. *Frontiers in Psychology* 8 (1236), 1–12.

Smyser, H. (2016) The Goldilocks of variability and complexity: The acquisition of mental orthographic representations in emergent refugee readers. Unpublished PhD dissertation, University of Arizona.

Sonnenschein, S. and Schmidt, D. (2000) Fostering home and community connections to support children's reading. In L. Baker, M.J. Dreher and J.T. Guthrie (eds) *Engaging Young Readers: Promoting Achievement and Motivation* (pp. 264–284). New York, NY: Guilford.

Spada, N. and Tomita, Y. (2010) Interactions between type of instruction and type of language feature: A meta-analysis. *Language Learning: A Journal of Research in Language Studies* 60 (2), 263–308.

Spiegel, M. and Sunderland, H. (2006) *Teaching Basic Literacy to ESOL Learners.* London: Learning Unlimited.

Stanovich, K.E. (1980) Toward an interactive-compensatory model of individual differences in the development of reading fluency. *Reading Research Quarterly* 16 (1), 32–71.

Stanovich, K.E. (1992) Speculations on the causes and consequences of individual differences in early reading acquisition. In P.B. Gough, L.C. Ehri and R. Treiman (eds) *Reading Acquisition* (pp. 307–342). Hillsdale, NJ: Erlbaum Associates.

Steiner, J. (2003) Aphasie. In M. Grohnfeldt (ed.) *Lehrbuch der Sprachheilpädagogik und Logopädie. Erscheinungsformen und Störungsbilder: Band 2* (pp. 205–218) Stuttgart: Kohlhammer.

Stockmann, W. (2006) Portfolio methodology for literacy learners: The Dutch case. In J. Kurvers, I. van de Craats and M. Young-Scholten (eds) *Low-educated Second Language and Literacy Acquisition: Proceedings of the Inaugural Symposium* (pp. 152–164). Utrecht: Landelijki Onderzoekschool Taalwetenschap.

Stowe, L.A., Haverkort, M. and Zwarts, F. (2005) Rethinking the neurological basis of language. *Lingua* 115 (7), 997–1042.

Street, B. (1984) *Literacy in Theory and Practice.* Cambridge: Cambridge University Press.

Strömmer, M. (2017) *Mahdollisuuksien rajoissa: Neksusanalyysi suomen kielen oppimisesta siivoustyössä.* Jyväskylä: University of Jyväskylä.

Strube, S. (2007) Bridging the gap in the LESLLA classroom: A look at scaffolding. In I. van de Craats and R. van Hout (eds) *Adult Literacy, Second Language, and Cognition: Proceedings of the 2014 LESLLA Symposium* (pp. 149-164). Nijmegen: Centre for Language Studies.

Strube, S. (2014) *Grappling with the Oral Skill: The Learning and Teaching of the Low-literate Adult Second Language Learner.* Utrecht: Landelijki Onderzoekschool Taalwetenschap.

Strube, S., van de Craats, I. and van Hout, R. (2009) Telling picture stories: Relevance and coherence in texts of the non-literate L2 learner. In T. Wall and M. Leong (eds) *Low-educated Adult Second Language and Literacy Acquisition: 5th Symposium* (pp. 52–63). Calgary: Bow Valley College.

Stubbs, M. (1987) An Educational Theory of (Written) Language. See https://eric.ed.gov/?id=ED346738 (accessed November 2019).

Suni, M. (2008) *Toista kieltä vuorovaikutuksessa. Kielellisten resurssien jakaminen toisen kielen omaksumisen alkuvaiheessa.* Jyväskylä: University of Jyväskylä.

Tammelin-Laine, T. (2014) *Aletaan alusta. Luku- ja kirjoitustaidottomat aikuiset uutta kieltä oppimassa.* Jyväskylä: University of Jyväskylä.

Tammelin-Laine, T. and Martin, M. (2015) The simultaneous development of receptive skills in an orthographically transparent second language. *Writing Systems Research* 7 (1), 39–57.

Tarnanen, M., Junttila, J. and Westinen, E. (2009) Kohti monimediaisia tekstitaitoja: mihin maahanmuuttajataustaiset aikuiset käyttävät tietokonetta ja miten he siihen suhtautuvat? In J. Kalliokoski, T. Nikko, S. Pyhäniemi and S. Shore (eds) *Puheen ja kirjoituksen moninaisuus. AFinLAn vuosikirja* (pp. 175–191). Jyväskylä: AFinLA.

Tarone, E. and Bigelow, M. (2005) Impact of literacy on oral language processing: Implications for SLA research. *Annual Review of Applied Linguistics* 25 (1), 77–97.

Tarone, E., Bigelow, M. and Hansen, K. (2009) *Literacy and Second Language Oracy*. Oxford: Oxford University Press.

Taylor, M. (1992) The language experience approach and adult learners. See http://www.cal.org/caela/esl_resources/digests/LEA.html (accessed November 2019).

Thomas, M. (2013) History of the study of second language acquisition. In J. Herschensohn and M. Young-Scholten (eds) *Cambridge Handbook of Second Language Acquisition* (pp. 26–45). Cambridge: Cambridge University Press.

Thornbury, S. (2002) *How to Teach Vocabulary*. London: Longman.

Tiefenthal, C. (2009) *Fast Mapping im Natürlichen Zweitsprachenerwerb*. Trier: WVT.

Tomasello, M. (2001) Perceiving intentions and learning words in the second year. In M. Bowerman and S.C. Levinson (eds) *Language Acquisition and Conceptual Development* (pp. 132–158). Cambridge: Cambridge University Press.

Tomasello, M. (2003) *Constructing a Language: A Usage-Based Theory of Language Acquisition*. Cambridge, MA: Harvard University Press.

Tomblin, J.B., Records, N.L., Buckwalter, P., Zhang, X., Smith, E. and O'Brien, M. (1997) The prevalence of specific language impairment in kindergarten children. *Journal of Speech Language Hearing Research* 40 (6), 1245–1260.

Treiman, R. and Zukowski, A. (1991) Levels of phonological awareness. In S.A. Brady and D.P. Shankweiler (eds) *Phonological processes in literacy: A tribute to Isabelle Y. Liberman* (pp. 67–83). Hillsdale, NJ: Lawrence Erlbaum.

Trupke-Bastidas, J. (2007) Phonics/Phonemic Awareness Activities for Teaching Low-level ESL Adults. Handout given at presentation at Minnesota Literacy Council (St. Paul, MN, February 2007).

Ullman, C. (1997) *Social Identity and the Adult ESL Classroom*. Washington, DC: National Center for ESL Literacy Education.

Ullman, M.T. (2001) The neural basis of lexicon and grammar in first and second language: The declarative/procedural model. *Bilingualism: Language and Cognition* 4 (2), 105–122.

Umbel, V.M., Pearson, B.Z., Fernandez, M.C. and Oller, D.K. (1992) Measuring bilingual children's receptive vocabularies. *Child Development* 63 (4), 1012–1020.

UNESCO (n.d.) Learning to live together. See http://www.unesco.org/new/en/social-and-human-sciences/themes/international-migration/glossary/migrant (accessed November 2019).

UNESCO Institute for Statistics. (2016) Literacy data release 2016. See http://www.uis.unesco.org/literacy/Pages/literacy-data-release-2016.aspx (accessed November 2019).

Unsworth, S. (2013) Assessing age of onset effects in (early) child L2 acquisition. *Language Acquisition* 20 (2), 74–92.

Upton, T. and Lee-Thompson, L. (2001) The role of the first language in second language reading. *Studies in Second Language Acquisition* 23 (4), 469–495.

Vainikka, A. and Young-Scholten, M. (1994) Direct access to X'-Theory: Evidence from Korean and Turkish adults learning German. In T. Hoekstra and B.D. Schwartz (eds) *Language Acquisition Studies in Generative Grammar* (pp. 265–316). Amsterdam: Benjamins.

Vainikka, A. and Young-Scholten, M. (1996) The early stages in adult L2 syntax: Additional evidence from Romance speakers. *Second Language Research* 12 (2), 140–176.

Vainikka, A. and Young-Scholten, M. (2005) The roots of syntax and how they grow: Organic Grammar, the Basic Variety and Processability Theory. In S. Unsworth, T. Parodi, A. Sorace and M. Young-Scholten (eds) *Paths of Development* (pp. 77–106). Amsterdam: Benjamins.

Vainikka, A. and Young-Scholten, M. (2011) *The Acquisition of German: Introducing Organic Grammar.* Berlin: de Gruyter.

Vainikka, A., Young-Scholten, M., Ijuin, C. and Jarad, S. (2017) Literacy in the development of L2 English morphosyntax. Paper presented at the 12th Annual Low-educated Second Language and Literacy Acquisition Conference (Granada, 8–10 September).

Valdés, G. (2000) Introduction. In L. Sandstedt (ed.) *Spanish for Native Speakers. Vol.1. AATSP Professional Development Series Handbook for Teachers K-16* (pp. 1–20). New York, NY: Harcourt College.

Valdés, G. (2001) Heritage language students: Profiles and possibilities. In J.K. Peyton, D.A. Ranard and S. McGinnis (eds) *Heritage Languages in America: Preserving a National Resource* (pp. 37–77). McHenry, IL: Delta Systems.

Valdés, G., Fishman, J., Chávez, R. and Pérez, W. (2006) *Developing Minority Language Resources: The Case of Spanish in California.* Clevedon: Multilingual Matters.

Van de Craats, I. and Young-Scholten, M. (2015) Developing technology-enhanced literacy learning for LESLLA learners. In M.G. Santos and A. Whiteside (eds) *Low Educated Second Language and Literacy Acquisition: Proceedings of the Ninth Symposium* (p. 129–150). San Francisco: Lulu.

Van de Craats, I. and van Hout, R. (2010) Dummy auxiliaries in the L2 acquisition of Moroccan learners of Dutch: Form and function. *Second Language Research* 26 (4), 473–500.

Van de Craats, I., Kurvers, J. and van Hout, R. (2015) Low-educated second language and literacy acquisition: Ten years on. In I. van de Craats, J. Kurvers and R. van Hout (eds) *Adult Literacy, Second Language and Cognition* (pp. 1–5). Nijmegen: Center for Language Studies.

Van Deusen-Scholl, N. (2003) Toward a definition of heritage language: Sociopolitical and pedagogical considerations. *Journal of Language, Identity and Education* 2 (3), 211–230.

Van Lier, L. (2000) From input to affordance: Social-interactive learning from an ecological perspective. In J.P. Lantolf (ed.) *Sociocultural Theory and Second Language Learning* (pp. 245–260). Oxford: Oxford University Press.

VanPatten, B., Williams, J., Rott, S. and Overstreet, M. (eds) (2004) *Form-Meaning Connections in Second Language Acquisition.* London: Lawrence Erlbaum.

Vermeersch, L., Drijkoningen, J., Vienne, M. and Vandenbroucke, A. (2008) Assessing adult literacy: The aim, use and benefits of standardized screening tools. In I. van de Craats and J. Kurvers (eds) *Low-educated Adult Second Language and Literacy Acquisition: Symposium Proceedings* (pp. 121–131). Antwerp: Landelijki Onderzoekschool Taalwetenschap.

Vertovec, S. (2007) Superdiversity and its implications. *Ethnic and Racial Studies* 30 (6), 1024–1054.

Vinogradov, P. (2008) 'Maestra! The letters speak': Adult ESL students learning to read for the first time. *MinneWITESOL Journal* 25 (1), 1–12.

Vinogradov P. (2010) Balancing top and bottom: Learner-generated texts for teaching phonics. In T. Wall and M. Leong (eds) *Proceedings of the 5th Low-Educated Second Language and Literacy Acquisition Symposium* (pp. 3–14). Cologne: University of Cologne.

Vinogradov, P. (2013) Defining the LESLLA teacher knowledge base In T. Tammelin-Laine, L. Nieminen and M. Martin (eds) *Proceedings of the 8th Low-Educated Second Language and Literacy Acquisition Symposium* (pp. 9–24). Jyväskylä: Jyväskylä University Printing House.

Vinogradov, P. and Liden, A. (2009) Principled instruction for LESLLA instructors. In I. van de Craats and J. Kurvers (eds) *Proceedings of the 4th Low-educated Adult Second Language and Literacy Acquisition Symposium* (pp. 133–144). Utrecht: LOT.

Vinogradov, P. and Bigelow, M. (2010) Using oral language skills to build on the emerging literacy of adult English learners. See http://www.cal.org/caelanetwork/resources/using-oral-language-skills.html (accessed November 2019).

Volterra, V. and Taeschner, T. (1978) The acquisition and development of language by bilingual children. *Journal of Child Language* 5 (2), 311–326.

Von Stutterheim, C. (1984) Der Ausdruck der Temporalität in der Zweitsprache. Unpublished PhD thesis, Freie Universität Berlin.

Von Stutterheim, C. (1987) *Temporalität in der Zweitsprache.* Berlin: de Gruyter.

Vygotsky, L.S. (1978) *Mind in Society: The Development of Higher Psychological Processes*. Cambridge, MA: Harvard University Press.

Wagner, J. (2015) Designing for language learning in the wild: Creating social infrastructures for second language learning. In T. Cadierno and S.W. Eskildsen (eds) *Usage-based Perspectives on Second Language Learning* (pp. 75–104) Berlin: De Gruyter Mouton.

Wagner-Gough, J. (1978) Comparative studies in second language learning. In E. Hatch (ed.) *Second Language Acquisition. A Book of Readings*. Rowley, MA: Newbury House.

Wang, M., Park, Y. and Lee, K.R. (2006) Korean-English biliteracy acquisition: Cross-language phonological and orthographic transfer. *Journal of Educational Psychology* 98 (1), 148–158.

Wang, M., Perfetti, C.A. and Liu, Y. (2005) Chinese-English biliteracy acquisition: Cross-language and writing system transfer. *Cognition* 97 (1), 67–88.

Wangru, C. (2016) Vocabulary teaching based on semantic-field. *Journal of Education and Learning* 5 (3), 64–71.

Warriner D.S. (2009) Transnational literacies: Examining global flows through the lens of social practice. In M. Baynham and M. Prinsloo (eds) *The Future of Literacy Studies* (pp. 160–180). London: Palgrave Macmillan.

Wartenburger, I., Heekeren, H.R., Abutalebi, J., Cappa, S.F., Villringer, A. and Perani, D. (2003) Early setting of grammatical processing in the bilingual brain. *Neuron* 37 (1), 159–170.

Watkins D., Biggs, J. and Regmi, M. (1991) Does confidence in the language of instruction influence a student's approach to learning? *Instructional Science* 20 (4), 331–339.

Watson, J.A. (2010) Interpreting across the abyss: A hermeneutic exploration of initial literacy development by high school English language learners with limited formal schooling. Unpublished PhD dissertation, University of Minnesota.

Wei, L. (2007) Dimensions of bilingualism. In L. Wei (ed.) *The Bilingualism Reader* (pp. 3–24). Oxford: Routledge.

Whong, M. and K.-H. Gil (2018) What is in the textbook and what's in the mind: Polarity item any in learner English. *Studies in Second Language Acquisition* 40 (1), 91–118.

Wiley, T.W., Peyton, J.K., Christian, D., Moore, S.C. and Liu, N. (eds) (2014) *Handbook of Heritage, Community and Native American languages in the United States: Research, Educational Practice and Policy*. New York, NY: Routledge.

Wilkins, D. (1972) *Linguistics in Language Teaching*. London: Arnold.

Williams, A. and Chapman, L. (2007) Meeting diverse needs: Content-based language teaching and settlement needs for low-literacy adult ESL immigrants. In M. Young-Scholten (ed.) *Low-educated Second Language and Literacy Acquisition: Proceedings of the Third Annual Forum* (pp. 125–136). Durham: Roundtuit.

Williams, R. (1986) Top ten principles for teaching reading. *ELT Journal* 40 (1), 42–45.

Williamson, E. (2013) Our lives press. Inspiring through the experience of others. *National Association of English and Community Language Teaching to Adults News* 101 (1), 5.

Woodward, A. (2000) There is no silver bullet for word learning. Why monolithic accounts miss the mark. In R.M. Golinkoff and K. Hirsh-Pasek (eds) *Becoming a Word Learner: A Debate on Lexical Acquisition* (pp. 174–179). Oxford: Oxford University Press.

World Demographics Profile (2018) Index mundi. See https://www.indexmundi.com/world/demographics_profile.html (accessed November 2019).

Wray, A. (2002) *Formulaic Language and the Lexicon*. Cambridge: Cambridge University Press.

Wright, C., Piske, T. and Young-Scholten, M. (2018) *Mind Matters in SLA*. Bristol: Multilingual Matters.

Wrigley, H.S. (1993) Innovative programs and promising practices in adult ESL literacy. See http://www.ericdigests.org/1993/promising.htm (accessed November 2019).

Wrigley, H.S. (2009) Serving low literate immigrant and refugee youth: Challenges and promising practices. In T. Wall and M. Leong (eds) *Low-educated Adult Second Language and Literacy Acquisition: 5th Symposium* (pp. 25–41). Calgary: Bow Valley College.

Wrigley, H.S. and Guth, G. (1992) *Bringing Literacy to Life*. Washington, DC: Office of Vocational and Adult Education.

Yaden, D.B., Madrigal, P. and Tam, A. (2003) Access to books and beyond: Creating and learning from a book lending program for Latino families in the inner city. In G.G. Garcia (ed.) *English Learners: Reaching the Highest Level of English Literacy* (pp. 357–386). Newark, DE: International Reading Association.

Yarbay-Duman, T., Blom, E. and Topba, S. (2015) At the intersection of cognition and grammar: Deficits comprehending counterfactuals in Turkish children with specific language impairment. *Journal of Speech, Language and Hearing Research* 58 (2), 410–421.

Young-Scholten, M. (2013) Low-educated immigrants and the social relevance of second language acquisition research. *Second Language Research* 29 (4), 441–454.

Young-Scholten, M. (2015) Who are adolescents and adults who develop literacy for the first time in an L2, and why are they of research interest? *Writing Systems Research* 7 (1), 1–3.

Young-Scholten, M. and Ijuin, C. (2006) How can we best measure adult ESL student progress? *TESOL Adult Education Interest Section Newsletter* 4 (2), 1–4.

Young-Scholten, M. and Strom, N. (2006) First-time L2 readers: Is there a critical period? In I. van de Craats, J. Kurvers and M. Young-Scholten (eds) *Low-educated Second Language and Literacy Acquisition: Proceedings of the Inaugural Symposium* (pp. 45–68). Utrecht: Landelijki Onderzoekschool Taalwetenschap (LOT).

Young-Scholten, M. and Naeb, R. (2010) Non-literate L2 adults' small steps in mastering the constellation of skills required for reading. In T. Wall and M. Leong (eds) *Low Educated Adult Second Language and Literacy: Research, Practice and Policy, 5th Symposium* (pp. 80–91). Calgary: Bow Valley College.

Young-Scholten, M. and Limon, H. (2015) Creating new fiction for low-educated immigrant adults: Leapfrogging to digital. *The International Journal of the Book* 13 (4), 1–9.

Young-Scholten, M., Faux, N. and Peyton, J. (2015a) 'Online teacher development delivered internationally: Can it be done?' Paper presented at the 11th LESLLA symposium (St. Augustine, FL, 11–13 November).

Young-Scholten, M., Sosinski, M. and Rubio, A.M. (2015b) Undergraduates' involvement in producing short fiction books for immigrant adult beginners in England and Spain. *Language Issues: The ESOL Journal* 26 (1), 55–60.

Zahedi, Y. and Abdi, M. (2012) The impact of imagery strategy on EFL learners' vocabulary learning. *Procedia – Social and Behavioral Sciences* 69 (2012), 2264–2272.

Zentella, A.C. (1999) *Growing up Bilingual*. Malden, MA: Blackwell Publishers.

Zobl, H. (1980) Developmental and transfer errors: Their common bases and (possibly) differential effects on subsequent learning. *TESOL Quarterly* 14 (4), 469–479.

Glossary

3D job: dirty, dangerous, demanding and dead-end job.

Abugida; abudiga script: a writing system in which characters are composed of a principal consonant symbol and vowel notation is secondary; also known as **alphasyllabary**. It comes from the first four letters of the Ethiopian name for the Ge'ez script.

Acquisition-learning distinction or **acquisition vs learning of a language**: attributed to Steven Krashen (1985), the idea that acquisition of a language is an automatic, subconscious process, whereas learning is an effortful, conscious process.

Adult learner: a learner who is beyond compulsory school age, usually age 16 or older.

Affective filter hypothesis: predicts that motivation, self-confidence, self-esteem and anxiety play a role in second language acquisition.

Affective strategies: concerned with emotions, feelings and attitudes, where the relevant strategies are responsible for building and maintaining self-confidence; e.g. through positive self-talk and self-assurance that the performance of a particular task is achievable for the learner.

Affordance: learning opportunity provided by the environment and perceived by the learner as worthwhile; e.g. to learn a specific language (see van Lier, 2004).

Alphabet: a type of writing system where graphemes represent phonemes.

Alphabetic literacy: literacy in a language that uses the Roman alphabet; e.g. English, German, Finnish, modern-day Turkish.

Alphabetic principle: graphemes are linked to phonemes in alphabetic orthographies.

Alphabetic stage in reading development: the reader starts to detect systematic associations between sounds and spelling before becoming proficient in reading unfamiliar words.

Alphasyllabary: a writing system which resembles both a syllabary and an alphabet in which characters are composed of a principal consonant symbol and secondary vowel notation; also known as **abugida script**.

Analogy model: word decoding is claimed to occur when the emergent reader applies memorized patterns to regularly and irregularly spelled words.

Analytical approach to literacy teaching: teaching that starts with the study of sentences or words and then continues with smaller units.

Ancestral language: the family language of heritage speakers.

Antonym: adjective pairs that denote opposite meanings; e.g. hot – cold, old – young, good – bad, true – false.

Aphasia: an acquired language disorder, caused by stroke, head injury, migraines, brain tumour or neurological conditions which adversely influence the knowledge and/or use of language.

Articles: determiners which can mark definiteness, where both speaker and hearer presuppose the existence of a unique entity and can mark specificity where the speaker refers to a unique entity (Ionin *et al.*, 2004: 5). In 'I was scared of the grey parrot flying above me'; 'the' has both definite and specific reference'; in 'The grey parrot can be found in Africa' 'the' has definite but not specific reference; in 'A grey parrot was perched on his shoulder' 'a' has specific but not definite reference; and in 'A parrot can be quite smart' 'a' has neither definite nor specific reference.

Aspect: distinct from tense, aspect is a grammatical category associated with verbs, which refers to how an action, event or state does or does not extend over time. Lexical aspect, which may or may not be grammatically marked in language, refers to a verb's (or predicate's) inherent properties, as in states 'own' vs. activities 'bake' vs. accomplishments 'bake a cake' and achievements 'arrive'. (See also **imperfective aspect, perfective aspect** and **infinitives**.)

Attention span: the amount of attention that an individual is able to give to a text, task or project for a period of time.

Atypical language development: divergence from the typical patterns of language development.

Audio Lingual Method: a foreign language teaching method developed in the United States in the 1950s by linguists at the University of Michigan. The method involves dialogue memorization and drilling, with the aim of eliminating L1 influence by preventing learners from speaking spontaneously.

Authentic texts: written texts from real life, sometime brought into class for reading and discussion.

Basic level (of conceptualization): a specific way of expressing the name of an entity; e.g. dog rather than animal, car rather than vehicle.

Basic Variety: Klein and Perdue's account of language learners' earliest linguistic system whose organization follows the core characteristics of human language rather than that of a fully fledged, complex language (Klein & Perdue, 1997). For example, adult second language learners with little or no L1 literacy or formal education, having started with the Basic Variety sometimes do not progress any further if their L2 exposure is limited.

Bare verb: a verb without any of the suffixes which would normally mark tense, aspect or agreement in a given language.

Bilingual-specific language impairment: language learning disabilities experienced by bilingual individuals.

Bottom-up approach to reading: aims at understanding a text by starting with its smallest units, words or even letters, and then moving to phrases, clauses, sentences, paragraphs and an entire text. An approach often used by and with inexperienced readers.

Breadth of word knowledge: the number of words a person has stored in his/her mental lexicon.

Can-do statements: refer to what a learner is able to do with a language they are learning, at different levels at which the learner listens, speaks, reads and writes. For example, the learner can understand, speak, and write about the main idea and some pieces of information on familiar topics in texts that are spoken or written.

Canonical word order: the order in which words appear in a main, declarative clause in a language; e.g. SVO (subject-verb-object).

Case study: a study with one or only a few research participants.

CHILDES (Child Language Data Exchange System): the child language part of the TalkBank online database. Established in 1984 by Brian MacWhinney and Catherine Snow (MacWhinney & Snow, 1985), it now contains hundreds of publicly available corpora in a range of languages.

Chomskyan tradition: work in generative linguistics, both in syntax and phonology, and their acquisition where it is assumed that the capacity for language is innate and knowledge of a given language involves mental representations separate from those pertaining to general cognition.

Cloze activity: a learning activity in which letters or words are omitted from a passage and students fill in the blanks.

Code switching: the use of two languages within a sentence or in discourse.

Cognate(s): words in different languages that are similar due to a common etymological origin (e.g. *father* in English and *Vater* in German).

Cognitive academic skills: skills needed for success in school.

Cognitive mechanisms: mental mechanisms which are used to process information. In the SLA literature, these may be expressed as 'general cognitive mechanisms' to distinguish them from what are held to be purely linguistic mechanisms.

Cognitive processes: thinking procedures in charge of processing the information that we receive from the environment.

Cognitive strategies: these support the comprehension and/or production of language as they contribute to learning and problem solving. Examples are elaboration, linking information to previous knowledge, and inferencing.

Cohesion: a means of explicitly linking parts of a text; sentence to sentence, paragraph to paragraph, topic to topic. Among these means are repetition, substitution and use of certain adverbs.

Co-hyponym(s): words on the same hierarchical level in semantic organization; e.g. breeds of dogs such as Labrador, Poodle, German shepherd, Chihuahua.

Collocations: words or phrases that frequently occur together; e.g. 'Free as a bird', 'doing the dishes'.

Common European Framework of Reference for Languages (CEFR): a six-point scale (A1, A2, B 1, B2, C1, C2), developed in Europe, that describes in the form of can-do statements, from A1 up to C2, what second language learners are able to do at each level in terms of reception (listening and reading) and production (writing and speaking).

Compensation strategies: make up for missing knowledge and comprehension gaps; for example, when a person uses contextual clues or gestures to infer the meaning of a new word in an utterance or text or when a person describes the meaning of a word when he/she doesn't know or can't retrieve the word form.

Competing Systems Hypothesis (CSH) (Rothman, 2008): predicts differences between the role of pedagogically derived metalinguistic knowledge and knowledge that is acquired in natural contexts.

Complementizer: a conjunction which marks a complement clause; e.g. 'that' in 'I know that he left the building early'.

Comprehensible input: language that the learner hears or reads and understands.

Connectionist model of reading: an account of word decoding that involves the reader gradually forming both simple and complex mental representations through the repeated interaction of orthography, phonology and meaning.

Consolidated alphabetic stage in reading development: the last stage in reading development, when the grapheme-phoneme associations are automatically applied to multisyllabic words and to unfamiliar words of all types.

Consonant cluster: a sequence of consonants in the same syllable, either at the start of the syllable (in the syllable onset) or at the end of the syllable (in the syllable coda). Not all languages have the complex onsets and codas found in English syllables such as in the monosyllabic word, 'skint'. But in a language such as Mandarin, only 'sin' and 'kin' could be words because it only allows only a single consonant in the onset and a single consonant in the coda, from a highly restricted set of possible consonants.

Construction grammar: a theory of syntax dating back to Lakoff in which constructions are the central unit and the grammar of a language is made up of taxonomic networks of families of constructions; see Goldberg (1995); Lakoff (1987); Tomasello (2003). Constructions include those that are lexically fixed, such as idioms, as well as form-function pairings whose meanings are conventionalized. In the usage-based account of language acquisition, the learner engages in generalization when confronted by recurring use of constructions.

Contrastive Analysis Hypothesis: Lado's (1957) prediction that similarities between the learner's L1 and the L2 being learned will facilitate learning, while differences between the L1 and L2 will result in difficulties.

Corpora: collections of words, texts, or utterances based on a range of criteria; e.g. word frequency, genre, theme, era.

Counter-factuals: complex linguistic and cognitive processes which provide information about a hypothetical condition.

Critical literacy: a reader's ability to analyse written texts in order to detect the author's perspective, purpose, ideology and possibly discriminative elements.

Critical period: a period of resonance with specific input (e.g. for language, primary linguistic data) in development of a particular behaviour (e.g. use of the language) beyond which time that behavior will no longer develop. Lenneberg's (1967) Critical Period Hypothesis predicts that the acquisition of language is only successful if input is received between the ages of two and puberty.

Cross-linguistic influence: the interaction between the languages of the bilingual individual or second language learner.

Cross-sectional study: in language acquisition, a study which involves collecting data at one point in time from different groups of learners, at different levels of development.

Cultural awareness: the knowledge and understanding that people from other countries and other socio-economic or religious backgrounds may be different in terms of their attitudes, values and knowledge.

Declarative knowledge: knowledge as a set of facts. In second language acquisition processes, this refers to learners' knowledge of rules and paradigms which teachers or textbooks have explained and knowledge of words with their dictionary definitions. (See also **explicit knowledge**.)

Declarative sentence: a sentence which declares or states something, as opposed to asking a question.

Decoding: establishing the relationship between print and its phonological representation; in an alphabetic script, the process of associating graphemes with phonemes to read a word; also involves word recognition.

Depth of Processing Hypothesis: the idea that the storage of vocabulary items in the brain depends on cognitive engagement (see Craik & Lockhard, 1972).

Depth of word knowledge: how well a person knows a word; e.g. concerning its context, possible synonyms, connotations, etc.

Derivational affix: a bound morpheme which is attached to the beginning (prefix) or end (suffix) of a free lexical morpheme to create a new word and, thereby, changes the word class; e.g. danger (noun), dangerous (adjective), dangerously (adverb).

Derivational morphology: the process by which a new word is formed by adding certain morphology such as a prefix or suffix; e.g. un- in 'unhappy' and or –ness in 'happiness' to a root word 'happy'.

Determiner: a morpheme which introduces a noun. Examples in English are the article 'a', the demonstrative 'this', possessive 'her' and quantifier 'some' as in 'a book', 'this book', 'her book' and 'some books'. In English only one of these can precede the noun; 'a this book' and 'her some books' are ungrammatical.

Devanagari script: a writing system used in India and Nepal; it is an example of an **alphasyllabary**.

Dialogic approach: an instructional approach in which the teacher and a student or students interact, rather than the teacher presenting without such student participation. The goal of this approach is to shift the power dynamic from the teacher to students, to promote student engagement.

Differentiated instruction: second language instructional activities that have simpler and more complex versions to meet the needs of learners at different proficiency levels.

Digraph: two graphemes which represent one phoneme, e.g. the digraph <ph> represents the phoneme /f/ in <photo>.

Direct language learning strategies: strategies that *specifically* support *language* learning (as opposed to indirect language learning strategies, that are general learning strategies that support language learning but also other types of learning); examples of language learning strategies are using a word list and a dictionary to learn specific words.

Discrete-item test: one test item at a time is presented for the learner to respond to.

Distractor: in a test, a distractor is used as an incorrect alternative to the correct answer in order to check whether those taking the test are able to differentiate between the target item and a similar item (e.g. a semantically or phonologically similar word). The use of distractors is intended to make it harder for the learner/participant to simply guess the correct answer.

Dominant language: the language in which a bilingual or multilingual speaker has the greatest proficiency or the language that is used more often.

Dual-language immersion school: academic settings where two languages are used orally and for literacy and academic content instruction for all students.

Dual route model of reading: the reader follows the phonological route for regularly spelled words (associating individual phonemes with graphemes) and memorizes irregular words as a whole.

Dummy auxiliaries: a helping verb with no meaning but which serves a grammatical function. English questions with main verbs, no modals, and no other auxiliaries are only grammatical with dummy 'do' as in: 'What do you see?' and 'Do you see him?' (vs. 'What can you see?' and 'Can you see him?' with the modal 'can'). This term is also used to refer to language learners' overuse of auxiliaries to mark a grammatical function which it does not mark in the target language.

Emerging reader: a person learning to read; usually refers to those at lower stages of the learning process, but not to absolute beginners.

Emergentist theory of language acquisition: the idea that language acquisition is a general cognitive process based on the interaction of biological pressures and the environment. Under this view, as distinct from the generative view, the properties of language emerge based on the human brain's perception and processing of the input received. (See also usage-based accounts, discussed in Tomasello, 2003; MacWhinney, 1999.)

Empty subject: or 'null subject' is a pronoun which is not phonetically realized, i.e. not spoken or written, in a finite clause. English does not allow null subjects; it requires an overt pronoun subject in a finite clause, as in the sentence, 'John says he has no money'. Spanish allows such subjects and the subject 'he' can be empty/null, as in *Juan dice que no tiene dinero*. The pronoun *el* 'he' not only can be null, but it should be unless there is special emphasis on the pronoun; e.g. to distinguish that it's he (*el*) rather than she (*ella*) who has no money.

Ethnography: a qualitative in-depth research method commonly applied in various disciplines focusing on cultural phenomena.

Evolutionist perspective of the history of writing systems: writing systems evolve over time and become more efficient; supporters of this perspective regard the alphabetic writing system as the most efficient and the most evolved.

Explicit knowledge: the result of explicit learning. (See also **declarative knowledge.**)

Explicit learning: takes place when we notice, focus on, and have our attention drawn to (for example) a new word in order to acquire its meaning (explicit memory strategies). It requires considerable attentional resources. This also refers to the conscious learning of rules, paradigms, and definitions from the textbook or teacher's explanations.

Executive Functioning system: the cognitive system which controls processes needed to regulate our thoughts and behaviours in many aspects of life.

Extensive reading: reading based on an individual's choice of text and decisions on when, where, and how to read that text. Also referred to as free voluntary reading and pleasure reading.

Eye gaze: where the speaker is looking while talking.

Eye tracking: an experimental technique which involves instruments which track a study participant's eye movements as they carry out a task. In language learning, the task may involve listening to words or sentences one by one while reading a text or viewing a visual display. The eyes are monitored or tracked to see, for example, where they first look, where they next look, and where they look for longer and shorter periods of time (usually measured in milliseconds).

Failed Functional Features Hypothesis: the belief that it is impossible for an adult L2 learner to acquire certain functional features which are not part of their L1; for example, English speakers confronted with gender marking on the articles which precede nouns in German (Hawkins & Chan, 1997).

Fast mapping: the ability to store meaning aspects of a word upon hearing it only once or just a few times.

Finite form: of a verb refers to syntactic patterns where the verb is marked for tense, aspect, modality, person or number.

First exposure studies: a relatively new line of inquiry (see Gullberg *et al.*, 2010) where individuals listen to an unfamiliar language for a short time (sometimes only a matter of minutes). This may often involve listening while watching a video depicting something otherwise familiar, such as a weather report. Researchers then examine what study participants have subconsciously picked up on, usually phonological properties or meanings of words in the unfamiliar language. Results show that second language learners, regardless of age, are able to break into the stream of speech, which in its aural form does not separate words from each other.

First language: the language to which the child is exposed from birth. Also referred to as **native language.**

Flash cards: cards with pictures/drawings or written forms of objects, used for instruction in the classroom.

Fluency: natural, smooth, often rapid, and effortless use of language (Crystal, 1987), with minimum hesitations and unfilled pauses (Chambers, 1997).

Foreign language learning: learning that does not take place where the language is commonly spoken (e.g. Spanish learned in Finland) but rather in formal learning environments (language courses) and quite often without any regular opportunities to use the language outside the classroom, in daily life.

Formal vs. informal register: 'register' refers to a speaking or writing style that is characteristic for a specific communication situation; a formal register is used for official, professional, or academic purposes. An informal register is used when communicating in a more personal context; e.g. when communicating with friends or family members.

Formative assessment: the evaluation of students' progress toward a goal, conducted at regular intervals, with the teacher issuing feedback to help the student improve their achievement. Also used by teachers to determine the next focus of instruction.

Formulaic language/sequences/speech: words that co-occur, as in idioms ('You hit the nail on the head', meaning 'You are absolutely right'), and also in frequent and conventionalized word-meaning pairings or grammatical constructions such as 'My name is…' and 'Do you know…' A language learner may memorize these and other frequent sequences as chunks without breaking them down into their constituent parts and functions. (See also **holistic chunks**.)

Free voluntary reading: another term for **extensive reading** or pleasure reading, where the individual chooses a text and then reads when, how, and where (in or outside of class) they decide to.

Frequency (of words): see **high-frequency words.**

Full alphabetic stage in reading development: when a reader has developed the awareness of phoneme-grapheme correspondences for all of the letters of an alphabet in order to decode familiar and unfamiliar words.

Full Transfer/Full Access hypothesis: the idea that the learner's starting point when acquiring a second language is the full transfer of their L1 syntax and as acquisition proceeds, he or she is able to go beyond their L1 with the help of full access to Universal Grammar.

Functional category; functional morphology: One of the two major categories, with lexical category, into which words can be grouped. Indicates a grammatical functional such as the –ed morpheme, which marks tense in English. Function words and morphemes (those which mark a grammatical function) are a closed class, to which new items are rarely added. Nouns, verbs, adjectives are an open class lexical category to which new words are regularly added.

Functional elements: items that carry the grammatical content of a sentence, such as auxiliary verbs, tense or agreement markers, without which a sentence is ungrammatical.

Functional grammar: originated by Halliday (1994), this theory is concerned with how the social and pragmatic functions of language determine a network of systems for making meaning through grammar.

Functional literacy/functional reading skills: being able to engage in the activities that require literacy for effective functioning in society and for developing needed skills and knowledge for oneself and the community.

General cognition: see **cognitive mechanisms**.

Generative approach, generative linguistics; generative view of language: a school of thought attributed to Noam Chomsky in the late 1950s, which assumes that the capacity for language and its acquisition are innate. (See also **Chomskyan tradition.**) Language involves a set of rules or principles that formally includes all possible expressions in a natural language and excludes all impossible ones, either in syntax or phonology. (For further elaboration, see, e.g. De Villiers & Roeper, 2011.)

Generative theme: topics of interest for new readers that provide a framework for the texts that are selected for use in a literacy class, based on Paulo Freire's 'generative word' method (Freire, 1970/1993).

Generative word method: a literacy teaching method in which learners learn words in context and generate the words that they will work with.

Grapheme: the smallest unit of a writing system of a language. A grapheme may or may not carry meaning by itself, and may or may not correspond to a single phoneme of the spoken language. Graphemes include alphabetic letters, typographic ligatures, Chinese characters, numerical digits, punctuation marks and other individual symbols.

Grapheme-phoneme conversion: the mental process in which a reader links phonemes (sounds) with graphemes (representations of those sounds).

Great Divide: the purported fundamental division in modes of thinking (e.g. pre-logical, pre-rational and concrete vs logical, rational, and scientific) and in sophistication (primitive vs. civilized) between non-literate and literate societies and the individuals within them.

Guest workers: the English translation of *Gastarbeiter*, referring to migrant workers who were granted visas for a limited period to work in then West Germany from 1955 to 1973.

Heritage language: a language spoken at home and in the immediate community and not widely used outside the home/community environment.

High-frequency words: words which occur very often in the spoken or written versions of a language.

Higher-level reading skills: top-down skills related to recognition and processing words in longer texts and text comprehension. Text comprehension is less automatic and more reflexive than with lower-lever skills.

Hiragana: Japanese syllabic writing used mainly for function words.

Holistic chunks: words consisting of more than one morpheme or expressions consisting of more than one word which are learned, stored, or used as if they were single words. (See also **formulaic language/sequences/speech.**)

Home language: the language learned in one's home country, one's country of origin and spoken at home.

Hsing Sheng: a type of Chinese writing in which a character combines meaning and pronunciation elements.

Hypernym: the superordinate word in a given hierarchy/taxonomy; e.g. 'flower' is a hypernym to 'rose', 'plant' is a hypernym to 'flower'.

Hyponym: the subordinate word in a given hierarchy/taxonomy, e.g. 'rose' is a hyponym to 'flower'; 'flower' is a hyponym to 'plant'.

Ice-breaker: an activity, usually done at the start of a group session, designed to get participants talking and acquainted with each other.

Immigrant: individuals who resettle in a country other than their country of origin, regardless of their status (e.g. asylum seeker, refugee, chain migrant), and have the expectation of remaining in the country.

Imperfective aspect: an event which extends over time or is habitual or repeated regardless of when this takes place, in the past, present, or future; e.g. in English, past – 'I was talking to my mother when you called'; present – 'I'm cooking dinner at the moment, and I'll have to call you back'; future – 'He'll be sleeping by 10:00, hopefully'.

Implicit knowledge: the end result of implicit learning of which a person is not consciously aware and may not be able to articulate to others. Overall linguistic competence, apart from knowledge of specific linguistic features, is an example of implicit knowledge. (See also **procedural knowledge.**)

Implicit learning: a process in which the learner acquires something, for example a word and its meaning indirectly, i.e. incidentally, without being instructed and possibly without even noticing that the word has been stored. It requires a sufficient amount of exposure.

Indirect strategies: support the learning process on a more general level (e.g. social or affective strategies) rather than processes that involve a focus on specific words or structures.

Inferencing: intelligent guessing, guessing the possible meaning of new words drawing on previous knowledge.

Infinitive: the form of a verb found in a non-finite clause. In English, for instance, infinitives are often marked with the auxiliary 'to', as in 'to walk' or uninflected forms of a verb, as in 'run' in 'John can run' in English.

Inflection/Inflected verbs: a process of word formation or the result of word formation where a morpheme is added to a word to mark tense and agreement; e.g. 'He looked at the picture' or 'He looks at the picture'.

Informal register: used when communicating in a more personal context; e.g. when communicating with friends or family members. (See **formal vs. informal register**.)

Initial state: a term used in theoretical second language acquisition research which refers to the starting point of learning an additional language; see also **Full Transfer/Full Access.**

Instruction: as opposed to uninstructed or naturalistic L2 acquisition, when input is from a textbook and teacher in the form of explicit explanation, presentation of paradigms and of words with their definitions, and which involves corrective feedback.

Integration training: orientation for immigrants in Finland to learn how to act and live in the country. It includes e.g. learning Finnish or Swedish, and becoming familiar with Finnish society.

Intensive reading: reading of texts, often short ones and performed in the classroom, with a clear pedagogical or academic purpose and usually with teacher guidance.

Intercomprehension: originally referring to the ability of speakers of languages belonging to the same linguistic family (for example Slavic, Romance or Germanic) to understand each other or understand written texts in the same family without knowing the language.

Interlanguage: the evolving system that the second language learner subconsciously creates in his or her mind in response to target language input that involves both influence of the native language and universals of language.

The International Adult Literacy Survey (**IALS**) and **Second International Adult Literacy Survey** (**SIALS**): international large-scale comparative assessments designed to identify and measure a range of adult skills; the IALS was conducted in 1994 and 1998.

Interrogative utterances: asking questions or making requests.

Inter-syllabic awareness: an individual's awareness that words have a syllabic structure and ability to detect and manipulate syllables in a word.

Intra-syllabic awareness: an individual's awareness that a syllable has onset and rime and ability to detect and manipulate onsets and rimes in a syllable.

Irregular past tense verbs: in languages such as English, verbs which mark tense not by adding the same morpheme; e.g. –ed as in 'talk' - 'talked' but rather by varying their form as in 'speak' – 'spoke'.

Kana: Japanese syllabic writing; **hiragana** and **katakana** are its variants.

Katakana: Japanese syllabic writing used, for example, for loan vocabulary and transcription of foreign words.

Kinesthetic activities: instructional activities that involve students in physically manipulating objects as a learning strategy.

Knowledge: see **declarative, procedural, explicit, implicit knowledge.**

Language: see **dominant, heritage, home, native language.**

Language Experience Approach (LEA): an instructional approach that engages learners in writing about an authentic experience or activity with the teacher's or tutor's help, often in the form of acting as scribe. LEA builds on students' life experiences as the context for beginning reading and writing instruction.

Language family: languages which developed from one ancestral language, i.e. share the same roots.

Language input/output: language that the learner hears or reads (input); language that the learner produces orally or in writing (output).

Language learning awareness: reflection on one's own learning process; e.g. on learning strategies.

Language learning strategies: see **direct, indirect, affective, cognitive, compensation, memory, metacognitive strategies.**

Language of origin: see **heritage, home, native language.**

Language processing: a language speaker/user subconsciously makes sense of aural or written language in real time.

Learned language: see **acquisition-learning distinction; linguistic competence.** Language proficiency that is gained through conscious effort as in a classroom, under instruction.

Learner-centred approach: an instructional approach that emphasizes learner agency and includes conducting a needs assessment and involving learners in the choice of instructional topics, activities and expected outcomes.

Learner-friendly definition: a modified dictionary definition which is adapted to the learner's current language level.

Learning centres/stations: classroom centres where learners can choose what they want to do and work toward mastery of specific skills.

Learning strategies: cognitive, social, or affective operations and actions that aid the language acquisition process.

Lemma: contains all of the semantic and syntactic information about a word.

Lexeme: contains all of the phonological and morphological information about a word.

Lexical access: a mental process through which the basic sound/letter-meaning connections of language, lexical entries, are activated and retrieved from the long-term lexical/mental memory of language speakers.

Lexical entry: includes the lemma and the lexeme. These are connected by lexical pointers.

Lexical field: see **word field.**

Lexical pointers: According to Levelt (1989), lexical pointers link the two parts of a lexical entry, i.e. lemma and lexeme.

Lexical principles: guide first guesses as to what a given object word refers to. Markman (1989) distinguishes the whole-object assumption (as a default, children, in particular, take words to refer to objects in their entirety and not their colours, shapes or parts), the taxonomic assumption (words refer to objects of like kind) and the mutual exclusivity assumption (children prefer to know/use one word per object).

Lexical relations: include hyponymy, synonymy, antonymy; one word may simultaneously participate in a number of lexical relations; e.g. 'sad' is a hyponym of emotion and an antonym of 'happy'.

Lexical sets: groups of words that are related in meaning.

Lexicon: the vocabulary of a language.

Liberal adult education: studies that are provided by adult education centres, folk high schools, sports institutes, summer universities and study centres to improve adults' civic skills and to offer social studies, general education studies and studies for hobby-based or interest-based information and skills acquisition.

Linear text: horizontal text written row by row.

Linguistic competence: the subconscious knowledge which enables intuitive use of language. See **linguistic competence – learned linguistic knowledge distinction**.

Linguistic competence-learned linguistic knowledge distinction: the acquisition-learning distinction, as expressed in Schwartz (1993). Linguistic competence refers to knowledge that does not come from an explicit or conscious process. Learned linguistic knowledge, which draws on general cognitive mechanisms, involves conscious learning, typically in a classroom where rules are explained and errors are corrected.

Linguistic properties: core characteristics of a language.

Literacy: all reading and writing competencies. In a broader sense, includes attitude toward reading, the ability to use abstract language and competent ways of dealing with different media.

Literacy learner: an adult who is learning to read and write for the first time in a new language.

Logographic stage in reading development: when the reader recognizes logos, brands and signs by visual shape and has memorized sight words which are treated similarly to these.

Logographic writing system: a single written character represents a word or a larger unit; e.g. Chinese, Egyptian, Mayan.

Logogram: a written character that symbolizes a whole word in a logographic writing system.

Longitudinal study: a study carried out over a period of time; e.g. a year or several years, during which data are collected on a regular basis. Because such a study can result in a considerable amount of data, the number of participants is usually limited. In language acquisition studies, this can be as few as one individual.

Lower-level reading skills: bottom-up skills related to decoding, recognition of letters/graphemes; they are the basis of reading ability, need to be automatized in order for learners to gain fluency in reading, and are automatized in proficient readers.

Majority language: the language usually spoken by a majority of the population in a country or in a region of a country which is generally considered the official or the high-status language.

Meaning first vs. form first: two different ways of introducing a new word. Meaning first refers to the idea of introducing the meaning of the word before its pronunciation and spelling are introduced. Form first refers to introducing pronunciation and possibly spelling before meaning.

Meaning making: determining the meaning of a written text, using pictures, vocabulary and visual organization as guidance.

Memory strategies: individual strategies that help to store and retrieve newly gained information.

Mental lexicon: part of a person's long-term memory, where word knowledge is stored and organized.

Mental representation of language: syntactic, morphological, phonological, phonetic and semantic information that is stored in the human mind.

Metacognitive strategies: help to regulate our cognitive processes through focusing on, planning and evaluating our own processes of learning and problem solving.

Metalinguistic awareness: the ability to think and talk about the structure and characteristics of language. This awareness enables manipulation of the forms, structure and characteristics of language independently of their meaning.

Minimal pair: two words that differ by only one morpheme (or phoneme); e.g. in English, 'sip' and 'zip'; 'bus' and 'buzz'.

Morpheme: the smallest unit in a language – both words and affixes – which conveys meaning. For example, 'deregistered' is a single word, but it contains three morphemes: the derivational prefix 'de-', the root 'register' and the inflectional suffix '-ed'. Only 'register' is a free morpheme. The other two are bound morphemes.

Morpheme accuracy: one way in which language acquisition was measured in the cross-sectional studies of children by de Villiers and de Villiers (1973) and a study of L2 adults by Bailey *et al.* (1974).

Morphological awareness: a sub-category of metalinguistic awareness, related to thinking and talking about and manipulating morphemes.

Morphological knowledge: knowledge about how words are built in a specific language; e.g. how to indicate tense, number, and case or how to change the meaning or word class by adding derivational affixes.

Morphology: derivational, inflectional: derivational morphology - words to which the addition of an affix changes its word class or meaning; e.g. in English, register vs. deregister, meaning change; registration, word class change. **Inflectional morphology** involves the marking of grammatical functions through affixation, as in the '–ed' in 'register' vs. 'registered'.

Morphosyntactic development: the acquisition over time of word order in combination with functional morphology.

Morphosyntax: an area of grammar which includes morphology, syntax and the relation between those two areas.

Mother tongue: a person's first language/L1 and native language: the language a child learns from birth.

Multilevel classes: those with students with varying language and literacy skills, at varying levels.

Multiliteracies: the many ways that people practice literacy in their everyday lives in and outside of formal school settings; being literate in more than one language.

Multi-word chunks: group of words that are usually used together.

Mutual exclusivity assumption: there is a preference for one label per object.

Naming insight: young children's understanding that every object, action, or idea can be named and referred to with a word or an expression (see also **symbolic function**).

Native language: first language, L1, mother tongue: the language the child learns from birth.

Native speaker (NS): an individual who is indistinguishable from other members of their speech community in terms of their morphosyntax and phonology.

Naturalistically acquired: acquisition of a second or additional language without instruction.

Nature vs nurture debate: focuses on whether biological or genetic predispositions or input from and interaction with the environment determine human traits and behaviours, including language. (See, e.g. Bynum, 2002, on the 19th century origin of this binary.)

Neurobiological representation of language/neurolinguistic investigation: in neurolinguistics, the study of the human brain's mechanisms underlying the abstract knowledge of language and its comprehension and production. The study of the brain has advanced considerably since Broca published in 1865 findings from autopsies of 12 patients in his paper 'Localization of speech in the third left frontal cultivation' (see Berker *et al.*'s 1986 translation), inspiring others to locate various additional functions of language in the brain's right and left hemispheres.

Newcomers: recently arrived immigrants.

New literacies: literacy skills which have arisen with the rise of new technology, such as digital literacy.

Non-finite verbs: verb forms that do not show tense, person, or number. Typically, they are infinitive forms with and without 'to' (e.g. 'to go', 'go'). Refers to a verb that cannot appear on its own in a main clause, or to a clause without a finite verb. In English, the participle 'going' and infinitive 'go' are non-finite verbs, as in 'Going to school was something that she enjoyed' and 'I want him to go'.

Non-native speaker (NNS): someone who has started to learn a second language as a child, adolescent or adult after learning their mother tongue as a baby.

Non-referential pronoun: one which does not refer to a specific noun, as it would in a statement such as 'He wrote the book' and the speaker has already used that person's name in discourse. Pronouns such as 'it' and 'there' do not refer to specific nouns in uses such as 'It is cold outside' and 'There is a book on the table'.

Non-target-like: a learner's production that does not entirely match the L2.

Nordic Alfa Council: Nordic network of teachers and researchers working with L2 adults and adolescents with little or no native language schooling

Norm-referenced test: the scoring on such a test reveals how those who take it perform in relation to the average score, the norm. Performance is compared for test takers assumed otherwise to be equal; e.g. the same age or the same year/grade in school.

Noticing Hypothesis: Richard Schmidt's (1990) idea that learning the grammatical features of a new language requires noticing as the starting point of acquisition, for intake to occur.

Object pronouns: a type of personal pronoun that is used as a grammatical object, either as the direct or indirect object of a verb (e.g. 'He called him' or the object of a preposition (e.g. 'Give it to him'). In a full pronoun, all vowels and consonants are pronounced; e.g. 'him'. In a **reduced pronoun,** used in casual speech, vowels or consonants may be deleted or altered; for example, 'him' is produced as a single consonant, 'We saw 'm'.

Onset: the beginning element of a syllable; precedes the rime; e.g. 'str' in 'strike'.

Opaque (or deep) orthography: in languages such as English, in which in its written form there are words with no direct relationship between sounds and the graphemes that represent them; e.g. <f> and <ph> 'fantasy' and 'pharmacy'; <u>, 'umbrella' or 'Utah'.

Operational factors in instruction: focus on curriculum and subjects taught in school; materials available and used in the language; students' initial literacy; languages used in assessments; and involvement of teachers, parents, and community members.

Oral recasts: a language learner makes an error, and the conversational partner (e.g. a teacher or researcher or other interlocutor) repeats the utterance, producing the target, correct form.

Organic Grammar: the idea that the learner starts with rudimentary syntax (a bare VP) which in second language acquisition is based on the learner's L1. Under OG, continued access to Universal Grammar helps the learner posit functional projections over time as he or she receives more input. These projections are not based on the learner's L1.

Orthographic depth: the strength of the phoneme-grapheme (sound-symbol) correspondence of a language, usually depicted on a continuum of shallow to deep, or transparent to opaque. See **opaque orthography** and **transparent orthography**.

Orthographic knowledge: how written language represents spoken language. This may refer to knowing letter-sound correspondences (alphabetic writing systems), knowing and recognizing orthographic patterns, and storing whole orthographic representations of words.

Orthographic representation: the written form of a word, sentence or text.

Orthographic stage in reading development: when alphabetic processing becomes automatic and morphological awareness embellishes proficient reading.

Orthography: a written spelling system.

Outcome factors: these are concerned with expectations regarding ultimate proficiency in a language, subject matter mastery and sociocultural maturity.

Overextend: use of words to refer to a wider range of objects or ideas than a proficient or native speaker would use; e.g. using the word 'dog' to refer to all four-legged animals rather than just to dogs.

Overgeneralization: in language learning, the application of a rule when it is incorrect to do so; for example, use of '–ed' to form the past tense with irregular verbs that are already in the past tense; e.g. 'wented'.

Partial alphabetic stage in reading development: when a reader starts to make grapheme-phoneme correspondences to decode words.

Perceptual salience: during visual or aural information processing, attention is especially drawn to an object or stimulus that stands out in some way.

Perfective aspect: a bounded event or action which has been completed; e.g. 'She baked a cake'.

Phoneme: the smallest abstract unit in the phonology of a language; also see **minimal pair**.

Phonemic awareness: ability to detect and manipulate phonemes; awareness that syllable onsets and rimes consist of individual consonant and vowel phonemes.

Phenomenon of substantial generality: the order of language development found in the study conducted by Brown (1973) which can be applied to all children acquiring English and is evidence of children's innate predisposition for learning language.

Phonics: a bottom-up approach to language instruction that begins with the alphabet, sounds and syllables, with a focus on learning those, gradually building to working with longer texts.

Phonological awareness: the conscious realization that words are made up of syllables, that syllables consist of onsets and rimes and that these are made up of phonemes.

Phonological route model of reading: an account of word decoding by matching a grapheme or its combinations with corresponding phonemes and then blending them. In this model, the reader analyzes sequences of sounds into graphemes or grapheme combinations corresponding to a single phoneme.

Phonology: the branch of linguistics that deals with abstract systems of sounds at both a segmental (consonants and vowels) and suprasegmental (syllabus, rhythm, stress, intonation) level in a language or across languages.

Pictograph: a graphic/pictorial symbol for a word or phrase.

Pidgin: a system of communication which is syntactically simpler than natural languages and that may develop among groups of adults who do not share a common language.

Polycentric: has emerged independently in different places or has more than one centre.

Pragmatic knowledge: how language is used and interpreted in context by other speakers of a speech community. We know, for example, that the word 'dog' can be used as an insult in certain contexts or cultures, that a written text may serve a special purpose, or how to ask a question politely, depending on the relationship we have with the person or group we are talking to.

Pragmatics: the branch of linguistics focused on language in use and the contexts in which it is used, including such matters as deixis, the taking of turns in conversation, text organization, presupposition and implicature.

Prefix: a bound morpheme which is attached to the beginning of a root to create a new word. In derivational morphology, this can, for example in English, change its meaning as in 'pre-' in the word 'prefix' and 'precede'. (See also **derivational affix**.)

Pre-alphabetic stage in reading development: when the reader does not associate phonemes with graphemes and does not detect differences between words with similar visual shapes.

Print awareness: awareness of the functions and uses of print, the letters of the alphabet (in an alphabetic writing system), and the meanings of high-frequency words.

Pro-drop languages: languages such as Finnish, Spanish and Turkish which allow subjects to be empty or null in finite clauses.

Procedural knowledge: subconscious knowledge of how to do something, without always being able to articulate this knowledge. Procedural knowledge includes the knowledge that enables us to ride a bicycle and can include subconscious knowledge of language.

Processability Theory: Manfred Pienemann's (1998) approach to the development of morphosyntactic knowledge in the L2, where the learner restructures his/her L2 knowledge system based on processing principles and certain ideas from cognitive linguistics.

Processing time: how long it takes a listener or reader to process aural or written language in real time.

Productive vocabulary: the words someone can produce orally and in writing by using multiple aspects of word knowledge.

Program for the International Assessment of Adult Competencies (PIAAC): a large-scale program of assessment and analysis of adult skills; e.g. literacy, numeracy and problem solving.

Program for International Student Assessment (PISA): 15-year-old students' skills in reading, mathematics and science are assessed in all OECD countries every three years.

Project-based learning: a teaching method in which students gain knowledge and skills by working for an extended period of time to investigate and respond to an authentic, engaging, and complex question, problem or challenge.

Prosody: all the elements of a language associated with the rhythm, stress and intonation of speech.

Proto-writing: systems of symbols used to transmit concepts rather than representing them with letters/graphemes. Examples are the cuneiform writing of the Sumerians, Egyptian hieroglyphs, Cretan hieroglyphs, Chinese logographs, Indus script and the Olmec script of Mesoamerica.

Psycholinguistics: a branch of linguistics that studies the relationships between the language and certain aspects of human psychology; e.g. processing.

Pull-out model: program or classroom design in which students requiring additional help are separated or 'pulled out' for more intensive instruction.

Quantifier: a determiner that indicates quantity; in English, words which can precede nouns such as 'all', 'some', 'many', 'few', 'a lot' and 'no'.

Rapid profiling: collecting oral questions produced by second language learners as a form of assessment. An application of Pienemann's Processability Theory (1998) to assess second language learners using the oral questions and other expressions they produce; its use requires training in working with oral samples of spontaneous speech.

Reading: getting information by decoding written symbols.

Realia: common objects that are used as scaffolds for language learning.

Rebus principle: the use of existing written symbols to represent their sound.

Recasts: see **oral recasts**

Receptive vocabulary: the words that one is able to understand while reading or listening.

Register: see **formal vs. informal register**.

Reliability: the degree to which a measurement of behaviour is consistent and gives the same results when used on repeated occasions under the same conditions.

Rhyme: words whose final sounds use the same vowel (and consonant); e.g. 'balloon' rhymes with 'moon'.

Rime: the final part of a syllable; composed of a nucleus (with a vowel or vowels) and sometimes a coda (with a consonant or consonants).

Roman alphabet spelling systems: orthographic writing systems based on the Roman alphabet.

Salience: an object or stimulus which draws, for example, the listener's attention by being longer or, for second language learners, is the same as or similar to a word in their L1.

Scaffolding: the learning process of giving students assistance with skills or knowledge, which helps them learn at a faster rate than they would have if they were left on their own.

Scripts: see **abugida**, **davanagari** and **logographic scripts/writing systems**.

Second International Adult Literacy Survey (SIALS): see **International Adult Literacy Survey (IALS)**.

Second language: any new language learned after the first one has been used or mastered in early childhood.

Second language learning: learning an additional language in addition to the one that the person knows and uses.

Semantics: the study of the literal meaning of words, phrases and sentences as well as their relationship to each other.

Semantic mapping: a method to visually support the word learning process. Objects (new words) and their relations to each other are graphically represented.

Semantic processing: analysing the meaning of an item and relating it to previous knowledge.

Sensitive period: a weaker version of the critical period with its absolute termination at puberty. It allows for the possibility of acquiring a second language after puberty although not necessarily to native speaker competence in all areas.

Sequencing activity: a language instructional activity in which students identify and or manipulate beginning, middle, and ending sounds to change the meaning of words.

Sight words: frequent words the beginning reader memorizes by sight and recognizes as a whole, without decoding.

Simultaneous bilingualism: learning two languages at the same time, from a very young age, typically from birth. It usually occurs in the family when two languages are spoken in the home.

Situational factors: factors that influence language learning and acquisition, including students' social and linguistic backgrounds, population diversity, language policies of the country, the role of the languages in school, the status of the languages in the society and the costs of providing bilingual education.

Skills-focused instructional approaches: literacy teaching approaches that emphasize the importance of skills and abilities needed to become literate; e.g. phonological awareness.

Social-focused instructional approaches: teachers act as facilitators of group discussion and cooperative learning. It includes peer-assisted learning and student-centred discussions in which students participate and learn from their classmates in order to deepen their understanding of the material.

Sociocultural aspects of literacy: literacy is conceptualized as a culturally and socially embedded practice that is infused with beliefs and ways of knowing within a particular context, rather than a set of isolated, transferable skills.

Sociocultural theory: based on Lev Vygotsky's (1978) ideas on learning as a mental, socially shared process facilitated by interaction with other people and the surrounding culture.

Sociolinguistic competence: the ability to use language appropriately in social contexts; competence regarding when to speak, when not to speak, what to talk about with whom, when, where and in what manner; e.g. regional or social dialect, standard language, technical language.

Specific language impairment: a language disorder that influences the mastery of language skills in children who have no hearing loss or any other diagnosed developmental delays.

Speech stream: the steady flow of language with no immediately detectable boundaries between items; e.g. between words. Babies segment the speech stream during their first year of life to identify word boundaries.

Spelling: representing sounds with letters; putting words together with letters.

Standardized tests: tests in which all participants answer the same questions in the same way, which are then scored in a standard way to allow comparison across individuals and for successive cohorts. Standardized tests are usually connected to large-scale tests given to large populations of learners; e.g. the TOEFL test in the United States.

Students with limited or interrupted formal education (SLIFE): for economic, political or social reasons, they have not participated in schooling during the age of compulsory schooling.

Subject-verb agreement: the marking of number (singular or plural) and person (first, second, or third) of the subject on the verb; in German, *Ich geh-e* 'I go' vs. *Er geh-t* 'He goes' and *Wir geh-en* 'We go'.

Subordinate words: words which represent an inferior category (within a system of classification); e.g. Labrador, poodle, German shepherd or Chihuahua are all subordinates of dog.

Subordination: joining of two or more clauses not with a coordinating conjunction such as 'and' or 'but' ('John saw the book and it was a novel'), rather with a complementizer such as 'that' ('John saw that the book was a novel').

Successive/sequential bilingualism: learning a second language after the mother tongue/home language, usually after the age of 4 or 5. This frequently occurs when a child learns one language at home and is exposed to another language at school.

Suffix – derivational, inflectional: a bound morpheme, which follows its root. An example of a derivational suffix is –able, which attaches to verbs to create adjectives as in 'doable'. The past tense –ed is an example of an inflectional suffix, which attaches to verbs but changes their function, not their meaning, as in jump-ed.

Super-diversity: a range of changing variables surrounding today's global migration patterns, their interrelations and social complexities in migrant communities.

Superordinate words: words which represent a superior category within a system of classification; e.g. dog is the superordinate of different breeds of god, such as poodle and German shepherd.

Suppliance/non-suppliance in obligatory context: a morpheme is either supplied or not supplied in a given linguistic environment, obligatory context. Brown (1973) was able to determine when the three children in his study had acquired a set of 14 morphemes by looking at when they supplied them in obligatory contexts.

Syllabary writing system: a writing system where a character represents a syllable.

Syllable: minimally a vowel, but typically a vowel along with one or more consonants, that forms the whole or part of a word; e.g. 'pop', 'prop', 'Proust', 'pro-test'.

Symbolic function: gives us the insight that a word, a sign, or an icon refers to some entity in the world: a specific object, a particular action, or a quality. We can refer to children's development of this as the **naming insight**.

Synonyms: words that have very similar but not identical meanings, which usually differ in terms of register (to start – to commence), regional use (fall – autumn) or grammatical context (almost – nearly).

Syntactic knowledge: knowledge of how words can be combined to form grammatical sentences. Syntactic knowledge tells us, for example, that 'dog' is a noun and the direct object in the sentence, 'I love my dog' or that *'The shape of this painting looks dog' is ungrammatical.

Syntactic projections: the syntactic representation of lexical information in terms of heads of phrases in the hierarchical structure of a sentence. See Hawkins (2001 or 2018) for an introduction to these ideas in syntax as applied to SLA.

Syntax: the rules which words follow to form the phrases, clauses, and sentences that make up language, particularly in terms of their internal order, order with respect to each other, and the various positions in which they can appear.

Synthetic approach to literacy teaching: a method of teaching that starts with the study of individual sounds and letters and then continues with larger units.

Tactile learning: use of objects (e.g. magnetic letters) to promote the learning process.

Target language: the language one aims to learn/acquire. Often used synonymously with second language.

Target-like: language that comes close to that of a proficient user of the language.

Taxonomic assumption: the assumption that words refer to objects of like kind.

Taxonomic knowledge: the knowledge that objects or animals can be hierarchically ordered into higher and more abstract categories. Eagles, sparrows, and blackbirds are birds. Birds are not amphibians or mammals, but they belong to the category of *sauropsida*, which in turn, is a subcategory of animals.

Taxonomy: a semantic hierarchy; e.g. 'plant – flower – rose – Rogue Valley Rose'.

Temporal contiguity: learners pick up the meanings of new words better or more easily when speakers point to an object and simultaneously use the word for that object. Pointing to a ball and uttering the word 'ball' at the same time is believed to be more helpful for young children than pointing to the object first and then uttering the word without the pointing gesture.

Tests: see **discrete-item**, **norm-referenced** and **standardized tests**.

Theory of Mind: the ability to attribute mental states such as beliefs, desires and intentions to oneself and to others, and to predict and interpret the behaviour of others depending on these mental states.

Threshold level: degree of linguistic competence that is enough to understand a text.

Tip of the tongue phenomenon: a state in which one cannot quite recall a familiar word but can recall words of similar form and meaning (Brown & McNeill, 1966).

Top-down approach to reading: the reader starts with expectations about the whole text and then checks those expectations with increasingly smaller units.

Transitional bilingual education: educational programs which focus on transitioning learners from their mother tongue into the mainstream language in the community or the country.

Translanguaging: multilingual individuals' strategic ways of using two or more languages as part of the meaning-making process; also a pedagogical orientation valuing the flexible, parallel use of different language resources in the classroom.

Transparent orthography: orthography with direct letter-phoneme correspondence.

Trigraph: three graphemes which represent one phoneme; e.g. the trigraph <sch> represents the phoneme /ʃ/ in <schilling>.

Typical language development: language development processes of normally developing children with no linguistic impairment.

Typological perspective of the history of writing systems: classifies writing systems on the basis of how and which linguistic units are represented; e.g. words, syllables, phonemes.

Underextension: use of a word or words to refer to a narrower range of objects and ideas than would be done by a proficient language user; e.g. using the word 'dog' exclusively for the family dog and not dogs in general.

Unitary Language Systems Hypothesis: holds that until the age of two, bilingual children cannot differentiate between their two languages, and they mix lexical elements from their two or more languages. They gradually move from an initial one-system phase (lexically mixed stage) into eventual lexical and structural differentiation between the languages (Volterra & Taeschner, 1978).

Universal Grammar: in generative linguistics, UG is the hard-wired, innate system of categories, principles and parameters accounting for human language and its acquisition.

Usage-based theory of language development: the key idea that language structure emerges from language use, introduced in Tomasello (2003).

Validity: a measure that tests the phenomenon it purports to test.

Variety: a set of human speech patterns also referred to as a dialect associated with standard and non-standard language use, geographical area or a social group.

Venn diagram: a diagram consisting of two or more (overlapping) circles; shows all possible relations between a finite number of different words and ideas.

Verb raising: the explanation given to account for the different positions of non-finite and finite verbs in languages such as French and German.

Visual route model: an idea that explains that word decoding occurs when the orthographic representation of a whole word is matched with its phonological representation.

Vocabulary: see **productive, receptive vocabulary**.

Voicing: variation in vibration of human vowel cords that distinguishes voiced phonemes (e.g. /d/) and voiceless phonemes (e.g. /t/).

Whole Object Assumption: the word learner's assumption that words refer to entire objects rather than their parts or substances.

Word family: group of words that share the same base (sleep, sleeps, sleepless, etc.).

Word field: a group of words that belong to a particular area of knowledge; e.g. words connected to animals.

Word knowledge: see **breadth, depth of word knowledge**.

Word recognition: the process of making a fast association of graphemes with phonemes (the written form of a word and its spoken form), and of comprehending syllables and words; also known as **decoding**.

Word stem: the part of a word which is present in all inflected variants of the word; e.g. 'do' in 'doing', 'doable', 'undoable', 'done'.

Working memory: part of the cognitive system that provides temporary storage, processing, and manipulation of information necessary for complex cognitive tasks such as language comprehension, learning and reasoning.

Working memory capacity: upon receiving raw acoustic information, we either forget it or transform it into a more useful form. The average person's capacity to briefly retain information is seven (minus or plus two) letters or numbers.

ZISA study: *Zweitspracherwerb italienischer und spanischer Arbeiter* 'Second language acquisition of Italian and Spanish Workers' project, which also included Portuguese speakers and looked at the acquisition of German using a cross-sectional study of 45 adults, a one-year longitudinal study of three 8-year-old children, and a two-year longitudinal study of 12 adults.

Zone of proximal development: the difference between what a learner can do without help, and what they can do with the assistance of a teacher, more knowledgeable other or some type of scaffolding.

Index